AF518611

RAJA RAO'S

KANTHAPURA

A CRITICAL STUDY

RAJA RAO'S
KANTHAPURA

A CRITICAL STUDY

Edited by
Suman Bala
Ranu Uniyal

asia book club
an international publishing house

Published by
Asia Book Club
C 3/1, Janakpuri
New Delhi 110 058
Ph. 9818755529
Email: asiabookclub@gmail.com
Website: www.asiabookclub.com
ISBN: 81-7851-027-8

Copyright: Editors, 2007

All rights reserved. No part of this book may be reproduced or utilized in any form or by any means, electronic or mechanical, including photocopy, microfilm, microfiche, recording, e-mail, web publication, or any information storage and retrieval system, without the written permission of the copyright owners.

Printed at Chaman Offset Press, New Delhi 110 002

Contents

Broader Themes

Women in *Kanthapura*

Story-Telling

A Comparative Approach

The Novelist Extraordinary
A Tribute to Raja Rao

Raja Rao, a pioneer of Indian English fiction, passed away on Saturday 8 July 2006 at Austin in U.S.A. As for the history of Indian literature, his death marks an end to an era of literary excellence. Raja Rao was born on 8 November 1908 in Hassan, Mysore, to a Brahmin land-owning family. He had a brilliant academic career. In 1925, he entered Aligarh Muslim University and studied English with Eric Dickinson and French with Jack Hill. From 1926 to 1929, he attended Nizam's College, Hyderabad, where he graduated with a B.A. in English and History. His interest in literature flourished as he received the Asiatic scholarship to attend the University of Montpellier. His sojourn in France inspired him to take deep interest in his native language, Kannada, and also in his native scholarly research on the Indian influence on Irish literature. The comparative approach to literature widened Rao's outlook towards life and society. He was open to various literary and political movements that were sweeping Europe during those times. It was in 1938 that he published his classic novel *Kanthapura* that established him as a formidable novelist. The story of the novel, narrated by Achakka, was mostly written in the 13th century castle of the Dauphine in the heart of Alps. The novel made such a strong impact on Indian psyche that during last six decades, since it was published, it has intensely gripped the minds of the readers, in India and abroad.

In 1964, Raja Rao was awarded the prestigious Sahitya Akademi Award (National Academy of Letters) for his philosophical novel *The Serpent and the Rope*. In 1959, he joined the University of Texas as Professor of Philosophy, a position he held till his retirement in 1980. In recognition of his services to art, literature and philosophy, the Government of India conferred on him the award of the Padma Bhushan (The Order of the Lotus). He was honoured with several titles and fellowships. In 1972, he was made Fellow of Woodrow Wilson International Centre, Washington. The Modern Language Association of America (MLA) elected him as Honorary Fellow. Back home, he was awarded Fellowship by the Sahitya Akademi, New Delhi. In his Acceptance Speech on 24 March 1997 in Austin, Raja Rao expressed his wish to write in his native language: "To have been born in India and not have written in Sanskrit, or at least in Kannada, is, believe me, an acute humiliation. But I still dream of writing in Sanskrit—one day."

Raja Rao has been widely published, in India, England and America. His publications, including novels, stories, essays, exceed 125 in number. He was not as prolific as his peers Mulk Raj Anand and R.K. Narayan were, but each of his work was received with great enthusiasm and gusto in the literary circles. Whenever he visited India, he met scholars and saints in various ashrams. He had a great faith in Indian culture and Hindu religion. He was politically alive too. During the Quit India movement launched by Mahatma Gandhi in 1942, he was associated with the underground activities of the young Socialist leaders. During 1943-44, he edited with Ahmed Ali, a journal called *Tomorrow*. His great work *Kanthapura* was written when he was twenty-one, though it was not published till 1938. Interestingly, though he was adept in Kannada and French languages, he preferred English, 'the language of our intellectual make-up.' He was so successful in presentation that he produced a body of work that spanned seven decades. His first novel remains the most influential in the entire gamut of Indian fiction written in the first half of the 20th century.

Raja Rao has had interactions with eminent literary figures of the world. In his essay on E.M. Forster, included in the book *E.M. Forster: A Tribute* (edited by Natwar Singh), he narrates an interesting episode regarding his meeting with Forster. He states: "The same evening, I wrote a letter to Forster: 'I have abandoned literature for good, and gone over to metaphysics; I am not a writer any more. I do not know on what grounds I could come to see you.' Forster immediately sent me a reply: 'You have, you say, abandoned literature for metaphysical inquiry. I have abandoned literature for nothing at all. So please let us meet.'" Raja Rao often met Mulk Raj Anand when they were in Paris and discussed literary and political matters of mutual interest. Interestingly Raja Rao introduced Jawaharlal Nehru to Andre Malraux in Paris in the early part of 1936. In his tribute in *The Legacy of Nehru*, Raja Rao describes his encounter with Nehru in the Black Forest in Germany. Nehru's wife, Kamala Nehru, was in a sanatorium there. Nehru had been instantly released from jail to be with his desperately ill wife. Nehru took Raja Rao to meet Kamala. The trialogue is both entertaining and memorable. It shows varied interests of the personalities involved. Metaphysics, Raja Rao's fortè, was not Nehru's cup of tea. He asked Raja Rao: "Do you always speak like this?"

Raja Rao's knowledge of religion, mysticism, metaphysics has kept all the readers spellbound all these years. Scores of books and theses have been written to explore the thought-content of Raja Rao's writings. To some, he was an enigma, to others a guru, and to a large reading community a literary genius who fused matter and manner in a highly dexterous fashion.

In a grove of live oaks and flowering myrtles under a clear Texan sky, Raja Rao ended his long journey that had begun almost a century ago in a small unknown village in South India much like Kanthapura. It is perhaps a cliché to state that Raja Rao, along with.Mulk Raj Anand and R.K. Narayan, was maker of the great Indian English fiction. The three ventured into the Indian novel in the 1930s and took the literary world by storm. The first six years of the 21st century have taken a huge toll by claiming the lives of the three writers: RKN died in 2001 at 94, MRA in 2004 at 99 and now Raja Rao at 96. All of them played long but significant innings. They put Indian fiction on the road to success. Adieu, Raja Rao! We shall always cherish your memory with each reading of *Kanthapura*!

SUMAN BALA

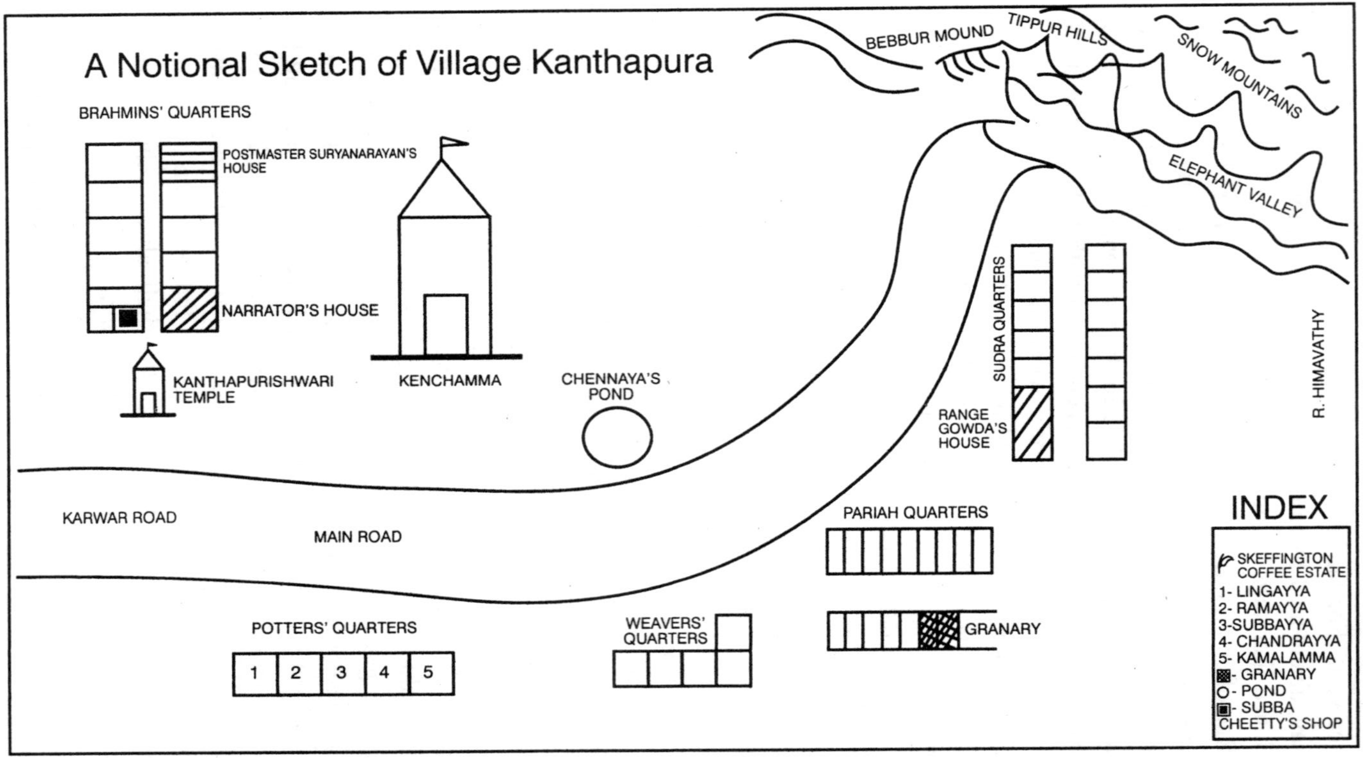

A Notional Sketch of Village Kanthapura
BRAHMINS' QUARTERS
POSTMASTER SURYANARAYAN'S HOUSE
NARRATOR'S HOUSE
KANTHAPURISHWARI TEMPLE
KENCHAMMA
CHENNAYA'S POND
BEBBUR MOUND
TIPPUR HILLS
SNOW MOUNTAINS
ELEPHANT VALLEY
SUDRA QUARTERS
RANGE GOWDA'S HOUSE
R. HIMAVATHY
KARWAR ROAD
MAIN ROAD
PARIAH QUARTERS
GRANARY
POTTERS' QUARTERS
1
2
3
4
5
WEAVERS' QUARTERS
INDEX
SKEFFINGTON COFFEE ESTATE
1- LINGAYYA
2- RAMAYYA
3-SUBBAYYA
4- CHANDRAYYA
5- KAMALAMMA
- GRANARY
O- POND
- SUBBA CHEETTY'S SHOP

Raja Rao's *Kanthapura*: An Introduction

SUMAN BALA
S.B.S. College, University of Delhi

Life and Works

Eldest son of an ancient brahmin family, Raja Rao (1908-2006) was born in the village of Hassan in Mysore. After matriculating from Hyderabad, he went over to Aligarh for higher education. There he came in contact with Professor Eric Dickinson who inspired him to study French language and literature. He took his B.A. degree from Nizam College, Hyderabad. He was awarded government scholarship by the Hyderabad university which enabled him to continue his study of French literature in France. First, he studied at the University of Montpellier and then received his Ph.D. degree from the University of Sorbonne under the supervision of Professor Cazamian. In France, he married Camille Morley, a highly-educated French woman. From 1928 to 1939, he lived in France and returned to India on the outbreak of World War II. He spent some months in Gandhi's Ashram at Sabarmati in 1941. In 1946, he again went to France. His first novel *Kanthapura* (1938) was written in France, thousands of miles away from India. It is a vivid and realistic portrayal of the Gandhian struggle for the freedom of country. Most of the stories included in his next work *The Cow of the Barricades* (1947) were also written in France.

His second novel *The Serpent and the Rope* has France as its scene of action. It has been called the spiritual autobiography of the novelist and has received wide acclaim. Termed as the best novel ever written, it won Raja Rao the Sahitya Akademi Award.

Raja Rao visited the U.S.A. for the first time in 1950 and was fascinated by American culture and way of life. He lectured at various American universities and taught Buddhist and Vedantic philosophy at the University of Texas. In 1965, he married an American stage actress Katherine Jones and had a son by her.

In 1965, Raja Rao published *The Cat and the Shakespeare: A Tale of Modern India*. It is a curious mixture of fantasy and realism and its setting is provided by the famine of 1942. His next novel was *Comrade Kirillov* (1976) which delves into the ambiguous life of an orthodox brahmin Communist. In 1978, he published *The Policeman and the Rose and Other Stories* (1978). The title piece is a novella. One of the finest pieces in this collection is "India: A Fable." *The Chessmaster and His Moves* (1988) was awarded the prestigious Neustadt Prize for Literature by the Oklahama University. *On the Ganga Ghat* (1989) is a collection of short stories which present a glimpse of Indian life.

The World of Kanthapura

Raja Rao's *Kanthapura* narrates the stirring times when the soul of our oppressed nation was fired by the call of the Mahatma, and thousands sacrificed themselves for the sake of our motherland. Discussing *Kanthapura* as a Gandhi novel, it is imperative to explore its literary framework. In *Kanthapura*, Raja Rao has written a historical Indian novel not by linear but by the 'mythic,' or 'cyclical' time perspective. It is not a historical novel like Bankimchandra Chatterjee's *Durgeshnandini*, nor is it a traditional epic like the *Mahabharata*. In his *Foreword* to the novel, Rao contests the Western notion that India is lacking in a sense of history. Explaining the nature of his novel, Rao states:

> There is no village in India, however mean, that has not a rich *sthala-purana*, or legendary history, of its own. Some god or god-like hero has passed by the village—Rama might have rested under this pipal-tree, Sita might have dried her clothes, after her bath, on this yellow stone, or the Mahatma himself, on one of his many pilgrimages through the country, might have slept in this hut, by the village gate. In this way the past mingles with the present, and the gods mingle with men. . . . One such story from the contemporary annals of my village, I have tried to tell. (5)

Adhering to this statement, Rao has created in *Kanthapura* a veritable *sthala-purana*, a legendary history out of the Indian life in the pre-Independence era.

Rao has drawn the raw material of his novel essentially from history. But he has moulded the subject in a mythical framework, aptly suited to the Indian mind. Both his novelistic technique and the novel's content reiterate the theme—freedom of India from the British rule, a freedom sought in a unique way under the leadership of Mahatma Gandhi.

Rao presents his story in a highly conversational style, deriving significantly on the folklore. The combination of folklore with the vigorous tradition of Indian story-telling goes back to two thousand years, to the *Ramayana* with all the vigour and resonance this implies, which allows the novelist suppleness and variety in rendering the response of the villagers to the theme of *Kanthapura*. The end product is so natural and acceptable to the readers that they never feel that something is being imposed on them. Events that take place during the course of the story are given the colour of a puranic myth and in this process, in the words of the author himself, "the past mingles with the present, and the gods mingle with men." (5)

At this point, one can compare Raja Rao with Mulk Raj Anand, a contemporary of Raja Rao, who was greatly influenced by Gandhi in his writings. There is a clear distinction between the two great writers. While Anand was influenced by the humanistic aspect of Gandhian thought, Rao imbibed its spiritual and metaphysical aspect. In his novels like *Coolie* and *Untouchable*, Anand explores man's relationship to society. Raja Rao, on the other hand, moves from the humanistic to the spiritual viewpoint.

Mulk Raj Anand, like Charles Dickens in English and Premchand in Hindi, is passionately concerned with the recognition of fundamental principles of human living. The Indian life that he depicts in his novels is that of the lowly and the lost. He relentlessly advocates the need to raise the living standards of the untouchables, the peasants, the coolies and the oppressed sections of the society. In *Untouchable*, a Gandhian novel, published in

1935, Anand tells us the story of one Bakha, a sweeper, a cleaner of latrines, considered as an outcaste by the society. He is highly frustrated with the ways of the world as he is constantly harassed and tortured. At the end of the novel, he goes to listen to the speech of Mahatma Gandhi which has a great impact on him. The novel succeeds in presenting the predicament of the poor and the outcaste in Indian society. *Untouchable* is thus a thesis for social justice, and Mulk Raj Anand a great social chronicler.

Raja Rao, on the other hand, is an intellectual writer. He is guided mainly by the spiritual and metaphysical aspects of life. He therefore takes refuge in religion and culture. In this respect, he draws a great inspiration from Gandhi. Though a common man, Gandhi was a great genius, one who could feel the pulse of the nation. He realized that it was impossible to revolutionize the nation without drawing upon the resources of its religion.

Gandhi invoked the traditional Indian culture with a view to presenting a contrast to the Westernization brought in by the British. Traditional India, he realized, was essentially religious. His aim was to liberate the country from the clutches of the alien rulers. How could he possibly do it? He could do it by blending religion with politics. In fact, he did not find a dichotomy between religion and politics.

> My own devotion to Truth has drawn me into the field of politics; and I can say without the slightest hesitation and yet in all humility, that those who say that religion has nothing to do with politics do not know what religion means.

With this view in mind, Gandhi used religion as a mean to revitalize the lost and demoralized generation of the times. He knew that only by revamping the indigenous resources, Indian milieu could be awakened from the slumber.

Gandhi had intense faith in the philosophy of Karmayoga of the *Gita* where action is part of man's dharma. According to this philosophy, man can achieve spiritual fulfillment only through his activity in this world. In this respect, Rao's own point of view is akin to Gandhi's: "For me, literature is Sadhna . . . my writing is mainly the consequence of a metaphysical life."

Although Rao employs apparently the theme of political domination and organized revolt against it, it represents implicitly a conflict between the possessor of power and claimants of human rights and dignity which are absolutely denied to the inhabitants of Kanthapura and the rest of the country. Considered in religious terms, it is a perpetual war between evil and good.

It is his faith in Gandhian thought that had led Rao to idealize Mahatma Gandhi as a true saint. In *Kanthapura*, he depicts Gandhi as an emblem of true divine power. Gandhi is presented, metaphorically, as an incarnation of Lord Krishna who will assuage the sufferings of the oppressed Indians.

Rao elevates the Gandhian movement to a mythological level. Mother India, who is the Goddess of sapience and well-being, portrays the enslaved daughter of Brahma and so Siva incarnates Gandhi to liberate Mother India from the bondage of foreigners. Rao alludes to a fine analogy of Rama and Ravana—Rama for Mahatma Gandhi and Ravana for the British government. In the novel, Mother India or freedom is compared with Sita, Gandhi is presented as Rama and Jawahar Lal Nehru is considered to be his brother, Bharata. The novel thus lays emphasis on the notion of identity in terms of its spiritual foundations. In it, Rao makes an attempt to depict the theme of liberation of Indian spirit by Gandhian ideas.

The Text

The novel opens with the description of a small unknown village in South India: "Kanthapura is its name and it is in the province of Kara. High on the Ghats is it, high up the steep mountains that face the cool Arabian seas, up the Malabar Coast is it, up Mangalore and Puttur." (7) In the village, there live people of all communities. Though for centuries it has remained cut off from the live centres of civilization, it has a life of its own in its conservative atmosphere and its traditional manner. Section one describes the simple life of villagers in Kanthapura. Their strong religious life reflects their inner harmony. The arrest of Jayaramachar, a follower of Gandhi, leads to the burning of foreign clothes by the young men of Kanthapura.

Historical Beginning

The novel starts with invocation to the Goddess Kenchamma, "Kenchamma, Kenchamma, Góddess benign and bounteous," (10) urging her to protect them from famine and disease, death and despair, and ends with the same faith in goddess: "Protect us, Mother!" (258) Within these two invocations, Raja Rao tells a powerful story that captivates the readers and takes them to the stirring times when it was written. It presents a phase of Indian history through the story of a small south Indian village in the nineteen thirties with a unique force of evocative and interesting details. The development of events in *Kanthapura* represents all that was happening in every village at that time: Kanthapura is thus not one village but every village in microcosm.

The strings of the narrative are given in the hands of an unnamed grandmother who had herself participated in the freedom movement. Since she had witnessed everything with her own eyes and had been an ardent admirer of Gandhi's philosophy, her narration is quite credible. She is all the more convincing because in India, the art of story-telling is traditionally associated with women.

The grandmother casts such a spell on the reader that he is absolutely taken off his feet. The use of a woman narrator is a remarkable achievement. That makes this novel a precursor of feminist literature. In its women-centred recital of India's history, the novel gains both in its authenticity and dimension.

As the story begins, we are told about the geographical location and the population of the village Kanthapura. We are told that in this village on Karwar Road, there existed a small Kanthapurishwari's temple which became the centre of villagers' life. It was from here that the entire Gandhian movement was controlled. Towards the end of the novel, it beeomes a place of refuge for the villagers participating in the freedom struggle. Here religious discourses were organized on various festivals like *Sankara-jayanthi* and *Ganesh-jayanthi*. *Harikatha* was very popular; these were stories of God, taken from Indian legends.

Sastri, the poet, was regarded a grand *Harikatha*-man. He recited eloquent poetry and kept the audience under spell for several hours every time. After the *Sankara-jayanthi*, Moorthy suggested that they should have *Harikatha* regularly. He knew the *Harikatha*-man Jayaramachar who lived in the city and was much honoured even by the Maharaja. Moorthy said that he could bring Jayaramachar to the village if cart and railway fare could be arranged. He went from house to house and collected money for the expenses. He went to the city and brought Jayaramachar to Kanthapura.

In his *Harikathas*, Jayaramachar blended his religious discourse with the Gandhi movement which was gaining momentum at that time. While giving the story of Shiva and Parvati in penance, he compared Gandhi, its leader, with Siva: "Siva is the three-eyed . . . and Swaraj too is three-eyed: Self-purification, Hindu-Moslem unity, Khaddar." (20) He also made into legend the birth of Gandhi:

> There was born in a family in Gujerat a son such as the world has never beheld. As soon as he came forth, the four wide walls began to shine like the Kingdom of the Sun, and hardly was he in the cradle than he began to lisp the language of wisdom. You remember how Krishna, when he was but a babe of four, had begun to fight against demons and had killed the serpent Kali. (22)

Siva himself has incarnated on the earth in the form of Mohandas Gandhi to free Lord Brahma's beloved daughter India from her enforced slavery. Gandhi was going from village to village to slay the serpent of the foreign rule. Jayaramachar was all praise for the Mahatma. Explaining the cause for which Gandhi stood, he tells the congregation: "If you spin, he [Gandhi] says, the money that goes to the Red-man will stay within your country and Mother can feed the foodless and the milkless and the clothless. He is a saint, the Mahatma, a wise man and a soft man, and a saint." (22-23) The *Harikatha* about the birth of Gandhi had great effect on the villagers: "and so Kittu and Srinivas and Puttu and Ramu and Chandru and Seenu, threw away their foreign clothes and became Gandhi's men." (23) The news of *Hari-*

katha being used as political propaganda reaches the government officials and Jayaramachar is arrested.

Thus, Raja Rao goes to the past to find parallels for the present and the past is used to glorify the present. The *Harikatha* glorifies Gandhi and raises him to the level of Siva, Rama and Krishna who fought the demons as Gandhi was fighting the Redman.

Moorthy

In Kanthapura, Moorthy does his best to popularise the Gandhian thought. He goes from house to house, to neighbours and friends, and asks them to throw away their foreign clothes and become Gandhi's men. After the arrest of Jayaramachar, he again goes to the city and returns a few days later with the necessary instructions. From the Karwar Congress Committee office, he brings publicity material, spinning wheels and cotton wads and distributes them free to the residents. Henceforth, he is seen constantly going to Kannayya House where he would remain for hours together. It was soon apparent that the big house had become the office of the village Congress Committee or the Congress House.

Moorthy and other educated boys of the village go from door to door distributing free spinning wheels and explaining the advantages of spinning to the people. Moorthy encourages the women to become self-sufficient by spinning. He convinces the women of Kanthapura that spinning every day will bring them some extra money: "You see, you have nothing to do in the afternoons after the vessels are washed and the water drawn, and if you spin just one hour a day, you can have a bodice-cloth of any colour or breadth you like, one bodice-cloth per month, and a sari every six months." (28) He lucidly explains the message of Gandhi to the ignorant village-folks. He gives them reasons why Mahatma Gandhi wanted Indians to spin:

> Because millions and millions of yards of foreign cloth come to this country, and everything foreign makes us poor and pollutes us. To wear cloth spun and woven with your own God-given hands is

> sacred, says the Mahatma. . . . Our country is being bled to death by foreigners. We have to protect our Mother. (29)

When Nanjamma asks him if Mahatma practises what he preaches, Moorthy says:

> The Mahatma, sister? Why, every morning he spins for two hours immediately after his prayers. He says spinning is as purifying as praying. (32)

Moorthy gets a rousing welcome at the Pariahs' quarters where each member carries a charkha home. They are delighted to have a brahmin amidst them to explain the ethics of spinning. They are fully convinced and plan to "spin and spin" and hope to have "clothes to wear, blankets and shirts and loin-cloths. . . . It was all of the Mahatma!" (33) All this shows that Moorthy, the protagonist, is a true Gandhiite.

Soon we get to know of Moorthy who had been to the city and "he knew things we did not know." Moorthy, who had organized the *Harikatha*, was calm and saddened. The arrest of the *Harikatha*-man Jayaramachar makes Moorthy a Gandhi-man in the right earnest. As a college-student in the city, Moorthy had heard Mahatma Gandhi speaking in a public meeting. His encounter with the Mahatma was highly emotional. He "sat beside the platform, his head in his hand, and tears came to his eyes, and he wept softly, and with weeping came peace. . . . And suddenly there was a clapping of hands and shouting of '*Vande Mataram, Gandhi Mahatma ki jai.*'" (53) Moorthy was fully moved by Gandhi's words which seemed to come from his very heart and so went deep down into the heart of the audience. After the speech, Moorthy went upto Gandhi and offered himself as a servant and devotee. He fell at the feet of the Mahatma, saying: "I am your slave." (53) The Mahatma lifted him up, and said, "What can I do for you, my son?" Moorthy said, like Hanuman to Rama, "Any command." (53) Gandhi advised him to discard foreign clothes and go to villages and work among the dumb millions. The vision of Mahatma Gandhi in his dreams brings Moorthy back to the village to fight against colonial oppression. He gives up his studies in the city.

When he came back from college that evening, he threw his foreign clothes and his foreign books, and walked out, a Gandhi's man. He took to wearing khadi-kurta and dhoti and became a devoted follower of the Mahatma. But this did not much further the cause so dear to the Mahatma.

Moorthy acquires spiritual power in his very first visit to Gandhi, who imparts instruction to him in shaping his political ideology. Says Moorthy, "There is in it something of the silent communion of the ancient books." (52) He comes under complete impact of Gandhian philosophy, and states: "There is but one force in life and that is Truth, and there is but one love and that is the love of mankind, and there is but one God in life and that is the God of all." (52-53) Moorthy thus explicates his faith in Gandhism and acquires self-realization after catching a glimpse of Mahatma Gandhi.

Moorthy is an embodiment of Gandhism, in all its facets. The readers see him as though he were a spirit of the Mahatma: sometimes they find him a full-blooded, energetic young man working with full commitment among the village-folk. Most of the villagers feel convinced by Gandhi doctrines, advocated by Moorthy. Postmaster Suryanarayana, for example, is already a Gandhian. He asks for two charkhas to spin. Everyone in the village adores Moorthy. The city advocate Sankar says about him: "I love him as a brother, and have found no better Gandhian," to which Rangamma remarks: "he is the saint of our village."

Moorthy's mixing with the pariahs creates resentment among brahmins. In the beginning, Bhatta takes keen interest in Gandhi bhajans but he turns hostile to the Gandhi movement after one of his visits to the city. While the villagers are swayed by the liberation talk, and celebrate their endeavours into the Gandhi-bhajans, Bhatta is the only one who would have nothing to do with these Gandhi-bhajans: "'What is all this city-chatter about?' he would say; 'we've had enough trouble in the city. And we do not want any such annoyances here.'" (34) Bhatta, we are told, is a greedy, moneyed man, the first brahmin of

Kanthapura. He owns thirty-seven acres of dry land in all the villages.

Bhatta does not like Moorthy, for he sees no money in social and political activities started by Moorthy. He has married a minor girl of twelve-and-a-half years. Further, he condemns pariahs's admission in colleges for studying Sanskrit, and throwing open temples to them. Bhatta criticizes Gandhi for adopting a pariah girl as a daughter: "He is a Vaisya and he may do what he likes. That does not pollute me." (44) He has a narrow vision of life; money rather than principles matter to him. He is tactful and scheming: "With his smiles and his holy ashes, we said he would one day own the whole village." (35)

Bhatta is on the side of the Swami who rules from the city, one who has been trying to influence the innocent and credulous villagers. He vehemently opposes Mahatma Gandhi for his efforts to remove untouchability. We are told that the Swami is "worried over this pariah movement, and he wants to crush it in its seed, before its cactus-roots have spread far and wide." (44)

Bhatta becomes a government agent to work against Moorthy and other Gandhi men of the village. He goes around the Brahmin quarter telling people that the Swami in the City of Karwar would ex-communicate all of them if Moorthy does not stop going to the Pariah quarter and mixing with the pariahs. Bhatta represents the government repression let loose by the British once the Gandhi movement started gaining ground.

Moorthy, who has seen in his vision the Mahatma as sober, wise and impressive like Rama, decides to play the role of Hanuman to his leader, Mahatma Gandhi. He allows himself to eat from his own kitchen like a pariah. He continues to mix with pariahs and works for their social uplift.

Moorthy has to pay a price for what he is doing: mixing with the downtrodden and working for their betterment. He soon learns that he is to be excommunicated from his brahmin community on the recommendation of the Swami; he has been charged of mixing up with the untouchables. This news is highly distressing for Moorthy's mother. In the beginning, she is depicted as a proud mother and feels flattered because her son is being sought after by quite a few people and she receives several proposals of marriage. She feels dejected when Moorthy rejects all proposals, saying that he did not want to marry. Earlier, Mother had felt disappointed when Moorthy had given up his college education and shattered her dreams regarding Moorthy's bright and glorious career. But when she is threatened by Bhatta that her son would be excommunicated if he does not stop mixing up with the pariahs, she trembles and big tears roll down her cheeks. She strongly rebukes Moorthy:

> Oh! to have a son excommunicated! Oh! to have gone to Benares and Rameshwaram and to Gaya and to Gokurna, and to have a son excommunicated! I wish I had closed my eyes with your father instead of living to see you polluted. Polluted! Go away, you pariah! (61-62)

Moorthy tries to make his mother understand and not to be misled by others. And he refuses to be cowed down by the Swami and his threats. Says Moorthy: "Let the Swami do what he likes. I will go and do more and more pariah work. I will go and eat with them if necessary. Why not? Are they not men like us." (63) From that day on, mother and son did not speak to each other again. He sat and ate his food on the kitchen doorstep and she in the kitchen. Moorthy started visiting the pariah quarters more frequently. When Bhatta saw that his threats were of no avail, he announced that the Swami had excommunicated Moorthy, his whole family and all the generations to come. The news of her son's ex-communication fills Moorthy's mother with shame and she dies. That very night, Narsamma falls down unconscious in a field and is found dead in the morning. She is cremated where she lay because Bhatta refused to perform her funeral rites. That very night Moorthy leaves for some unknown destination where the last rites are performed.

On his return to the village, Moorthy lives at Kannayya House. He is treated as a pariah and is served food at the kitchen door. However, despite several oppositions, Moorthy persists with his work and frequently visits the pariahs. He continues teaching the pariahs to read and write. In the meantime, the movement spreads and infuses the villagers with new courage to defy the cramping conventions and stale social customs.

While all this goes on, we are given a graphic picture of Skeffington Coffee Estate which is situated in the neighbourhood of Kanthapura. The events at the Coffee Estate serve to constitute a sub-plot in the novel, joined to the main theme by the association of Moorthy with the suppressed labourers of the Estate as well as by their participation in the Non-cooperation Movement launched by Moorthy under the instructions of Congress headquarters. Here is a place which draws coolies and labourers from the nearby villages from below the ghats. They are shabbily treated by the English masters: "a four-anna bit for a man and a two-anna bit for a woman." (68) Since they have no resources, no definitive jobs, they are agreeable to accept low wages. Their working conditions are so bad that these labourers are often insulted and tortured. They are told by the English masters: "if you work well, you will get sweets and if you work badly you will get beaten—that is the law of the place." (70)

The labourers at the Coffee Estate are put to hard labour and insults are heaped on them. The employers had the audacity to demand any woman for their sexual gratification. The new Sahib of the Estate, we are told, is a pastmaster in human relations. He does not beat the coolies, like his uncle earlier did, nor does he refuse to pay advance money. But "he will have this woman and that woman, this daughter and that wife, and every day a new one and never the same two within a week." (82) Very often the workers, helpless as they are, offer their wives or daughters to the English masters. But when some refuse to do so, they are roughed up, beaten or even killed. One such incident has been fully described:

> The master got so furious that he came down with his revolver, and the father was in the back yard and the young son shouted out, 'The Sahib is there, the Sahib,' and as Seetharam hears that, he rushes to the door, and the Sahib says, 'I want your daughter Mira' and Seetharam says, 'I'm a brahmin. I would rather die than sell my daughter.'—'Impudent brute!' shouts the Sahib, and bang! the pistol-shot tears through the belly of Seetharam. (83)

However, it so seemed that such a situation would not continue for long. Even coolies and workers start drawing inspiration from Gandhi. This awareness helps them to face the problem and take a bold stand. This has been possible as they have become conscious of their rights. They realize that the pariahs must learn to read and to write, and when they can do this, they can speak straight to the English master and ask for their legitimate rights: money, material and holidays. They wonder: "Why should not Pariah . . . learn to read and to write? They shall. . . . What is a policeman before a Gandhi's man? Tell me, does a boar stand before a lion or a jackal before an elephant?" (84) The followers of Gandhi like Vasudev and Gangadhar come from the city and take the pariahs of the Skeffington Coffee Estate to Kanthapura. They inspire the coolies to participate in religious activities. The presence of Moorthy is felt in the village of Kanthapura. A social transformation has set in.

When Moorthy goes to Skeffington Coffee Estate to teach the pariahs, the policeman Badè Khan tries to stop him. He refuses to let Moorthy enter the Estate. There is a lot of cursing and hurling of abuses. A fierce fight follows; there is whipping and pulling of hair and beards. The women fall upon the foreman and Badè Khan and would have torn them to shreds if Moorthy had not shouted: "No beatings, in the name of the Mahatma." (88) The foreman whips the coolies up the Estate path while Vasudev takes Moorthy to Kanthapura. Moorthy's resistance leads to violence. Rachanna is expelled from the Estate for he had raised his voice against the police. The next morning, Rachanna, his wife and their grandchildren are thrown out of the hut at the Skeffington Coffee Estate. They are given shelter by Patel Rangè Gowda and they start living in Kanthapura.

Moorthy begins his 'Don't-touch-the-Government' campaign. In the short span of his leadership, Moorthy becomes the most venerated figure of the village. He holds himself responsible for creating chaos inside the Estate. He tries to atone for his sins by fasting and meditation. Like Gandhi, he observes fasts as a means of purification and in order to build will power. He decides to fast for three days and to take nothing except salt water thrice a day. He finds such a fast necessary because he feels that he has not lived upto the teaching of the Mahatma. He himself is not pure and that is why so much violence has taken place at Skeffington Coffee Estate. He wants to purify himself to be able to practise love, Truth and Ahimsa as taught by the Mahatma.

Moorthy begins his fast in the temple. At night-fall when there is no one else in the temple, Rangamma tries to offer him a banana but Moorthy firmly refuses it. On the third day, he feels so weak that he cannot go to the river. He feels dizzy when he tries to stand and has to sit down. But there is peace within his soul which irradiated with ineffable bliss. A number of villagers come in the evening and sing bhajans. The next morning, Moorthy breaks his fast. He feels lighter in limb and lighter in soul. A certain change takes place within him and he begins his struggle against the government with greater enthusiasm.

Moorthy realizes that it is not possible to build a movement against the foreign rule until women in the village extend their cooperation. He seizes an opportunity in Rachanna's central veranda. Addressing them, he says:

> Sisters, from today onwards I want your help. There is a huge Panchayat of all India called the Congress, and that Congress belongs to the Mahatma, and the Mahatma says every village in this country must have a Panchayat like that, and everybody who will become a member of that Panchayat will spin and practise ahimsa and speak the truth. (105-6)

The women are thoroughly convinced and agree to join the movement. All men and women start regarding Moorthy as the Mahatma of the village: "He is our Gandhi. . . . Moorthy, who has been caught in our knees playing as a child, is now grown-up and great, and he has wisdom in him and he will be our Mahatma" and they all said, "So he is!" (109)

Moorthy launches a vigorous campaign to enroll villagers in the Congress, a party of Indians that stand firmly against the British rule. He propagates the ideals of truth, non-violence and untouchability. He proposes to the like-minded friends: "We shall start a Congress group in Kanthapura, and the Congress group of Kanthapura will join the Congress of All India. You just pay four annas or two thousand yards of yarn per year, and that is all you have to do, and then you become a Congress member. And you must vow to speak Truth, and wear no cloth but the khadi cloth." (101) If the villagers were to become Congressmen, they had to adhere to the tenets of truth and simplicity, advocated by Gandhi.

With the blessings of the Patel Range Gowda, the Kanthapura Congress Committee is formed. In a meeting, Moorthy is elected as its President, Rangè Gowda as the Protector and twenty-one others as ordinary members. They all vow to spin everyday, to practise Ahimsa and to seek Truth. The membership fee at the rate of four anna per member is duly collected and sent to the Provincial Congress Committee. When the news of the formation of Kanthapura Congress Committee is published in the newspapers, the joy and pride of Kanthapurians knows no bounds. They begin to spin more and more everyday and Moorthy sends bundles of yarn to the city. Moorthy informs them that Gandhi was very pleased with their work.

When Bhatta learns that Moorthy's following has grown in the village, and it is soon going to have a panchayat, he says to himself: "Now this is a bad business." (112) As revenge, he decides to charge much higher rates of interest from those who join Congress. He decides to ruin them by attaching their farms for non-payment of taxes. He derives satisfaction from the fact that there are others too in the village who are opposed to Moorthy.

In the meantime, as Moorthy's 'Don't-touch the Government Campaign' gets more intensified, the police become strict with the inhabitants of Kanthapura. They harass public and conduct midnight arrests. Late one night, the police reaches Kannayya House to arrest Moorthy. Moorthy is questioned by the police inspector to embarrass him. Books, spinning wheels and other items are thrown on the floor and the trunks are laid open and boxes are slit through. Moorthy is absolutely unmoved: "The voice of the Police Inspector is not heard. But now and again we see Moorthy's head nodding: he merely nods and nods and seems to smile at nothing." (121)

While Moorthy's questioning is going on, the sympathizers gather outside, hearing whispers in Moorthy's room and suspicious movements of the policemen. When the Inspector orders Badè Khan to arrest Moorthy, Rachanna comes forward and asks them not to bind their master. When the police threaten to beat them, he shouts: "Mahatma Gandhi ki jai." The cry is taken by the crowd and repeated several times. The police use their lathis to disperse the crowd but the slogan-shouting continues.

The police, sensing trouble, kick them in the back, on the head and in the stomach. Such a callous beating does not pacify them. They feel highly agitated and shout: "Mahatma Gandhi ki Jai!" (122) Even in such trying circumstances, Moorthy keeps his calm. He takes permission of the police inspector to pacify his sympathizers and addresses the crowd:

> Brothers, in the name of the Mahatma, let there be peace and love and order. As long as there is a God in Heaven and purity in our hearts evil cannot touch us. We hide nothing. We hurt none. And if these gentlemen want to arrest us, let them. Give yourself up to them. That is the true spirit of the Satyagraha. (122)

Moorthy exhorts his sympathizers to remain quiet and allow the police to arrest him. But they do not budge from there and oppose the police operation tooth and nail. As soon as he says, "The Mahatma has often gone to prison," (122) the Inspector slaps him on the face. This enrages the crowd and the police are attacked. The policemen mercilessly beat them on their knuckles and even spit into their mouths. Old Ramanna and Dorè come forward and say, "We too are Gandhi's men, beat us as much as you like." (124)

Moorthy's arrest and the raid at Rangamma's house form the central core of action. People resist the police force and in turn they too are arrested. Moorthy and seventeen others are taken away to Santur police station. The others are given a sound beating and released the next day. But Moorthy is taken to Karwar and imprisoned for three months. The people are stunned and pray to God to help Moorthy.

A case is recorded against Moorthy. The students form a Defence Committee and organize a huge meeting to raise funds. Rangamma, an advocate, comes forward to defend Moorthy in the court, but Moorthy is reluctant to accept it. Truth is on his side and Truth needs no advocate. The Mahatma has taught him that Truth is his God and Moorthy says: "Between Truth and me none shall come." (125) Rangamma tells Moorthy that he cannot get justice in the whiteman's court: "the English are not for the brown skin but for the white, and the Government is not with the people but with the police." (125) Sadhu Narayan gives him a long sermon, requesting him to understand the reality of the situation, and showers his blessings on him. Moorthy falls at his feet and shows his grateful respect to him.

Another person who interacts with Moorthy at this juncture is Advocate Sankar, Secretary of the Karwar Congress Committee. He is an experienced advocate devoted to Gandhian principles. He puts on Khadi coat and a rough yarn turban. Since he does not own a car, he is popularly known as 'walking advocate.' He does not attend a marriage party if all those who attend do not put on Khadi dress. Though he offers legal help to Moorthy, he agrees to the latter's view that he needs no help: "Well, Moorthy, if such is your decision, my whole soul is with you. Gandhiji says, a Satyagrahi needs no advocates. He is his own advocate. And how many of us did go to prison in 1921 and never had touched the shadow of an advocate. I am an advocate for only those who cannot defend themselves." (126)

On Advocate Sankar's suggestion, Moorthy agrees to meetings being held for him. The Congress Volunteers set to work and go from Bazar to Bazar to tell people that there would be a public meeting that evening in the Gandhi Maidan. A large meeting is organized where the atmosphere is filled with the shouting of slogans: "Mahatma Gandhi ki jai." A number of speeches are delivered about the noble qualities of Moorthy, about Hindu-Muslim unity and the untouchables. Advocate Ranganna speaks last of all: "Choose between a saint like Mahatma Gandhi who has given up land and lust and honours and comfort and has dedicated his life to the country, and these fattened brahmins who want to frighten us with their excommunications, once the Government has paid them well." (132) At this, the Police Inspector comes and arrests him. Immediately afterwards, a procession is taken out and there are repeated shouts of "Mahatma Gandhi ki jai." When the procession reaches the Imperial Bank, it is violently dispersed by the policemen who are waiting there.

The Kanthapurians learn that the police is accusing Moorthy of arranging the attack of the pariahs on the police. They all pray to Kenchamma to help Moorthy. The English however would have their way. Two days later, we learn that the Red-man's judge has sentenced Moorthy to three months' rigorous imprisonment. People in Kanthapura are stunned; nobody in the village stirs out. They protest against the order in the Gandhian way: they all fast.

Gandhi ways are adopted not only by men but also by women in the village. Many girls, married women and widows join together and form a Women's Volunteer Corps or Sevika Sangha to fight against the British. Women begin preparing themselves for the struggle. Ratna and Rangamma take over the charge of reading and interpreting the Vedantic texts after Ramakrishnayya's death. Rangamma narrates to them the history of India: "Why sister, you need not be a man to fight. Do you know the story of Rani Lakshmi Bai, and do you know how she fought for India?" (149) She tells them stories of Rani Lakshmi Bai of Jhansi who fought the British so heroically, of the Rajput ladies who burnt themselves on the pyre of their husbands rather than surrender to the enemy and of Annie Beasant, Kamaladevi and Sarojini Naidu. She narrates the stories from Vedas and Puranas and correlates them with contemporary situation. Such an approach has a telling effect on women who put their heart and soul in the Gandhian movement. These discourses greatly enthuse women of Kanthapura and they start taking regular training in the courtyard of Rangamma's house. Rangamma teaches them not to neglect their household duties, and to remain absolutely non-violent if the police were ever to fall on them and beat them. Lathis and blows can affect only the body, but never the soul.

She tells them: "Well, we shall fight the police for Kenchamma's sake, and if the rapture of devotion is in you, the lathi will grow as soft as butter and as supple as a silken thread, and you will hymn out the name of the Mahatma." (154) They even organize an ovation to Moorthy when he comes back to the village from the jail by offering him 'aarti' (prayer).

Moorthy creates in the people an urge to struggle collectively against repression. He wants caste and religion to be set aside, if the villagers wish to achieve their goal. Unity, he believes, is basic requirement to forge a front against the British. Metaphorically, Moorthy proposes to build "a thousand-pillared temple, a temple more firm than any that had yet been builded." (170) He strongly feels that a single person cannot do wonders, it is the collective effort that makes a difference.

The scene now turns to Mahatma Gandhi who, we learn, has left Sabarmati with a small group of followers on a long march to Dandi beach to manufacture salt, and the villagers decide that they should also go on a similar pilgrimage. Some wonder: "Why should he [Gandhi] not take a horse carriage or a motor car?" (173) But Moorthy repeats: "No, no, sister, he will not take it. He says he likes our ancient ways and like the ancients he will make the pilgrimage on foot." (173) Moorthy keeps the people of Kanthapura informed of the course of events. The Mahatma is moving; at every village he is given a hero's welcome and more and more people begin to follow him. Hundred and seventy Patels resign their jobs. Moorthy asks the people of Kanthapura to swear to speak the truth, to spin their hundred yards of yarn everyday, not to practise untouchability, but to have absolute faith in the oneness of all, and to have love in their hearts for all and hatred for none.

The day Gandhi manufactures salt, Kanthapurians too sing and celebrate. They wait anxiously for Mahatma's call for action. As the villagers prepare themselves to receive Gandhi, they receive the news that Mahatma Gandhi has reached Dandi, has prepared a handful of salt and carried it home. Thereafter, people prepare cartloads of salt and carry it away. The result is that the government is compelled to take action. Gandhi is arrested and along with him thousands of people are sent to jail.

The news of Mahatma's arrest creates great excitement and people are filled with a greater need for action. Moorthy often talks to them and prepares them to face police lathis and repression in a disciplined non-violent manner. He explains to them that if he is arrested, they should follow the man who becomes their leader after his arrest, and the next one after him and so on. In this way, in Kanthapura as also in every other town and village of India, preparations are made for the great non-violent fight that lay ahead, before India could be free.

At last, the call for action comes. The message sent by the Congress Committee asks the people of Kanthapura to whip up their 'Don't-touch-the-Government Campaign.' They decide that they will not pay taxes to the Government, come what may. Explaining this to the villagers, Moorthy says:

> 'That's what I am going to explain, brother Rachanna,' and he talks of taxes that are not to be paid, 'even if the Government attaches the lands. . . . And we shall establish a parallel Government, and it is this Government that will rule not that.' (179-80)

All the villagers heed to the plan envisaged and decide to put up a brave front by defying the rules and regulations of the alien Government. A parallel government is formed with Rangè Gowda as its Patel. The people in Kanthapura refuse to pay their revenue dues. They plan to picket Boranna's Toddy Grove. Toddy is an evil in itself and also a means to corrupt and exploit the people. However, before the campaign begins, Moorthy asks them to purify themselves of all evil within them. They will not be soldiers-at-arms but soldier-saints. They pledge to harm no one and go to the end fearlessly. All of them will fight together, with no consideration of caste.

On the appointed day, men and women in thousands form themselves into a procession and march ahead with drums and horns in order to register their protest. As they reach the grove, they see the policemen on all sides. The Police Inspector warns them that they are forbidden to march to the grove because it is against the law. Moorthy and the villagers argue that they are following the instructions of the Congress and they will continue to do so till death. They continue to move on and a large number of carts and cartmen join them as they reach the grove.

They continue their protest as advised by Gandhi. Moorthy and Rangè Gowda open the gates of the grove and Rachanna climbs a toddy tree, shouting "Mahatma Gandhi ki jai." The police rush at him and bang lathis on his legs. Amidst shouts of "Vande Mataram" and "Mahatma Gandhi ki jai," more and more people enter the grove and climb the trees. The police rain blows after blows but to no avail. Even women and children bear the blows bravely. All of them try to tear out at least one toddy branch and break at least one toddy-pot. There are shrieks and shouts, cries and sobs. Their bangles break; their saris are torn; but they move on. Policemen try to pull down the people who have climbed the trees.

At last they are arrested and carried in waiting lorries to the Santur Police Station. Rachanna, Lingayya and Siddayya are sent to the lock-up. Others are taken away in three different directions in lorries and left at distant places to walk back on foot to Kanthapura. The women march back to Kanthapura after an adventurous journey. Whey they reach Kanthapura, they receive a hero's welcome. They are escorted to Kanthapura like victorious heroes returning from war. There ensues a clash between the processionists and the police. They are badly beaten by the policemen but keep chanting "Mahatma Gandhi ki jai."

Picketing at the Skeffington Coffee Estate forms the major core of action in this section. The coolies too join the people against the police. A few men are arrested. Next morning, a few more coolies from the Estate join the pariahs in Kanthapura.

Now begin the atrocities launched by the police. Very next morning, while the villagers sing the songs on the river path and behind the temple, we witness a strange scene as some people march into a slow-moving procession to the Skeffington Coffee Estate. Boys, men and women are whipped on the way, showing them who the real masters are. Are they Moorthy and Gandhimen or the atrocious ruling British? The policemen chase the people and brutally assault them. They insult women in every possible manner, even molest and rape them. We are given a graphic picture: "Women were beaten and beaten, and yet would not move till their brothers were freed and they cried 'Vande Mataram.'"[2]

Resistance against the British forces becomes prominent all over India. The people in Kanthapura fast and pray for the success of the Gandhian movement. The news of colonial oppression fills them with a greater need for resistance.

We now come to the next phase of the movement. It is at the time when a convoy of British officers come to Kanthapura to attach the fields of the villagers for their failure to pay the revenue despite the ultimatum. All the roads and lanes leading to Kanthapura are barricaded. Stones upon stones are piled on the road and tree upon tree is laid beside them. Canal-banks are dug and water is let through. Six policemen stand beside them with bayonets and bugles in their hands. Their chief is a tall white man.

In the afternoon, an announcement is made directing the people to pay the revenue due to them or face a punitive tax of one rupee and three pice per person. The government is determined to rule the country and those who create trouble are threatened with arrest.

During the night, Moorthy, Rangamma and Ratna go from door to door, to tell the people that the fight has begun and if any policeman enters the house, they should ring the temple bell to ask for help. Early the next morning, the policemen arrive to take the coolies back to Skeffington Coffee Estate from which they had fled earlier. Meanwhile, Moorthy, Rangamma and many others are arrested.

Over to Ratna

In the absence of Moorthy, the leadership of the Satyagraha goes to Ratna. But what can a lady do in the face of police force? In the absence of Moorthy, she is not able to take a firm stand.

The people of Kanthapura decide to take out a procession and go out of Kanthapura under the cover of the procession.

They make a cart ready, decorate it as if for Satyanarayana Puja. Ratna leads the procession towards the fields. Initially the policemen do not take any action since it is a religious procession. But when they start to shout slogans 'Vande Mataram,' 'Inquilab Zindabad' and 'Mahatma Gandhi ki jai,' the policemen rush at them and shower lathi blows on them. The procession throne, the god and the flowers fall down. Though the police tries to contain them, they repeatedly come out of their hiding, hoist the flag on the top of a pipal tree and shout:

> Lift the flag high
> O, Lift the flag high
> Brothers, sisters, friends and mothers,
> This is the flag of the Revolution. (238)

As the police rush at them, the boys take the flag and it leaps from hand to hand as they sing the song:

> O lift the flag high
> Lift it high like in 1857 again,
> And the Lakshmi of Jhansi,
> And the Moghul of Delhi
> Will be ours again.

Through a gap in the hedge, they see their fields lying below and the city coolies reaping the harvest by gas-light. As they rush to the fields, they see a large number of soldiers with bayonets in their hands. They turn round with shrieks and cries of fear as a shot is fired in the air as a warning. The terror-stricken crowd tries to find shelter and reach their fields. The repeated shouts of "Mahatma Gandhi ki jai" enrages the soldiers who order them to disperse. On their refusing to do so, a shower of bullets is fired in the air. The coolies in Skeffington Coffee Estate return their slogans.

The whole village is full of policemen who spread terror among the inhabitants of Kanthapura. One of them picks up a little boy by his leg, turns him upside down and beats him so violently that when he throws the child on the grass, only blood and sobs come from his mouth. Some others chase the women, throw stones at them and whip them and kick them. The seven-month pregnant Radhamma tries to run away from there but she collapses and twists with pain. She gives birth to a child right there. Ratna, on the other hand, is beaten in the Post-Office House. Her ankles are tied together and her bodice is all torn. Ratna suggests that all of them should go to the temple, which is a safe place to hide. On way, they see that Bhatta's house has been set on fire by the pariah women.

One of the women, Vedamma, has high fever and she trembles and moans. When Ratna tries to go out and bring blankets for her, she is chased by the policemen. She rushes to the safety of the temple and locks the door from inside. The policemen try to break in but fail. They seal it from outside so that none may go out. The result is that by afternoon they are all hungry and thirsty. To attract the attention of the villagers, they light the sacred fire and recite bhajans. But no one comes to their rescue.

In order to pass time as well as to encourage them, Ratna tells them stories of the women of Bombay and of other big cities who were bravely fighting the Red-man shoulder to shoulder with their menfolk.

When they come out of the temple in the morning, they discover that many of their men have been taken away by the police. Some of them have escaped as they had hidden themselves in the dense jungle bushes on the outskirts of the village.

The government does not stop with beating the people and arresting them. Those who do not pay taxes are declared rebels and their fields are to be auctioned. The people are gripped with feelings of being uprooted and becoming landless as their land is sold. The women feel terrified and they approach Ratna for directions. Ratna assures them that the help would come from the city. They decide to hold a *Satyanarayana Puja* which gives the city-boys an opportunity to come to Kanthapura and stop the government auction.

Raja Rao gives us an idea of the impact of the Gandhian movement through one of the volunteers who has come from the city and narrates the situation prevalent there:

> Yes, sister, yes, the Government is afraid of us, for in Karwar the courts are closed and the banks closed and the Collector never goes out, and there are policemen at his door and at his gate and beneath his bedroom window, and every white man in Karwar has a policeman beside him . . . and shops are closed and bonfires lit, and khadi is the only thing that is sold, while processions and songs and flag-salutations go through the streets, picketings and prabhat pheris, and the Police will beat and the soldiers open fire, and millions and millions of our brothers and sisters be thrown in prison, and yet go and ask them, who is our King? They will say, "Congress, Congress, Congress and the Mahatma," and hand in hand they go, shouting "Victory, victory to the Mahatma." (227-28)

He also tells that millions of the people have been thrown into prison: when the father comes back, the son is taken, and when the daughter is arrested, the mother comes out of prison.

In Peshawar, the satyagrahis and disciples of Mahatma conquer the city without a gun-shot. When the soldiers are sent to shoot them, they refuse to do so. As he says: "For after all, sisters, these soldiers, too, are Indians, and men like us, and they, too, have wives and children and stomachs to fill as we." (229) The narration by the Volunteer inspires and encourages the people in Kanthapura. It shows how the people were growing fearless—the greater the repression, the stronger the resistance of the people. The sufferings of the people had an impact on the Indian officers and led to change of their hearts. Many of them disobeyed the government orders or resigned their jobs.

In the evening, the coolies, who had been brought from the city, set to work and cut the rice growing on the fields. The harvest grown by the people of Kanthapura is taken away and their fields are occupied by the strangers.

The scene, at the end of the novel, shifts to Kashipura, close to Kanthapura. The narrator describes how the people have shifted to other areas, leaving the village bare. A year has passed ever since the trouble began in Kanthapura. The reading of Upanishads is continued in Kashipura. As in Kanthapura, here also everyday in the evening, Upanishads are read and *Harikathas* are delivered. The narrator's son Seenu is still in prison.

Those who were jailed for participating in the agitation clash with the Government officials and reach there. Though beaten mercilessly, they do not lose heart. They will do or die.

Change in Moorthy

Moorthy is finally released from the jail since the pact with the Viceroy has included the release of the Satyagrahis from jail. But Moorthy's mind has changed. He is unable to understand why the methods of Mahatma Gandhi are disastrous to the country. Says he:

> The Mahatma is a noble person, a saint, but the English will know how to cheat him, and he will let himself be cheated. (256)

He does not lose heart, and pins his faith in the younger generation: "Ratna, things must change. You know Jawaharlal is like a Bharatha to the Mahatma, and he, too, is for non-violence and he, too, is a Satyagrahi." (256-57)

As the novel comes to an end, the struggle for freedom is still on. In a letter to Ratna, Moorthy writes that though the Mahatma is a noble person and a saint, he is so simple that the English can easily make a fool of him. Further he is not quite sure whether independence is a panacea for all ills because self-government in the village has not been able to eradicate misery, corruption and callousness. Moorthy comes to believe that the only solution to the existing problems lies in removing social inequalities in society.

Narrator Achakka reveals that only Rangè Gowda ever went back to Kanthapura "to dig out his jewels." New houses are being constructed on the Bebbur Mound. There is not a familiar face in the village now. Bhatta has settled in Kashi. Rangè Gowda seeks Kenchamma's blessings asking her to protect all of them.

The novel ends with a grim note of pathos. The fight against the British is still on; the fruit of this fight will be reaped sometime later in history. A piece of subtle craftsmanship, *Kanthapura* is saved from a feeble ending as there is no hurried winding up of the plot with a positive note of reconciliation.

Kanthapura as a Gandhi Epic

A close study of *Kanthapura* has made it obvious that in this Raja Rao is fully committed to the larger spiritual and political significance of the Gandhian movement in the early decades of the twentieth century. Such a study further reveals that *Kanthapura* is no historical treatise; it is a work of art of great creative force and imaginative appeal. Its focus is on the spiritual impact that Gandhi exercised on the Indian mind; the novelist's commitment to Gandhian thought is unequivocal and strong even when Kanthapura is annihilated in the physical sense of the term, the village gains in terms of the awakening of the spiritual consciousness. The political revolution is transcended and assimilated into the web of myth and legend. Though the village is destroyed, but out of this debris of material waste, a new spiritual realization takes place. This precisely is the central concern of the novel.

We find the people caught in a vortex of struggle. What they fight for is the right to live free from the British oppression. The phenomenon of conflict is at the basis of all encounters with the rulers. The entire struggle is directed towards a certain path by Gandhi. His ideas not only guide the protagonist but also motivate the others to action. Though Gandhi remains in the background, his presence cannot be ignored. There is never a direct confrontation between him and Kanthapurians, yet we can see him permeating their conscious selves.

It is their commitment to Gandhi and the urge to fight which despite having uprooted them from their land and family does not kill their hope. The desire to struggle and resist remains in them even after the complete destruction of the village Kanthapura.

Gandhi's personality was so magnetic that it cast a strong spell on people. Many of them got converted to his way of thinking. As a result thereof, there emerged several mini-Gandhis who took upon themselves to carry Gandhi's message to every corner of the country. Moorthy in *Kanthapura* is one such Gandhi. He invariably preaches the Gandhian principles of non-violence, love of mankind, adherence to truth and abolition of untouchability. He is true image of Gandhi who remains an invisible living presence throughout the novel.

Moorthy is one of those thousands of young men who, having been inspired by Gandhi, gave up their studies, earned the wrath of the alien government, and became fighters for the cause of freedom for their motherland. He has an extraordinary capacity for work and a charming personality to inspire the village folks. He is an embodiment of self-sacrifice. This is evident in his attitude towards Ratna, a young widow. She is attractive as is clear from the attention which Moorthy pays to her. Love affair between the two has not been explicitly depicted by Raja Rao. But soft feeling for each other has been amply suggested. Ratna takes keen interest in the Gandhian movement and is a source of great inspiration to Moorthy. She stands for the educated, progressive womanhood whom Gandhi had enthused with his own ideals and imagination.

Gandhi was all for widows's re-marriage and for their active participation in life. Ratna is the female counterpart of Moorthy but the blossoming of their love fails to take place. This is deliberate on the part of the novelist. Rao is not writing a love story. As a matter of fact, he did not want to dilute the seriousness of purpose for which he was writing. That is why Moorthy is shown to undergo a spiritual progress, as is reflected in the transformation of his personality. As the events take place in the village of Kanthapura, he becomes sober, staid and overcomes lust and covetousness. That is perhaps why when Ratna comes to meet him, she finds some changes in his feelings towards her. Her smiles do not seem to attract him:

> That was why, when Ratna came to see him, he felt there was something different in his feelings towards her. Her smile did not seem to touch his heart with delicate satisfaction as it did it before. (94)

Moorthy's transcending the physical desire is essentially vedantic in import, for Hinduism recommends sexual containment as the means of spiritual attainment. His spiritual progression is reflected in his sexual abstinence, non-attachment to wealth and adherence to truth, all these traits are expressive of Moorthy's belief in Vedantic philosophy.

Kanthapura may appropriately be called a Gandhi-epic, for it conveys the very spirit of those stirring days of the Thirties when a single individual, Moorthy, could enthuse the people so vigorously that this could transform the entire nation.

NOTE

Raja Rao, *Kanthapura* (New Delhi: Orient Paperbacks, 1971).

Textual Analysis of the Novel

RANU UNIYAL
University of Lucknow

Raja Rao's *Kanthapura* is a novel depicting the Indian people's struggle for freedom from the British colonial rule. In the early 1930s Mahatma Gandhi's ideals of non-violence and truth gave a new direction to the national struggle. The British were being held responsible for creating social-economic barriers in the society. Gandhi not only stood by his people by encouraging and giving them a new dimension but also insisted on the reawakening of the national spirit and the restoration of lost identity.

Kanthapura is set against the pre-Independence background. The novel depicts ordinary rural commoners defying the colonial forces. As the people begin identifying themselves with the problems and demands of society they seek not only political freedom but also socio-economic and cultural refinement. They confront countless obstacles on their way such as threats, arrests and deaths yet none of these outer forces deter them. They do not waver from the aim of winning freedom

Mahatma Gandhi emerges as the icon of liberty. Moorthy, the protagonist of the novel goes through a period of uncertainty and doubts, but later, under the influence of Gandhi he chooses to fight not only the imperialist forces, but also those that are responsible for creating an ècart between man and man. The people of Kanthapura struggle unitedly for political freedom as well as for the preservation and survival of India's rich cultural values. They strive to create a bond of fraternity among the various sections of the Indian society.

In his other novels like *The Serpent and the Rope*, *Comrade Kirillov* and *The Cat and Shakespeare* too, Raja Rao is mainly concerned with the individuals who strive to explore their inner selves. The quest for freedom forms the basis of this need for self-exploration. Raja Rao's characters are men and women who are living in a particular set of conditions, vacillating between several doubts and conflicts. A certain feeling of *'entaussern'* grips them and they consciously fight against it.

A literary critic questions a text as to what it says and by doing so reveals a deeper meaning that points to its essential truth. Each text is complete in itself and is imbued with meaning. The present chapter aims at a careful reading of the text. It tries to lay bare the latent relationships which are not apparent in the first reading.

SECTION 1

Section one begins with a description of a small unknown village situated in the province of Kara. Carts full of merchandise and men pass through the roads of Kanthapura.

People pray to Kenchamma, the village Goddess to bless them with good luck and fortune. She had fought a battle and killed a demon ages ago. People pray to her and make several promises to her. She punishes the wicked and rewards the virtuous.

The narrator tells us that her village has twenty-four houses. The house of Patwari Nanjundia has a big verandah. The postmaster Suryanarayana has a 'double-storied' house. The other houses are small and some are not bad to look at. 'Kannaya-House people' have a big house and Rangamma, a widow, stayed in that house. Akkamma, another village woman has guests at her place. Coffee planter Ramayya is a cousin of Akkamma's sister-in-law and on his way to Karwar he has dropped in to see them. Several other people from the village are invited over by Akkamma. Dore, another villager has now become a 'Gandhi-man.' The narrator does not like him as much as she likes Moorthy, who is quiet and serene. Had she not been a daughterless widow, she would have offered her granddaughter to him. To the narrator Achakka, Seenu and Moorthy are like Lakshmana and Rama. Only a Sita is needed to make it complete. Moorthy's horoscope did not match with that of coffee planter Rammayya's daughter.

The village has a Pariah quarter, a weaver's quarter and a Sudra quarter too. Bhatta had begun his life with just a loincloth around him but would soon own the entire village. The potter's street is the smallest street in the village. The potter's business has flopped due to the introduction of modern Mangalore tiles and they turn to land. During the Gauri festival, Chandrayya makes festival pots for them. Rangè Gowda is the Patel of the village and his word is law in the village. Rangè Gowda helps the Pariahs whenever they are in trouble. The Brahmin Street is on the opposite side and the narrator's house is the first on the right.

Kanthapurishwari's temple has become the centre of their life. Moorthy has discovered a half-sunk linga and he, along with the city boys, decides to consecrate it. Bhatta performs the consecration ceremony. A grand feast is held and Sankara Jayanthi begins that very day.

Ramakrishnayya, Rangamma's father, reads out the Sankara Vijaya every day. People discuss the philosophy of Maya and then go home. Amidst bhajans and prayers Harikathas are held. Sastri is a grand Harikatha man. The day Sankara Jayanthi was over, the 'air looked empty.'

Moorthy decides to hold the bhajans daily and the people readily agree to it. Moorthy goes from house to house and collects money from the people. His going to the pariah quarter shocks the brahmins. Jayaramachar, the famous Harikatha man, comes and narrates the story of 'Bharatha'—how a land of wisdom is now being ruled by men from an alien land. The birth of 'Gandhi,' like the birth of 'Krishna,' heralds the death of evil. He asks people to spin and weave everyday. One evening, when he is about to light the camphor to the God, the police from Sankur comes and talks to Moorthy and Jayaramachar. From that day, people never see Jayaramachar again. The youth of the village give up their foreign clothes and become Gandhi's men. The first section ends with the arrival of the policeman, Badè Khan, in Kanthapura.

CRITICAL ANALYSIS

Kenchamma: Faith

Kanthapura is a small unknown village where the people have a deep-seated faith in Goddess Kenchamma. If ever there is drought, cholera or small pox they pray to her for respite. This faith in the Goddess signifies the strong trust which the people have bestowed on her. Kenchamma as a complete signifier stands for faith, trust, hope and strength.

House: Possession

The second part of the first section reveals the kernel situation. 'Kannaya house people' have a big house which is many generations old, it still looks as though it has been recently built. The fact of Rangamma being a widow and yet living in such a big house forms the central core of the conflict because it subtly touches the basic existential issue. Venkamma's disgust is revealed in the following ensembles:

> Why should a widow, and a childless widow too, have a big house like that? (11)
> And it is not her father that built it. (11)
> It's my husband's ancestors that built it. (11)
> I've two sons and five daughters, and that shaven widow hadn't even the luck of having a bandicoot to call her own. (11)
> And you have only to look at her gold-belt and her dharmawar sari. Whore! (11)

These ensembles signify Venkamma's desire to possess the other. A note of discord indicates the conflict here. We can see a complete proposition expressing a judgement. Rangamma's being a widow and that too a childless one poses the real problem. The two sets of signifiers being (a) widow: Rangamma (b) childless widow: Rangamma. One set of signifier signifying Rangamma's state of existence and the other as a complete signifier, showing her present status in society. Her being a widow and that too a childless one gives her no right to live in a big house.

'House' as a kernel semanteme stands for possession. The opposition between Rangamma's house and Venkamma's house is a significant one. Venkamma as the other, here questions the right of Rangamma to stay in a big house. The argument is evident to us from the satirical remarks of Venkamma. One can see in her the quest for possession. The desire of Venkamma is to annihilate the existence of Rangamma. Venkamma feels that since her husband's ancestors and not Rangamma's father had built the house it belonged to her. The fact that she has seven children whereas Rangamma has none further intensifies the situation. Her being a 'childless widow signifies barrenness.

'Bandicoot' is a carrier of plague, as a signifier signifies the barrenness of widow Rangamma. She cannot even call this harbinger of dirt and filth her own. Rangamma being a childless widow is a proposition which brings in progression the opinion of the other. The fundamental argument is related to the social context. Rangamma's widowhood also signifies curtailment of certain rights. She negates such restrictions as have been imposed on her by the society and sees to it that her wishes are not thwarted. Her living in a big house, wearing expensive Dharmawar saris and gold belt is an act of freedom and we can see that she chooses to live life according to her wishes. She endeavours to realize her being and her identity which has been made possible only through her willingness and strength.

'Dharmawar saris' and the 'gold belt' are both the signified meaning and the signifying sign. A sign of her love for good things in life and also a sign of her strength which encourages her to defy the norms of society that are imposed on a widow.

There is a fundamental dichotomy between the way she lives and the manner in which Venkamma, a member of society wants her to live. The society has imposed certain restrictions on widows. It has forbidden them to wear expensive saris and jewellery. Venkamma regards herself as the rightful owner of the house. She thinks that she being mother of seven children should be allowed to live in it. Constant conflict goes on as the problem emerges in full focus. The narrator herself says:

> Venkamma's own house was as big and strong as her sister-in-law's. But she said it was not large enough for her family. Besides, she could not bear the idea that it was occupied by Rangamma's father and mother, and when the vacations came Rangamma had all her younger brothers, and the children of the elder one from Bombay—'all those city-bred fashionable idiots'—to spend the summer. (11)

The contradiction does not solely aim at a relationship between the 'haves' and 'have nots' but also underlines the conflict between who should exist and who should not.

'City-bred fashionable idiots' signifies Venkamma's contempt for life and for the class of people which is not her own. To Akkamma who appears as a passive listener, Venkamma says:

> Why should our family feed theirs? If her parents are poor, let them set fire to their dhoti and sari and die. Oh, if only I could have had the courage to put lizard-poison into their food! Well that will come too. (11)

The final outburst presents the proposition in extension. Being poor, these people have no right to exist. As her desire remains unfulfilled it is transformed into violence.

Fire and Lizard-Poison: Annihilation

Fire and Lizard-poison as signifier signify the desire of one to kill the other. The annihilation of one, by the other i.e. Rangamma and her family is motivated by Venkamma's psychic component. It is not simply an emotional reaction of a subject to inflict violence or destroy the other. Venkamma's strong instinct is of self-preservation and her aspiration for greater attainment of wealth.

The narrative thus deals with basic existential issue of a right to exist despite being poor, right to live in luxury despite being a childless widow. Social issues like widowhood and poverty are highlighted. What emerges out of all this probing is the fact that society has its own foibles. Petty jealousies, contempt and hatred of one towards the other can result in thoughts of complete annihilation of the other. Rangamma's refusal to adhere to societal norms leaves her estranged from the others. Her actions prove that she is capable of transcending the problems posed by society. On the other hand, Venkamma's anger and vengeful attitude reveal her mental state wherein she is unable to bear the existence of the other.

The basic human predicament reveals the ècart which exists, due to several opposing and intimidating forces, in this section.

Sankara-jayanthi and *Harikathas*: Deep Religiosity

Holding of Sankara Jayanthi and rendering of Harikathas signify the growing awareness of their state of dependence in the people. The young men's giving up their foreign clothes signifies the beginning of a struggle in Kanthapura. Jayaramachar's arrest and the arrival of the policeman, Badè Khan, in Kanthapura reveal the government's attempt to suppress the voice of the people.

Thus the section slowly reveals the birth of the Gandhian movement in Kanthapura. By giving up the wearing of foreign clothes, the youth of the village show their dissatisfaction and hatred for the rulers. The entire section reveals to us the way an awareness of their existing status as slaves in the country makes the coolies react against it.

SECTION 2

Badè Khan cannot stay in Kanthapura as he is a Muslim and therefore Mr. Skeffington at the Coffee Estate arranges a hut for him where he settles down with a pariah woman.

Badè Khan's sudden arrival and then his disappearance give rise to several speculations. Venkamma is of the opinion that Gandhi-affair in Kanthapura is responsible for this trouble. She blames Moorthy for it. Moorthy's refusal to marry her second daughter and his frequent visits to Rangamma's house anger her. Moorthy speaks of Mahatma Gandhi and his spinning habits. He begins encouraging the people to spin. He also meets the pariahs and gives them spinning wheels to spin the yarn. The second section ends on a note of fear and doubt, as the people see Badè

Khan prowling on the platform and later on in the Brahmin Street.

CRITICAL ANALYSIS

Badè Khan: Authority and Force

Badè Khan is a Muslim and is therefore shunned by the entire village and is not allowed to stay in Kanthapura. The way he is treated by the Patel Rangè Gowda signifies the status of a Mohammedan in a small Hindu village. The fact that he does not belong to their caste and is also a policeman is the major cause of this indifference. The proposition reveals to us the cause of antagonism towards Badè Khan. The following ensembles reveal that Badè Khan's being a policeman has led to such antagonism.

> But the government does not pay me to find houses for the police. I am here to collect revenue. (25)

> "I know I have the honour of speaking to a policeman," the Patel answered in a singsong way. (26)

Speaking in terms of existential psychoanalysis the two ensembles—the police and the government signify power and authority, i.e. *ètre*.

The policeman symbolizes force and power. Rangè Gowda despite being a 'Representative of the Government' (25) defies the orders of the policeman. Badè Khan's settling outside Kanthapura on the Estate with a Pariah woman is a sign of his being rejected by the people in Kanthapura.

Red-men: Exploitation

The kernel situation deals with the exploitation of the villagers by the Red-men. Badè Khan's arrival and then his sudden disappearance creates several doubts in the minds of the people.

> Policemen do not come along like this in these civilized days. (27)

> I know why they have come. They've come because of this Moorthy and all this Gandhi affair. He with his kitchen she—friends and all this bragging city-talk! (27)

To Venkamma the policeman symbolizes power and civilization. She feels that they are living in civilized days. 'Civilized days' is signified by the British rule. Her talking of the 'Gandhi affair,' mixing with Rangamma and his refusal to marry her second daughter, all combine together and are responsible for this antagonism. The dialectics is evident to us in 'she had no particular love for Moorthy. He had refused her second daughter.' (27) One can easily visualize the feelings of jealousy, resentment and hatred for 'Gandhi affair' in Venkamma's heart. She is more concerned with personal gains like the expansion of wealth, the marriage of her daughters and is afraid of her being challenged by the society. She realizes that the 'Gandhi affair' thwarts the existence of the old pattern of society and her refusal to change is the cause of her mental conflict.

Foreign Cloth: Dependence
Spinning: Independence and Self-Reliance

Moorthy's thought-provoking attitude forces the people to think about their plight. He asks them to become independent by spinning. Jayaramachar's expulsion is a sign of the British trying to assert their power over the people by generating fear in them. Congress Committee in Karwar has strongly reacted to it. Moorthy's visit to Karwar is significant as it reveals several changes in his thinking. Moorthy's efforts to propagate spinning signify his growing faith in Mahatma Gandhi. Moorthy meets the people and tells them that the Congress provides free cotton and free spinning wheels to the people. Nanjamma's serious question is followed by an explanation from Moorthy:

> "And why should the Congress give it free?"
>
> "Because millions and millions of yards of foreign cloth come to this country, and everything foreign makes us poor and pollutes us. To wear cloth spun and woven with your own God-given hands is sacred, says the Mahatma. And it gives work to the workless, and work to the lazy. And if you don't need the cloth, sister—well, you can say, 'Give it away to the poor,' and we will give it to the poor. Our country is being bled to death by foreigners. We have to protect our Mother." (29)

The above ensemble reveals that Moorthy's thinking has however, been influenced by Gandhi's ideology.

'Foreign cloth' versus 'cloth spun and woven with your own God-given hands'—this opposition signifies denial versus gratification. "Foreign" stands for something which is not a part of one's own being but has been taken from outside, whereas cloth spun with 'own god-given hands' is a source of satisfaction and respect. Anything 'foreign' not only makes us 'poor' and 'pollutes' us but also fills us with a sense of dependence. Moorthy holds that 'foreign cloth' is responsible for poverty in India. Here 'being bled to death by foreigners' (29) signifies the domineering attitude of the rulers which has been responsible for creating several conflicts in the minds of the ordinary men. Industrialization has not only left the men jobless but has also made them a slave. He speaks of the importance of independent labour which alone can make man reject the assertiveness of the other, i.e. his rulers, and thus realize his existence in totality.

Feelings of resentment and anger which are directed toward the British are visible in this section. 'The Mahatma' is another potential force emerging and he seems to be directing Moorthy's way of thinking. The act of 'spinning' is something unthinkable for a simple and orthodox village brahmin like Nanjamma. brahmins do not spin, do they? She says: 'My son, we have weavers in the village. There is Chennayya and Rangayya.' (29)

Nanjamma's query that brahmins do not spin and why should they when there are weavers available in Kanthapura is a logical one. It reveals to us the division of labour which took place on the basis of the caste system. A brahmin 'spinning the yarn' is unthinkable as the weavers are there to do the work. Moorthy tells her that 'our money' is being taken from India to the West. 'Our money,' 'our country,' 'our gold' and 'our cotton' signify things which belong to the people of India and therefore no outsider ought to have claims over it. There is a conflict visible between the 'exploiters' and the 'exploited' and it is because of this exploitation that there is a demand for conscious awakening. Moorthy speaks of the way mill agents coming from Bombay offer tempting rates and buy paddy from the farmers.

Later, using their own machines, they husk and prepare the rice and sell it to the Banias like Ramanlal and Chotalal. This realization by the villagers that they have no rice left for their daughter's wedding compels them to buy rice at heavy prices from Subba Chetty. So the money instead of being given to Rangi is taken by the Red-men.

The entire proposition in extension reveals to us the way in which labour of the working class is usurped by the British, i.e., the ruling class.

Even in the years in which the harvest is good, the villagers are being lured by the British to sell it. For the villagers looking after the rice is a real problem for they have to keep it safe from rats, worms and the cattle, and later, Bhatta's interest and the revenues are to be paid, the result being that the 'granary is empty as a mourning-house.' (31) The entire proposition reveals the way people allow themselves to be cheated by the foreigners. When 'Husking Rangi' asks when should she come for paddy, the villagers answer that 'we've still last year's rice' leaves her unimpressed for she knows the truth. She, with her husband, has to work on the fields. The fundamental opposition emerges as her children starve whereas the foreigners thrive on profits. The entire proposition in comprehension highlights the way exploitation of farmers has been going on by the rich bourgeoisie. With the arrival of modern machines and technology from the West landless labourers like 'Husking Rangi,' who are dependent on the farmers for work, are left unemployed. 'Husking Rangi' signifies the presence of men who are totally dependent on the rich for their existence.

The dichotomy which is visible between the city and the village is further extended in the novel. The city people bring clothes, sugar and bangles that have been manufactured abroad and sell it to the rural Indian folk. The purchase of these imported perfumes and soaps has made Indians poor. Except for men like Bhatta and Subha Chetty, the rest will become poorer day by day. Moorthy makes them realize the gravity of the situation and the consequences it would lead them to. He voices his anguish at their ignorance and suggests that the act of 'spinning' not only makes one independent but also purifies the human soul. The 'Mahatma' spins everyday.

Thus we can observe that 'spinning' not only brings about the fulfilment of human needs but also the spiritual regeneration. It purifies and elevates the soul to a higher level of perfection. 'Spinning yarn' with hands as against using cloth manufactured by machines abroad signifies the attempt of being to reject the authority of the other. Spinning is an act of self-reliance and independence whereas the use of imported cloth is the acceptance of economic dependence and dominance of the British. Moorthy's reaction to the whole situation reveals his inner conflict which has been aggravated by his rational being.

The Congress provides free spinning wheels to all. The 'Charkha' is a symbol of Gandhi's non-violent revolutionary movement. It embodies an important spiritual truth. The objective of spinning your way to independence can be attained only if you know how to spin yourself into the hearts of your enemies through love.

One notices Moorthy successfully influencing the villagers to spin. The brahmins finally relent and agree to do so. He then goes to the pariah quarter. The pariahs are overwhelmed on seeing a brahmin among them and willingly agree to do as he wishes.

The Pariahs who have been alienated by the other sections of society warmly receive a brahmin who approaches them. The last paragraph of the second section significantly announces the appearance of the policeman in Kanthapura. His presence is symbolic of the fact that trouble lies ahead.

Thus the kernel semanteme in this section shows what exactly 'spinning' stands for. People are made aware of the fact that they are being exploited by the foreigner and this awareness instils a desire of freedom and economic self-reliance. 'Spinning' as a complete signifier not only stands for economic independence but also for self-purification. The 'wheel' represents dharma, the unity of moral law, and it also represents the 'Sunayata' or the 'Nirvana.'

Moorthy, through the signifiers 'spinning' and 'Charkha,' tries to bring about a kind of harmony and self-restraint into the hearts of people. It fills them with love for their fellow men and thus inspires them to work for independence. Everything foreign makes us poor and pollutes us, says he to the villagers. A perpetual conflict goes on in the mind of an Indian like Moorthy who has begun realizing the extent to which the Indians are being exploited by the foreigners to achieve their selfish ends.

SECTION 3

The third section begins with a portrayal of Bhatta's feelings towards 'Gandhi-Bhajans.' Earlier he used to listen to *My Experiments with Truth*, with great interest but his last visit to the city has made him resentful towards the Gandhi-business.' He begins lending money to the people in the city. As a money-lender he is always 'smiling and ready.' His going to the city quite often is the main reason for his non-availability during the obsequial dinner. Ramanna, the second brahmin assisted him in performing the ceremonies. His wife would cook no meals but 'dal-soup and rice' knowing that the master would bring some odes after the ceremony once at home. Bhatta would count the money he received and put it in his casket. After the death of his wife he is flooded with offers of marriage from the families of many young girls. Finally, a twelve and a half year old is betrothed to him. The marriage is a grand affair. Bhatta is no more a pontifical brahmin but has become a landowner. He arranges for the advocates and settles disputes among people. He also sends 'Fig-tree-house Ramu,' a distant relative of his to the city for studies. The narrator Achakka is surprised at his dislike for 'Gandhi-bhajans.'

The second paragraph introduces Bhatta's visit to Rangamma's house. He expresses his grave concern at the change in the society as result of 'Gandhi-business.' Rangamma is unable to influence Bhatta whose beliefs are strengthened by his visit to the swami in the city. Kamlamma's arrival with her daughter Ratna to Rangamma's house makes Bhatta uncomfortable and he goes away. Ratna's way of living is however not appreciated by Bhatta.

Moorthy's mother Narasamma is completely ignored by the women at the riverbank and no greetings are exchanged. Narasamma is a pious woman and of her six children, Moorthy is the youngest and the only son. She loves him the most and has pinned high hopes on him.

The 'vision of Mahatma' in his dreams inspires Moorthy to give up his studies and join the Gandhi movement. His return from the city and his calling schools 'corrupt' shocks Narasamma. His refusal to marry and his constant mixing with the pariahs shocks her intensely. Venkamma's spiteful attitude and shocking revelation that her son would be 'excommunicated' leaves Narasamma weeping incessantly.

CRITICAL ANALYSIS

Bhatta: Accumulation of Wealth

The problematics in the third section is a deep-seated one. Bhatta's growing hatred for 'Gandhi-business' is due to several reasons. His visits to the city and meeting the swami influence him deeply. Bhatta has rigid beliefs. Being a brahmin and a moneylender too, his interests are somehow challenged as he visualizes the emergence of the pariahs i.e. the untouchables and the growth of their movement of human rights and civil liberties in the society. The following ensembles reveal the change which has come about gradually in Bhatta's economic status:

> Bhatta began life with a loin-cloth at his waist, and a copper pot in his hand. (35)
>
> With his smiles and his holy ashes, we said he would one day own the whole village. (35)

The death of his wife Savitharamma in an accident results in several new proposals coming up for Bhatta. His marriage to a rich man's daughter from Alur takes place in a grand way. His marriage to a young girl of barely thirteen years signifies the socio-religious conditions of a society where minors are married off without any qualms.

'Bhatta became richer and richer. He could lend out more money. And now he was no more a pontifical brahmin. He was a land-owner.' (38) His status has changed and he goes to the river accompanied with friends like Temple Rangappa and Front-house Suranna. With the passage of time it can be seen that Bhatta's role is no more confined to conducting obsequial ceremonies but his being a moneylender and a settler of disputes as well makes him a prominent figure in Kanthapura. The fact that he never charges more than Chetty brothers, is forever smiling, and has sent 'fig-tree house Ramu' to the city for further studies, reveals the other side of his personality:

> this Bhatta who has been a pontifical brahmin cannot be on the side of the pariahs. . . . I shall speak to our people. . . . And that is why I've come to see you. (45)

He justifies the reason behind his visit to Rangamma's house. Bhatta is afraid of his existence which is endangered by the change running through the society. His visiting Rangamma and arguing against 'Gandhi business' shows his fear and contempt for change. The conflicts have been going on in his mind for long.

> What is this Gandhi business? Nothing but weaving coarse hand-made cloth, not fit for a mop, and bellowing out bhajans and bhajans, and mixing with the pariahs. Pariahs now come to the temple door and tomorrow they would like to be in the heart of it. They will one day put themselves in the place of brahmins and begin to teach the Vedas. (42-43)

The conflict is further intensified as Bhatta is found influenced by the Swami: "The Swami says he will outcaste every brahmin who has touched a pariah" (45)

His saying later, "I see no fault in khadi and all that. But it is this pariah business that has been heavy on my soul," (46) further clarifies the real conflict going on in his mind. Rangamma is an educated woman who does her own thinking and reading. She is, therefore, not influenced by Bhatta's viewpoint. She tells women about countries where 'air, vehicles moved' and 'speech that goes across the air' and a country where 'men and women work together' women are given 'three months' holiday during child-birth,' the State provides the children with milk, education, jobs and homes, all free of cost. She speaks of the equality which exists there between men and women: 'there were neither the rich nor the poor.' (47) The proposition reveals that ideas of socialism are being propagated in the papers published from the city. Thus, the people are made aware of their state of dependence, oppression and humiliation under the foreign rule.

Ratna's meeting Bhatta at Rangamma's house is significant for in Ratna's presence Bhatta could never feel comfortable.

Ratna: Rejection

Ratna has defied the norms of widowhood by living according to her wishes:

> She still kept her bangles and her nose-rings and ear-rings, and when she was asked why she behaved as though she hadn't lost her husband, she said that that was nobody's business, and that if these sniffing old country hens thought that seeing a man for a day, and this when one is ten years of age, could be called a marriage, they had better eat mud and drown themselves in the river. (48-49)

The proposition reveals to us that Ratna's act of defiance, her living life as she wishes, despite being a widow, is a sign of her rebelliousness. Her wearing ornaments on her body is a sign of rejection and non-acceptance. She thinks and acts according to her wishes. Her reason does not permit her to live a life full of restrictions. Therefore, one can see Ratna transcending the limits of her being and thus realizing her being. The opposition presented by the two signifiers, brahmins and pariahs, signifies the presence of pure, holy, high caste people on one hand, and direct, impure, unholy, low caste beings on the other. The socio-religious context of the period in which this novel was written is revealed here.

Kaliyuga: Perversion and Suffering

Satamma's statement, "it is the Kaliyuga-floods . . . and the pollution of progeny," (43-44) reveals the entire problem. The conflict is not just personal; it has a wider connotation. brahmins like Bhatta and Satamma are afraid not only of their own existing status but also that of the entire community. Intermixing with different castes is strictly prohibited in Hindu mythology. "Kaliyuga" signifies the period of complete degeneration of human values. It stands for total loss of faith in God and therefore, results in famine, hunger, insecurity, unhappiness and misfortune.

Untouchability: Discrimination and Impurity

Bhatta is afraid that once the distinction between the brahmins and the pariahs is removed, his own existence would be that of a nobody. He is driven by a terrible sense of insecurity. Rangamma's remaining uninfluenced by Bhatta's remarks reveals that she is a rational being. It is untouchability which has created barriers among people. Narasamma is shocked to hear of "excommunication".

She nurtures high hopes for her son and wants him to be a high official. But the truth dawns upon her that after leaving his studies he has refused to marry and is likely to be excommunicated from the brahmin caste. The vision of Gandhi inspires men like Moorthy to give up their struggle for selfish ends, and, join the bigger struggle for freedom.

Venakamma: Rigidity and Self-Preservation
Excommunication: Rejection

A strong conflict is visible between the two sets of people. On one hand there are Venkamma and Bhatta who prefer clinging to old values and beliefs as it suits their interest and on the other there are Moorthy, Ratna and Rangamma who realize the serious repercussions of such evils which are responsible for social inequality.

Being a staunch brahmin, her caste is important to Narasamma and the fear of excommunication grips her. The dialectics is concerned with the mixing of Moorthy with Pariahs.

SECTION 4

The fourth section begins with the description of a morning in Kanthapura. As the day sets in, dust starts flowing and carts from the other areas enter the village. Moorthy, too, comes on one of them carrying a bundle of khadi and books in his arms. He walks round Boranna's toddy grove to Seethamma's back-yard in search of Ratna. Finally, after keeping his bundles in Rangamma's Congress room he goes home to see his mother, expecting a warm response from her. But she pushes him away saying that unless he seeks "Prayaschitta" from the Swami he should not show his face to her.

Narasamma rushes from her home towards the river-side and as she washes the clothes, her anger subsides. And she comes back home to cook and waits for Moorthy.

The news of her son's excommunication hastens her death. Nobody is willing to officiate over the obsequial ceremonies. Moorthy leaves Kanthapura and when he comes back he lives on in Rangamma' s house. He, along with Seenu, the narrator's son, continues teaching the Pariahs to read and write.

CRITICAL ANALYSIS

Pariahs: Pollution

The kernel semanteme of the section is in the last paragraph. Moorthy's s refusal to obey Bhatta and also the Swami is a sign of defiance.

Swami: Self-Assertion

The Swami is a symbol of cruelty and selfishness. Moorthy questions the existence of the Swami and calls him "a self-chosen fool". The Swami may be highly learned and well versed in Vedas but "has no thinking power" and "no heart."

Gandhi: Change and Pollution

The proposition in extension reveals that Bhatta and Narasamma hold city life and Gandhi responsible for the pollution. To them, city life is primarily responsible for dirt, pollution, chaos and change. The unrelenting attitude of her son shocks Narasamma and she says in a moment of helplessness: "Oh, this Gandhi! Would he were destroyed!" (65)

Had it not been for Gandhi, Moorthy would not have given up his studies and joined the fight for freedom and equality. Had it not been for Gandhi Moorthy would never have questioned the status of Swami or favoured the pariahs saying: "Are they not men like us?" (63)

Gayatri Mantra: Self-Purification
Mother's Death: Loss of Hope and Identity
Moorthy: Rejection and Change

To Narasamma her community is very precious and excommunication is disgraceful. Narasamma recites "Gayatri Mantra" to pacify her soul and cool her temper. She asks Moorthy to do "prayaschitta" which signifies purificatory rites that are to be performed by his defiled soul. Narasamma is unable to accept Moorthy's ideas of change, reform and liberation. According to the Vedas, no worse fate can befall a Hindu, as excommunication is symbolic of the loss of identity. The death is a negation of ideas and change. Life has become meaningless for there is no hope left.

Moorthy openly rejects the caste network by freely mixing with the Pariahs. He also offers his condolences at the death of Puttaya's wife. He even carries the body for a while. "Oh, he's lost," (65) said the brahmins.

Bhatta, a superstitious brahmin, refuses to officiate in an obsequious ceremony of Narasamma saying: "You can offer me a king's daughter, but never will I sell my soul to a pariah." (66)

Thus we see that the cultural situation points to those moments which are responsible for such a conflict.

SECTION 5

Coolies coming from Godavery never go back to it. The exploitation of women at the hands of new sahibs continues. Seetharam prefers death and refuses to give his daughter to the Sahib. A case is filed against the sahib who has shot Seetharam dead. He, however, escapes, for the Red-man's court forgives him. But after this incident, the master stops harassing the women.

The arrival of Badè Khan has pleased the sahib. The brahmin clerks Vasudev and Gangadhar begin taking the pariahs to Kanthapura for bhajans. They also encourage the pariahs to read and write.

CRITICAL ANALYSIS

Estate: Perfect Harmony and Better Treatment

The problematics in this section emerges at the Skeffington Coffee Estate. There is an aura of mystery around the Estate for nobody knows its exact area or when it was founded. The coolies are hired from several parts of the country to work in the Estate. There lies a conceptual opposition, between what they are promised and what they actually get. We can see their hopes being raised as the maisitri leads them towards the Estate. The following ensemble reveals the way maistri lures them:

> there he came and offered a four-anna bit for a man and a two-anna bit for a woman, and they all said, "Is there rice there?" and he said, "There is nothing but rice around us"; and they all said, "That is a fine country, for here, year after year, we have had neither rain nor canal-water, and our masters have left for the city." (68)

The 'Estate' signifies life full of perfect harmony happiness and contentment. It signifies an endless supply of food and amenities to the coolies:

> and when the children cried, the mothers said, "I'll leave you here with the tigers; but if you don't cry, I'll take you over the mountains where you can have milk like water—just like water," and the child stopped crying. (69)

Estate: Misery, Oppression

The hopes of the coolies are slowly belied as they become victims of fever and oppression. The 'Estate' becomes a cage for them. The life inside this cage is full of misery and oppression as against what had been promised to them. The attitude of the maistri also changes as he enters the Estate with them: 'And the nearer they came, the harder became the road and the stiffer the maistri.' The Other who attracted and lured the coolies now used them as mere Objects.

Rain: Inactivity; Fever: Death and Despair

The 'rain' and fever' are the two prominent signifiers which are related to each other. The rain signifies the period of destruction and misery. Not only does it bring fever but it is also a harbinger of sorrow and death. Despite having left their past behind, the coolies still hope for a better future. Several coolies die due to fever, yet hopes of others remain alive. They are waiting anxiously for the day when they would receive their wages and then proceed towards their home.

Siddayya: Submission; Seetharam: Resistance, Protest; Sahib: Lust, Brutality

There is a conceptual opposition between the two coolies Siddayya and Seetharam. Having stayed in the Estate for ten years, Siddayya signifies the presence of a Being who, without raising any hue and cry has submitted himself to the Other. He has neither protested against nor resisted the oppression of the women by the master. His acceptance and attitude of servility make him a passive being. The given ensembles reveal his familiarity with the things as they were in the Estate: "He knew that when one came to the Blue Mountain one never left it." (81) "This much I know, nobody who sets foot on the Blue Mountain ever leaves it. That is her law!" (82) He appears before us a man who has accepted things as they are in the Estate. Siddayya does not have the strength to fight against the oppressive forces. It is the Estate and the rulers inside the Estate who determine his life and that of the other coolies.

However, Seetharam is a character in contrast. Exploitation of the women folk by the new sahib provides another conflicting situation in the section. 'Sahib' signifies the presence of lust and brutality: "I want your daughter Mira." (83) There is in him a desire to crush and oppress the weak. Seetharam refuses to bow down to the sahib's wishes. The following ensemble reveals his strong sense of integrity: "I am a brahmin. I would rather die than sell my daughter." (83) Here 'brahmin' as a potential signifier stands for the presence of a being who places his pride above every other thing. His refusal to 'sell' his daughter is a sign of protest:

> "Impudent brute!" shouts the Sahib, and bang! the pistol-shot tears through the belly of Seetharam. (83)

Despite being poor he refuses to sell his daughter and accepts death. The 'death' of Seetharam signifies two important truths. On one hand, it is the physical death of a being who has resisted the rape of his wishes by not offering his daughter to the sahib, on the other, it stands for the victory of the brave. Though the court forgives the sahib, yet he has been defeated by the coolies:

> But everybody in the Skeffington Coffee Estate knows now he'll never touch a brahmin girl. And when a pariah says "No," he hardly ever sends the maistri to drag her up at night. (83)

The atrocities, the violence, the constant conflict between the oppressor and the oppressed creates major existential situation. Seetharam struggles to maintain his honour and refuses to be treated as a mere commodity by the other. His acceptance of death not only elevates him to a higher level as a being but also brings a certain change in the affairs of the Estate. He could not annihilate the oppression yet his attempts to do so make him an active being. His refusal is an attempt to claim the right of an individual which has been usurped by the other. He chooses death and thus makes a vehement attack on the psyche of the Other. This single act of Seetharam is not only a mere sacrifice but it also brings an end to further repression of the women.

SECTION 6

The people at the Estate are anxiously waiting for Moorthy one night. The vessels have been cleaned and 'the embers put out.' Badè Khan can be seen guarding the Estate.

The people get restless as time passes. Some feel he will not come that night. As Moorthy enters the Estate, Badè Khan forbids him do so. Moorthy pays no heed to his warning and insists on his right to go in. As he forces himself inside, Badè Khan hits him. The people are unable to watch it silently and they fall upon Badè Khan and beat him up. The maistri intervenes and Moorthy asks the people to be non-violent. The women, in a state of anger, refuse to obey him and keep on attacking the policeman and the maistri.

The next morning Rachanna is asked to leave the Estate. He refuses to do so unless his seventy-six rupees are paid, as a result of which he is beaten up by Badè Khan and the butlers. He is driven out of the Estate along with his wife and children. As they reach Kenchamma's grove, they prostrate before the Goddess and move towards Kanthapura. Moorthy takes them to Patel Rangè Gowda who arranges for their minimum requirements. But Moorthy has become more calm and sorrowful after the incident and begins his "Don't-touch-the-Government" campaign.

CRITICAL ANALYSIS

Estate: Authority

The kernel situation revolves around the Estate. The conflict evolves as we see Badè Khan guarding the Estate. The people at the Estate are gladly awaiting Moorthy's arrival. It is an exciting moment for the Pariahs. The problematics is revealed to us as we see Badè Khan refusing to let Moorthy enter the Estate. The kernel semanteme is the 'Estate.' It signifies authority and restraint.

The following ensemble reveals Moorthy's reactions: "I am a free man, Police Sahib. I can speak." (87) His fearlessness and undaunted courage is shown in his action as he forces himself through the gate. "Free man you may be in your palace. But this is the Skeffington Coffee Estate. And these are Skeffington Coffee Estate coolies. You'd better take care of your legs. I've orders." (87)

Badè Khan's threat to Moorthy signifies the power which is being misused by the policeman. Badè Khan signifies the presence of the other who believes in repression through sheer muscle power. His statement in extension reveals the fact that within the boundaries of the Estate each coolie is owned by the Estate and has no right to disobey the law. One can see the way the labourer is alienated from his own self.

Free Man: Estate; Coolie: Estate

A 'free man' according to Moorthy signifies the right of an individual to speak and move. Moorthy strongly objects to Badè Khan's statement by saying: "Coolies are men, Police Sahib. And according to the laws of your own Government, and that of Mr. Skeffington no man can own another. I have every right to go in. They have every right to speak to me." (87)

The confrontation between free man and Estate suggests an opposing force. 'Estate' signifies that no man has a right to remain free inside it. The Estate curbs the right of the individual to express himself. The coolies are not treated as 'men' but as mere commodities in the hands of the rulers. The coolies have become the slaves of the Estate, partly due to the work here and partly because they receive the means of subsistence. Their two levels of existence as coolies and as free men, on the Estate, are in conflict with each other. On one hand is Badè Khan who being a policeman claims he has orders not to allow Moorthy to enter the Estate and speak to the Pariahs and on the other is Moorthy who insists on his right to speak to them. Moorthy's forcibly entering the Estate is a sign of his defiance of authority. The Gandhian ideology, that each individual possesses the liberty to speak and act is projected here. Moorthy's "I shall" to Badè Khan's "you will not cross this gate" (87) is a sign of defiance. Badè Khan tries to assert his authority by beating up Moorthy and the others. The coolies on realizing that injustice cannot be borne silently for long, resort to action.

Expulsion: Repression; Refusal: Defiance; Silence: Submission

Rachanna's expulsion from the Estate and his refusal to leave unless his wages are paid to him, is a sign of resentment and protest at the exploitation. The use of force to overpower the Being who resists exploitation clearly signifies the brutality of the ruling class and its desperate need to assert itself over the others. The dialectics is revealed in the last paragraph where Rachanna is beaten up and none of his friends come to help him.

In the process of trying to resist the police force and the ruling class, we find the labourer is alienated from his own people. Afraid of the capitalist who controls the power structure, the labourers refuse to support their own friend and watch his ordeal silently.

The ruling class believes in complete annihilation of those who protest or refuse to comply with its wishes. The silence of his fellow workers while Rachanna is being beaten up shows their submission to authority.

Campaign: Non-Acceptance, Rejection

Moorthy being a 'Gandhi man' decides to begin a "Don't-touch-the-Government" campaign. His decision to begin this campaign signifies his refusal to accept the society as it is. It is a sign of protest of a human being who seeks to establish his identity through such an action. The protagonist, through the campaign, shows his unwillingness to yield to apparently overwhelming forces. There is only one choice before him and that is to clear his way by renewed action.

SECTION 7

Moorthy holds himself responsible for violence which took place at the Estate and decides to go on a fast for three days in the temple. He begins his fast by reciting the 'gayathri-mantra.' Rangamma and the others persuade him not to give up food but they fail. So deep is the influence of Gandhian ideology that he firmly decides to follow it. A kind of peace permeates his being as he sings the bhajans of Kabir.

While he is meditating he remembers his childhood days when he had a vision of Hari. As a child he had a deep faith in God and had asked his mother to throw him down the mountains, confident that Hari would save him from all dangers. Once, during the floods he prayed to Himavathy as a result of which the waters had abated. Ratna comes to see him and he asks her to pray. The realization that he had once thought of her as any thing but a sister, shocks and mortifies him. Moorthy's refusal to eat makes him weak. He tells Rangamma that only by giving up hatred can one become stronger and it is only through love that one can convert the enemy.

The next day he feels weaker and Bhatta mocks at him alleging that he is pretending to be pious.

On the third day he feels very light, his eyes grow dim and his entire body begins reacting to the surroundings. Ratna and Rangamma take care of him. As the evening draws nearer Moorthy asks for bhajans to be recited. Very few brahmins come for the bhajans. Next morning he breaks the fast, 'feeling lighter in limb and soul' and then he walks out to preach the 'don't-touch-the-Government' campaign.

CRITICAL ANALYSIS

Fasting: Repentance and Salvation

Moorthy's decision to fast signifies his desire for repentance and salvation. He holds himself responsible for the violent confrontation which took place between the coolies and Badè Khan. The people of the village react variously to his fast, thus revealing the opposition which constitutes their being. The people like Rangamma and Ratna persuade him to give up the idea for it would make him weak. Whereas Venkamma and Bhatta's attitude signifies their mockery and hostility, Venkamma's statement expresses her contempt: "Ah, the cat has begun to take to asceticism . . . only to commit more sins. Hè, son! when did you begin to lie to your neighbours? As though it were not enough to have polluted our village with your pariahs! Now you want to pollute us with your gilded purity! Wait! Wait! When you come out of this counting of beads, I shall give you a fine welcome with my broomstick." (91)

Moorthy says: "The fault of others, Rangamma, is the fruit of one's own disharmony." (90) Here we find a situation of conflict, guilt, dissatisfaction and disharmony. Moorthy is suffering from an acute sense of guilt and he feels that the violence committed by others has been due to his own state of disharmony. 'Disharmony' here suggests the protagonist's sense of loss and failure. It also reveals the *ètre* between what the people want and what they get from life. 'Disharmony' makes the protagonist realize the bitter truth that nothing is in accord with his being. It also reveals Venkamma's growing unease at the changes taking place in the village. Moorthy's free mixing with the pariahs has made him unholy in the eyes of Venkamma. Her reaction to Moorthy's fasting reveals her own sense of insecurity. She is dissatisfied with those who seek change and therefore cannot help but condemn them.

To Moorthy 'fasting' is the only means of purifying his body, mind and soul. 'Fasting' signifies his desire for purification and repentance. Through 'prayer' and 'meditation' he wishes to give up hatred and thus redeem himself. 'Fasting' as a tool becomes necessary, for without it Moorthy is unable to get rid of extreme distress and restlessness. It appears as a means of ordering his thoughts:

> "I shall love even my enemies. The Mahatma says we should love even our enemies," and closing his eyes tighter, he slips back "into the foldless sheath of the Soul, and sends out rays of love to the east, rays of love to the west, rays of love to the north, rays of love to the south." (92)

Moorthy is deeply influenced by the Gandhian philosophy. Gandhi symbolises a permanent source of love and non-violence. 'Fasting' signifies a restraint in diet as also a restraint in thought and speech. He feels as if his entire being is transformed, his repeating the words, "Sivoham, Sivoham. I am Siva. I am Siva. Siva am I," (92) gives him strength. "I am the Absolute," an expression of total non-dualism, and later on 'vision of Hari' while he is meditating and the reminiscences of the past 'visions' collectively signify the inward communion with God which is what he is seeking.

Ratna: Feminity and Distance

As we examine the situation in progression we discover Moorthy and Ratna are deeply attached to each other. Meditation and fasting make him realize the final truth that love should not be restricted to physical relationship only:

> Her smile did not seem to touch his heart with delicate satisfaction as it did before. She seemed something so feminine and soft and distant, and the idea that he could ever think of her other than as a sister shocked him and sent a shiver down his spine. (94-95)

Moorthy while meditating reflects over the man-woman relationships. Moorthy's analysing his contingence and his attempt to think of Ratna as a sister signifies his refusal to possess or be possessed by any one. He consciously tries to assert his supremacy over his unconscious desires.

A. Prayer: Purification; B. Prayer: Prostration

While correlating the signifying ensemble A and B, we can see what prayer means to two different individuals:

A. "Pray with me that the sins of others may be purified with our prayers" (95) says Moorthy.

B. "She could hardly grasp his idea. She was but fifteen. Praying seemed merely to fall flat before the gods in worship. So she said she would make ten more prostrations before the gods." (95)

The comparison between A and B suggests what 'prayer' as a complete signifier means to Moorthy. To him it is a way of seeking communion with the divine. It is an evocation of that divinity within his heart which would enable him to love even his enemies.

Though 'prayer' seems a powerful tool to Ratna, the difference lies in the objectives and understanding. Prostrating before the Gods is the only way of praying to her. As we examine the proposition in extension we find that Ratna's prayers are for Moorthy. She prays for his welfare as her world revolves around him.

> "God, God," she said, "keep him strong and virtuous, and may he rise out of this holier and greater; God, I shall offer ten coconuts and a kumkum worship. God, keep him alive for me." Then she rose and fell prostrate before the gods in the sanctum. (98)

The above ensemble on one level signifies her unconscious desire to be possessed by him; on another level, it signifies her love and complete devotion to Moorthy. Her utter simplicity is reflected as she prostrates before the Gods.

SECTION 8

The first person Moorthy goes to see is Rangè Gowda. Moorthy seeks his help saying that the number of brahmins attending the bhajans is getting fewer day by day, for the fear of ex-communication has gripped them. Waterfall Venkamma, Temple Rangappa, Patwari Nanjundia, school Master Devaryya and Bhatta are the ones showing disinterest. Rangè Gowda prefers being with the Mahatma and he thinks that the laws of God are the same for all. Moorthy talks to Rangè Gowda about the formation of the Congress group in Kanthapura. One would have to pay four annas, or two thousand yards of yarn per year to become a Congress member. The only condition would be that he must promise to speak the truth and wear nothing but Khadi cloth. It is difficult to get Rangè Gowda's consent for he feels that without being beaten, the pariahs do not agree to work.

Moorthy tries to convince him by saying that he is an esteemed elder of the community and if he followed the ways of the Congress, the others too would follow him. Finally Rangè Gowda agrees to do what Moorthy says. Then Moorthy goes to the Weavers' Street and the Potters' Street. The elders are ready to be with the Patel and the Panchayat.

Moorthy rushes towards the pariah quarters to see Rachanna. Rachanna's wife greets him and he enters the house rather hesitatingly. He can smell the 'stench of hide and pickled pigs.' She offers him a cup of milk. Moorthy takes a sip and puts it aside. The news of Moorthy's arrival to a pariah quarter spreads fast and soon all the women of that quarter come to greet him. His attempts to make them promise that they would spin everyday are to no avail. Rachanna's wife says she would spin only if her husband asks her to do so. Moorthy, feeling desperate, leaves the place and on entering the temple seeks the blessings of the Goddess and then goes to talk to Rangamma.

As he is going up the steps, he remembers his having gone to the pariah-home and the tumbler of milk, so he calls out for

Rangamma from outside. He goes to the backyard and after having a bath purifies himself with the Ganges water.

In the evening he goes to the pariah-night-school and talks to Seenu about the formation of the Congress Committee. Finally, Moorthy is successful in influencing the Pariahs, the Potters and the Weavers. Rangamma and Ratna too, along with Seethamma, welcome the idea of the Congress Committee.

The next evening, bhajans are recited and vows are made. Moorthy is declared the 'Gandhi of Kanthapura.' The Congress Panchayat is formed. While Moorthy is made its President, Rangè Gowda, Rangamma, Rachanna and Seemu are the other members of the Committee.

Two days later, a list of twenty-three members is made by Moorthy and sent to the provincial Congress committee. Moorthy's photograph in Rangamma's 'blue paper' fills the people with pride and they agree to work for him. Soon they are all spinning bundles of yarn and making the saris, bodice cloth and dhoties for themselves. Moorthy tells them that the Mahatma is pleased and people wish that he would remember and commend their efforts.

CRITICAL ANALYSIS

Moorthy: Brahmin: Superiority
Moorthy: Gandhian Ideology

The problematics here is that Moorthy, despite being an ardent follower of Gandhi, is acutely aware of his superiority. Being a brahmin, he is in a state of confusion and indecision, when Rachanna's wife invites him to sit down. He had never before entered a pariah's house. The following ensemble signifies his mental state:

> and Moorthy, who had never entered a pariah-house—he had always spoken to the pariahs from the gutter-slab—Moorthy thinks this is something new, and with one foot to the back and one foot to the fore, he stands trembling and undecided, and then suddenly hurries up the steps and crosses the threshold and squats on the earthen floor. (104)

The conflict goes on in the mind of the protagonist whether he should enter the house or not. His entering the hut is a sign of his boldness. Though he has entered the house he is unable to get over the feelings of dirt and filth with which the brahmins tend to associate the pariahs.

> But Rachanna's wife quickly sweeps a corner, and spreads for him a wattle mat, but Moorthy, confused, blurts out "No, no, no, no," and he looks this side and that and thinks surely there is a carcass in the back yard, and it's surely being skinned, and he smells the stench of hide and the stench of pickled pigs, and the roof seems to shake, and all the gods and all the manes of heaven seem to cry out against him, and his hands steal mechanically to the holy thread, and holding it, he feels he would like to say, "Hari-Om, Hari-Om." (104-5)

All that has been said above signifies the dilemma of the protagonist. It reveals the proposition that his religious brahminical upbringing revolts at the sight of 'carcass being skinned.' (105) The society he has lived in has always looked down upon the pariahs. The caste to which he belongs is the superior one. Therefore the dilemma which he faces while entering a pariah-house is reflected in his actions. It is a strange experience for him.

Holy Thread: Strength and Faith

The 'holy thread' signifies the presence of a guiding force, which brahmins wear to prevent themselves from committing sins. While Moorthy is in a state of confusion and fear, he seeks strength in the holy thread and touches it with his hands. The presence of holy thread signifies the strong religious ethos.

"Hari-om, Hari-om" expresses the strong urge in him to communicate with the divine. "Hari-Om, Hari-Om" (105) as a signifier stands for peace and solace which Moorthy is seeking at that precise moment. According to the Indian religious scripts 'Om' is the first sound which came out when 'Ishwara' or God made his first movement away from himself in order to create the universe.

Milk: Acceptance

The proposition creates stronger conflict in the mind of the protagonist as we see the pariah woman offering him a tumbler of milk. The signifying ensembles like:

> "Accept this from this poor hussy!" (105)
>
> "I've just taken coffee, Lingamma" but she interrupts him and says, "Touch it, Moorthappa, touch it only as though it were offered to the gods and we shall be sanctified"; "and Moorthy, with many a trembling prayer, touches the tumbler and brings it to his lips, and taking one sip, lays it aside." (105)

The above ensembles reveal the two sets of signifiers—pariah: Moorthy and woman: Moorthy. His being a brahmin and then entering a Pariah-home is enough to raise several voices of protest in the entire community. We can see the protagonist going through several phases of indecision, confusion, fear and doubt. His own being realizes the gravity of the situation and for a moment he is unable to decide whether he should accept the offer or not. The dialectics is evident to us as we see the mind of the protagonist undergoing several conflicts. The self has started asking whether what he is doing is right or wrong. His being a brahmin has aggravated the tension in the mind of the protagonist.

The opposition between the pariah woman and Moorthy signifies the struggle going on between the two individuals. It signifies Lingamma's desperate need to be recognized and identified. Her offering him a glass of milk and persuading him to take just a sip expresses her strong need for affiliation. She has been aware of the painful rejection i.e. the pariahs being rejected by the brahmins.

Moorthy's touching the tumbler and bringing it to his lips is a sign of acceptance of one by the other.

Ganges Water: Putrefaction

Moorthy, after he goes back to Rangamma's house, remembers his visit to the pariah-home. His entering the house through the backyard and purifying himself with a 'bath' and 'Ganges water' signify his inability to accept Gandhian ideology in totality. His refusal to change the 'holy thread' reveals his desire to overcome his weaknesses: "Now that I must go there every day, I cannot change my holy thread every day, can I?" (107) We encounter another existential situation as we see Moorthy accepting the 'Ganges water' "and taking the Ganges water he feels a fresher breath flowing through him, and lest anyone should ask about his new adventure, he goes to the riverside after dinner to sit and think and pray. After all a brahmin is a brahmin, sister!" (107)

The 'Ganges water' signifies purity and holiness which Moorthy's soul is seeking. His preaching that all castes are equal, and on the other hand his hesitation while entering a pariah-home, his confusion as he accepts the milk tumbler and later on his act of purification with 'Ganges water' reveal the predicament which has not yet been resolved.

The proposition in comprehension reveals the fact that despite being a 'Gandhi-man' Moorthy is unable to give up the 'samskaras' which are too deep-seated in him. The protagonist, however, realizes that it is this untouchability that separates one man from another and creates an ècart between human beings.

Moorthy's going to the riverside after dinner indicates his desire to escape the queries of the people. It also signifies his quest for freedom, his inner need to purge his heart of the taint of untouchability. The struggle within his heart is metaphysical one. His consciousness makes him aware of *Nèant*, the discrepancies present in the society between a pariah and a brahmin. He is repeatedly drawn into active confrontation between the old "samskaras" and the new ideas. It is this tension between varying attitudes that creates contradictions and conflicts.

SECTION 9

Bhatta decides to increase the rate of interest for every Congress member. He realizes that Moorthy's excommunication has not been able to deter from his Congress business. In fact, Moorthy's sway over the people has increased. He decides to arrange a match for Venkamma's daughter and make her conform to whatever he says. The advocate Seenappa who has just lost his wife seems a suitable match to him. As he makes further plans, he feels elated.

The women at the riverside plan to dress elegantly and sing songs at the wedding of the daughter of Venkamma. Earlier Venkamma had thought she would not invite the widows to her daughter's wedding, but as the marriage day draws closer she compromises on her rigidity and invites all. The women feel that their daughters have not had such good luck as Venkamma's. As the procession comes nearer, they see that the 'advocate groom' is a middle-aged man with 'two fallen teeth and a big twisted moustache.' Venkamma says that he is only twenty-five and had got married at the age of seventeen and his daughter is merely seven. But Bhatta tells them he is about thirty and owns quite a lot of land. Every woman is given a French sovereign each, and "every pariah and cur," in Kanthapura is happy at the grand reception. They now have second thoughts about Venkamma and Bhatta and think that they are not so wicked after all.

Moorthy wanders by the riverside the whole day long. As the evening comes, he goes back to Rangamma's place deeply disturbed. 'How, how is one an outcaste?' he ponders.

CRITICAL ANALYSIS

Wedding: Security and Rejection

The problematics here is that a young girl is married to a man old enough to be her father. The kernel semanteme is the wedding. Bhatta has become so afraid of the changes taking place due to Gandhian influence that he decides to mobilize people like Venkamma towards his side: "I shall find a bridegroom for her daughter, and she will be always with us, and what with her tongue and her tail, she will set fire where we want." (113) This shows that Bhatta suffers from a sense of insecurity. It has intensified as a result of Moorthy's excommunication. Moorthy's holding sway over the people fills him with fear. Venkamma is worried about her daughter's marriage and when Bhatta brings in the proposal of Seenappa, she accepts it joyfully.

The proposition is the wedding of Ranga. Bhatta's devious mind reveals the problematics rather clearly to us. He is thinking of making Venkamma his follower and therefore makes plans for convincing Venkamma:

> After all Venkamma, what does it matter whether it is first marriage or a second marriage? What we ask is that your daughter will have enough to eat, and be blessed with many children, and perform all the rites, isn't it? Seenappa is thirty-four, but you would say he is twenty-one if you saw him, and he has only three children, and one of them is soon to be married and will go away to her mother-in-law's, and your daughter will have the two god-like children to live with. (113)

The contradiction is evident to us as we see a young girl getting married to a middle-aged, widowed brahmin.

Marriage as a complete signifies stands for permanent security and rejection. It also indicates that the girls are considered a burden on the families and parents are keen on getting rid of them as soon as possible. Getting married to a rich man, howsoever old, is regarded fortunate. On one hand we have example of Bhatta and Seenappa who are getting married to girls young enough to be their daughter and on the other, the society looks down upon young widows like Ratna if they transgress the limits of decorum. This hypocrisy reveals the basic set-up of the society which has different norms and rules for the two sexes.

Bhatta's handling the matter reveals his authority over the brahmins. The proposition in extension reveals the reaction of the other women. The following ensembles throw light on the other's reactions:

> "Venkamma's daughter, Ranga, has *at last* found a husband, sister!"—"Where does he come from?" asks Nose-scratching Nanjamma of Satamma.—"Oh, it seems he is from a well-to-do family. May the goddess bless the girl. If not, what should we have seen before we closed our eyes?"—And people say, "Well, Venkamma is going to have a rich son-in-law." (115)

One can see that the settling of the marriages is not based on the merit of the boy or the girl. The caste and material conditions of the boy, irrespective of his age, are the main criteria. Whereas a girl who is soon going to attain puberty 'come home in a few weeks' time,' (113) is considered suitable for marriage.

Ranga's marriage is held in great splendour. The 'French sovereign' signifies the prosperity of the bridegroom's family. In the ensemble, 'every pariah and cur in Kanthapura was satisfied' (117) 'satisfied' signifies the treatment they receive at Venkamma's house during her daughter's wedding. It signifies contentment and bliss. Their being received with warmth at her place makes them accept Venkamma and Bhatta as good individuals: "This Bhatta and Venkamma are not so wicked after all." (117) The above ensemble also signifies their change of attitude.

SECTION 10

Kartik, the festival of lights, is celebrated with real gusto in Kanthapura. The lamps are lit. Kartik, being a month of gods, children wait to see them moving about.

When the Kartik lights fade out, hushed voices of men and women are heard enquiring as to what's wrong. Policemen have come to Rangamma's house and are talking to Moorthy.

Moorthy's arrest creates a furore among the people and they resist the attack being made on them. Finally, seventeen men from different quarters are taken to the police station and after a sound thrashing, all except Moorthy, are released, After he is taken away to Karwar, people pray and fast for his release.

Moorthy refuses to accept the help of advocates. He believes that truth needs no defence. Advocate Sankara who is also the secretary of the Karwar Congress Committee appreciates Moorthy's decision saying that Gandhi too is of the opinion that a true satyagrahi needs no advocates. Sankara leaves the prison promising to hold meetings for Moorthy.

Volunteers dressed in 'Khadi Kurta and Gandhi cap' along with a huge crowd assemble at the Gandhi maidan. Speeches are made by Sankara, Ranganna and Dasappa and they speak about the incorruptible qualities of Moorthy, Hindu-Moslem unity, charka and ahimsa.

A tall man dressed in 'durbar turban and a filigree shawl' speaks in favour of the British government. Being a Swami man, he is more afraid of the corruption wrought by casteism than the disorder in the material world.

Ranganna speaks of the way Swami tried to influence him, and later excommunicated him for opening his temple to the Pariahs. He asks people to choose between Gandhi who had sacrificed his comforts at the altar of the country and the rich exploiting brahmins.

Ranganna is arrested by the police while he is making his speech. He offers himself for arrest amidst cries of 'Vande Mataram' and 'Gandhi Mahatma ki jai.'

The people in Kanthapura read about the meeting and the arrest of Ranganna in the blue paper. They are shocked to know that the government tries to manipulate men like Swami and Bhatta, by offering them financial baits. Ramakrishnayya pacifies them and sends them home.

Besides Rangamma, more and more people start reading the newspaper. Each evening, the villagers listen to Ramakrishnayya's explanation of the 'Vedanta sutras' and discuss the government's activities.

The people going to Karwar bring news of Moorthy. Prayers are offered to Kenchamma for Moorthy's release. One pushya night, Rangamma and Nanjamma get ready to go to Karwar. On being informed that Sankar is looking after Moorthy's affair, Rangamma goes and meets Sankar. Sankar says that the police has alleged that Moorthy had arranged the assault of the pariahs on the police. The decision was still pending.

On her return to the village for corn distribution, Rangamma faces queries from the villagers about Moorthy's welfare. On hearing that the case is still pending they curse the government. The dismissal of Rangè Gowda from Patelship created an uproar in the village.

Rangamma stays at Sankar's place during her next visit to Karwar and helps him in the Congress work. The news of her staying with Sankar reaches Kanthapura and people like Venkamma criticise her vehemently. The others have faith in her as well as Sankar.

Sankar had refused to marry after his wife Usha's death. Sankar lives a simple life. He wears Khadi and speaks the truth and also insists on other villagers to do the same. He never takes up a false case. He takes the lowest fee and if the client is poor, he also pays for his stamps. Sankar works wholeheartedly for the Congress and insists on Hindi becoming the national language of India.

He speaks to his mother too in Hindi, confident that she would learn it one day. He has a 'little closed pot' and, if ever he utters an English word he drops a coin into it. He forces his friends to do the same. He is very active and punctual in his daily routine. Rangamma, too, has never looked so healthy as she is now.

The day Rangamma gave her first speech, she could not go beyond a few words and her eyes were filled with tears. But she is confident that if ever asked to speak again she would have no such fears.

Rangamma returns from Karwar for the Magh Cattle fair and two days later people hear the news of Moorthy being sentenced to three-months's rigorous imprisonment. That afternoon, the people remain inside their homes and fast.

The next day the rain set in, and Ramakrishnayya dies. The Pariahs work and prepare a 'mango pandal' and as the corpse is being tied up, the skies clear and the pyre is lit. Rangamma decides she would carry his bones to Kashi but all of a sudden the river begins to swell and sweeps the bones away. People pray to Kenchamma for protection. Bhatta leaves for a pilgrimage to Kashi soon after the harvest.

CRITICAL ANALYSIS

Arrest: Suppression and Authority

The kernel semanteme lies in the tenth section. Moorthy's arrest along with the seventeen men of Kanthapura reveals the proposition in extension. 'Kartik' signifies light and prosperity.

Moorthy's arrest expresses the desire of the one to dominate the other's existence.

The manner in which people resist the brutal forces suggests the growth of consciousness in the minds of the villagers. Their refusal to accept the authority leads to their arrest. The following ensemble signifies the conflict between men and the Red-man's government:

> and as the morning cattle were going out to the fields, and the women were adorning the thresholds for a Kartik morning, brahmins and pariahs and potters and weavers were marched into the Police Station—seventeen men of Kanthapura were named and locked behind the bars. (124)

This signifies a collective struggle in Kanthapura. People from different castes and sections of society court arrest. The 'bars' signify authority and the confrontation of *ètre* with *autre* i.e. the confrontation of the being with the other. The men of Kanthapura refuse to accept the Red-man's authority and this refusal leads to their imprisonment.

> And the policemen twisted their arms and beat them on their knuckles and spat into their mouths, and when they had slapped and banged and kicked, they let them out one by one, one by one they let them out, and they all marched back to Kanthapura, all but Moorthy. (124)

The signifiers 'twisted,' 'beat,' 'spat,' 'slapped,' 'banged,' 'kicked' signify the atrocities perpetrated on one by the other. They also signify authority and coercion. The arrest of the men is an act of vengeance especially on those who refuse to accept the British authority and disapprove of its existence. Later on, the men are released and their being 'let off' signifies the inability of the other to control the being for long. All but Moorthy are released. Moorthy's imprisonment and later transfer to Karwar signifies the desire of the other to crush the irrepressible being by inflicting a higher degree of violence on him.

Truth: Defence; Refusal: Defence

The proposition in comprehension shows the protagonist facing the atrocities with dauntless courage. The refusal to accept the authority leads to prison. The given ensemble reflects the strength which Moorthy has derived from Gandhi: "But if Truth needs a defence, God Himself would need one, for as the Mahatma says, Truth is God, and I want no soul to come between me and Truth." (126)

Truth: God; Truth: Moorthy

Moorthy's refusal to accept the help of the others, i.e. the advocates, signifies his truthful stance and his aspiration to come closer to God. By refusing to employ a defence, he asserts that truth alone triumphs and that it does not require any external help to vindicate its stand. It also expresses his urgent need to assure himself of his own strength and power.

Gandhi: Truth

'Gandhi' as a cult figure in this section can be seen as an external influence, which disturbs the inner pattern of Moorthy's life. The image of Gandhi is so portrayed that he no more remains a human being but transcends into a mythical figure. Though Moorthy has never met him personally, he has accepted the Gandhian faith and ideology. To him 'Gandhi' signifies the truth. The fact that the Mahatma has often gone to prison is enough to provide him with strength and he prepares himself for further eventualities. 'Gandhi,' as a source of sustenance, is also responsible for changing the thought pattern of Kanthapurians.

Moorthy: Gold; Moorthy: Saint

Moorthy symbolises goodness and perfection. He emerges as a hero who has sacrificed his life for a good cause. 'Why, he is the saint of our village,' (135) says Rangamma and Sankar said, 'Some day he will do holy deeds.' (135) 'I love him like a brother, and I have found no better Gandhist.' (135) Not only the villagers but the hopes of others too are pinned on him.

Brutal police force try to pull him down by levying false charges against him and accusing him of instigating pariah assault on the police. So strong is the people's faith in Moorthy that they refuse to believe the police. Moorthy's refusal to employ an advocate after his arrest shows the faith he has in his own self. The following ensembles reveal his state of mind:

> 'If Truth is one, all men are one before It.' (125)
> 'Between Truth and me none shall come.' (125)
> I shall speak that which Truth prompteth, and Truth needeth no defence.' (125)
> 'Judges are not for Truth, but for Law, and the English are not for the brown skin but for the white, and the Government is not with the people but with the police.' (125)

The following semiotic oppositions emerge: the brown skin: the white, Government: people. The brown skin signifies rejection. The English refuse to accept the brown men and their rules are in favour of the white. 'White' signifies domination and authority. The 'government' which is of the white men signifies repression of the wishes of the others.

'Our Moorthy is like gold—the more you heat it the purer it comes from the crucible.' (136) Moorthy's being compared to gold expresses the confidence which villagers have in him; gold symbolises permanence, purity and malleability. Like gold, Moorthy has accepted the changes taking place in society and yet he retains the old Indian tradition. Moorthy no longer remains an ordinary mortal but attains the heights of perfection. God-fearing women hope that the evil, which is perpetuated by the government, will be destroyed.

Imprisonment: Repression
Fasting: Purification and Negation

Moorthy receives three months's rigorous imprisonment. His 'imprisonment' signifies the desire of one to curb the freedom of the others. The imprisonment is followed by 'fasting.' 'Fasting' as a cultural code stands for purification of the mind and body. The decision of the people to fast is a sign of protest. 'Fasting' becomes a regular phenomenon as the movement gains momentum. It provides the people with necessary strength and a desire to unite and fight against the evil. A sign of purgation, it symbolises to the Hindus a powerful tool of struggle in life.

Rain: Death and Disaster

Ramakrishnayya's death signifies the end of the rich Indian past and the destruction of the good. The 'rains' are a sign of death and disaster. The death of Ramakrishnayya suggests his acceptance of freedom and the end of his struggle with life. It does not, however, kill hope but creates a new awareness in the people.

'Lord, may such be the path of our outgoing Soul.' (146)

The above ensemble expresses the wish of the villagers to meet their end as peacefully as he did.

SECTION 11

After Ramakrishnayya's death, Ratna begins reading the texts and Rangamma explains them with a reference to the British government and the atrocities perpetuated by them on the Indians. Inspired by Rangamma's example, several other women adopt the act of meditation. Yoga exercises lighten their hearts and fill their minds with a deep sense of spirituality.

Rangamma prepares the women folk for action by instilling courage in them. She tells them stories of Rani Lakshmi Bai who had valiantly fought against the British. Unlike Sarojini Naidu, Kamaladevi and Annie Besant who have joined hands with the Congress in this struggle for freedom, the thinking of the women of Kanthapura is limited to 'broomstick and the milking of cows.' The Sevika Sangha is formed in Kanthapura. Their workers are called the Sevis.

The men in the village resent women's joining the volunteer's corps. They beat their wives if they neglect domestic work. Rangamma after having talked to the men tells the women that their first duty is towards their home and husband. But nevertheless they decide to go picketing at cigarette and toddy shops. Not only the women but the children too are so fascinated with Lakshmi Bai's legend that they play her role with great fervour.

As Rangamma prepares the women to face the police, Nanjamma becomes so fear-stricken that even in her dreams she sees herself being attacked by Badè Khan. Rangamma says that once they are willing to face all atrocities for the sake of Kenchamma, the lathis that would strike them would be as 'soft as butter.' Venkatalakshmi's query whether Moorthy would be there or not reveals the simple faith and trust which these women have bestowed on him.

Seenu and Vasudev tell Rangamma that after the arrest of Moorthy the young men at pariah-school are refusing to come forward. They are afraid of the prison and police brutality. Vasudev and others decide to hold bhajans once again. Men, women and children rush towards the temple as they hear the conch blowing. Their hearts are filled with religious sentiments.

CRITICAL ANALYSIS

Change: Tradition

There is a reversal of the traditional role as we find women interpreting the holy scriptures. After the death of Ramakrishnayya, which signifies the complications in religious life of the people, there is a great change in Kanthapura. Women like Ratna and Rangamma have taken up the task of reading and explaining the Vedantic texts. This change in the society which has been brought about by the women is widely acclaimed. We find the women of Kanthapura no longer clinging to the images of Moorthy and Gandhi. The proposition in extension reveals to us the fact that the women are deriving strength from a past historical figure like Lakshmi Bai and the present cult figures like Kamaladevi and Annie Besant. Rangamma's attempt to identify herself with them is a highly connotative sign expressing her desire to be like them. Rangamma's presence acts as a vital force in the eleventh section for it has brought forth the participation of the women in the struggle.

Sevika Sangha: Collectivity

The formation of Sevika Sangha in Kanthapura signifies the need for action. It has created a new consciousness among the women. They no longer remain confined to their homes but the new ideas and thoughts seem to have enlivened their spirits. They become aware of what they are and what they want to be.

'Meditation' as a complete signifier is a significant spiritual code. It not only stands for self-control but it is also a powerful motivating force which goads them to action.

The 'Sevika Sangha' as a complete signifier stands for unity and collective action. It reveals their desire to strip away the old order and replace it with a new one. Its formation gives rise to several conflicts at home. Satamma's husband complains that his wife is not serving him meals on time. Rangamma's ability to influence the men signifies her strength. A new light of responsibility and services dawns upon them and they refuse to accept their secondary status any more. Their lives now take a new dimension. Their practising the yoga, meditation, and forming a Sevika Sangha are codes of actions which determine the growth of their thought processes. They feel that a great change has come over them. Rangamma's statement: "We should do our duty. If not, it is no use belonging to the Gandhi-group," (152) not only signifies the importance of Gandhian ideology but also attributes the difference in roles between the men and women. The women's statement, "We shall not forget our children and our husbands," (152) is an indicator of the fact that a woman's first duty is towards her husband and children and that each collective action should start from home.

"But how can we be like we used to be?" (152) reveals their existential predicament. It expresses their refusal to go back to the state they came from. What is happening to them at present is a highly complex change. Their husbands initially resent their active participation and preparation for struggle. But they relent when they see the enthusiasm of their women to reassert their identity for the national cause. Not only do the women decide on a further course of action but also prepare themselves for it.

Gita Karmayoga; Exercises: Preparing for Struggle

The *Gita* as a complete signifier not only stands for eternity but it also appears as a most significant tool in the hands of women. Through its sayings Rangamma instils courage in the women and dispels the fear which has gripped them. 'Exercises' as a complete signifier signify the need to be ready for the worse.

The proposition in comprehension shows the way women agree to fight against the police force. "Does not the Gita say, the sword can split asunder the body, but never the soul? And if we say, we shall not move a hair, we shall not move a hair." (153)

Rangamma's determination, her courage and her seriousness towards the entire movement have made her a pivotal figure. The *Gita* to her remains an infallible guide of conduct. Not only does the reference to *Gita* reveal the strong Hindu religious ethos but it also brings out the revelation that life, as a permanent phenomenon, resides in the soul. It is significant of the Hindu mythology which claims that 'Atma' is soul and is an eternal entity.

Gita as a mantic code not only leads us to the unknown but is an assimilation of the 'Karma Yoga' and 'Nishkam Karma.' It signifies that man must work hard for in 'Karma' lies the true essence of manhood. Both 'split' and 'move' are two contradictory forces. Rangamma quotes from *Gita* and interprets it by saying that though the body can be destroyed permanently by means of a sword, soul cannot be. 'Sword' as a mantic code is not only a sign of destruction but also that of violence. Her saying, 'we shall not move a hair,' signifies her indomitable spirit and convinces us of her deep involvement in the entire struggle. Here the most abstruse aspect of non-duality has been dealt with.

Lathi: Force; Moorthy: Home

Religion plays a vital role in bringing the women together and fighting jointly for a cause. The 'lathi' which contains the kernel semanteme has two conceptual oppositions. On one hand, it is a symbol of sheer brutality and force and on the other, it stands for resistance. The fear of the 'lathi' has deterred the women from action. The following ensemble elicits, reveals and develops the change in their attitudes.

> Well, we shall fight the police for Kenchamma's sake, and if the rapture of devotion is in you, the lathi will grow as soft as butter and as supple as a silken thread and you will hymn out the name of the Mahatma. (154)

Moorthy, the protagonist, though physically absent from the place is still a source of inspiration to the women. They hope that his presence would not only guide them but also guard them against all dangers. The predicament is completely exposed as Venkatalakshmi says: "But, sister, there will be Moorthy, too, and he will defend us." (154) The protagonist has receded into background after his arrest, yet, the fight which he initiated has not ended with his arrest. 'But Rangamma merely waves her hand and says, "We shall see, we shall see." (154) This constitutes a codified ensemble; it reveals her uncertain state of mind.

SECTION 12

Vaisakh is a period of ploughing the fields. Priest Rangappa determines the auspicious day for the people to yoke their bulls to the plough. Chenna informs the people about it by beating a drum. All the villagers have come to the temple to seek Kenchamma's blessings. Patel Rangè Gowda's presence is highly significant for then only begins the ceremony. Subba Gowda's bulls are the youngest and therefore tied to the yoke. Amidst the chanting of hymns and the breaking of coconuts, 'the plough cuts the earth.' The people feel happy and excited at the prospect that they would now till the earth.

The people ask for Kenchamma's blessings so that when Moorthy comes the crop would be ready. Elaborate plans are made to welcome Moorthy. The same afternoon, postmaster Subbayya informs Rangamma that Moorthy has been released.

Venkamma fixes up her daughter's wedding for Tuesday, the day of Moorthy's arrival. She asks women to choose between the two—a brahminic feast and a feast for Moorthy who has been ex-communicated. Women finally decide to go and bless the newly weds, afraid that if they tarried now, their own daughters might go unblessed in future.

Except for the brahmin women who go to Venkamma's house for the marriage ceremony, the rest of them gladly await Moorthy's arrival. The Pariah's the Potter's and the Weaver's quarters are decorated to welcome him. Seenu informs the people that Moorthy has already come and is in Rangamma's house.

People feel that they have been tricked wickedly and amidst cries of 'Vande Mataram,' 'Mahatma Gandhi ki Jai,' they voice their anguish. The police inspector's voice fails to pacify them. Finally Rangamma's plea calms them down and they leave for their respective homes. Moorthy is not allowed go out of Rangamma's house unless the marriage dinner at Venkamma's place is over. At midnight, the policemen leave the place. The younger Badè Khan has joined the elder one and he settles in the Estate too, in a hut with a woman. The next morning, people see Moorthy as unchanged as ever. His stay in the prison had hardly left any mark on him.

CRITICAL ANALYSIS

Soon after the rains have set in, worshipping of the bulls and the ploughing of fields take place amidst prayers. The offering of flowers, rice and coconuts to the Goddess signifies the Indian religious ethos. Such rituals signify the strong desire to come together by cutting off all barriers of caste and creed. The rituals held before the actual ploughing of the field signify a strong socio-religious code.

Wedding: An Attempt to Undermine the Other's Presence

The kernel semanteme is the 'wedding.' Venkamma's arranging her daughter's wedding on the same day when Moorthy is being released presents a conflicting situation. The women who have been anxiously waiting for Moorthy's arrival are placed in an extremely delicate situation. Venkamma's goading them to a decision is revealed in the following ensemble: "Well, choose between a brahminic feast and a feast for a polluted pig." (164) There lies an opposition between the two feasts. 'A brahminic feast' signifies a feast which is religious and sacrosanct in nature. The brahminic feast is held in honour of Venkamma's daughter's wedding, a very auspicious occasion. The 'feast for a polluted pig' signifies the holding of a grand welcome for a man who has been disgraced and is an outcaste. This decision of Venkamma to hold her daughter's wedding on the day of Moorthy's arrival expresses the jealousy and hatred which permeates her being. She has noticed people gladly awaiting his arrival. Unable to bear this, she connives with priest Rangappa and makes an attempt to ignore his arrival. She tries to impose limits on the freedom of others. Her psyche reveals the presence of being unable to bear the existence of the other.

Excommunication: Rejection

The brahmin women had forgotten all about Moorthy's being ex-communicated. "Why, of course, Moorthy was excommunicated, but how funny that we forgot all about it since he's been in prison!" (164)

Moorthy's excommunication is that socio-religious code which makes him an outcaste in his own society. The women had forgotten about it but Venkamma's painful reminder stirs their memory. Venkamma says: "That's it sister. You forget it. But this stomach that has borne eight children cannot forget it. If you had a daughter to marry, you would not forget it, would you?" (164) A significant conclusion which one can draw from her statement is that the existing circumstances have influenced her behaviour. Her resorting to vindictiveness suggests her selfish, monocentric obsession with her family's welfare at the cost of the village. One would not blame her totally for resorting to such means. Her acute sense of jealousy and inability to understand the necessity of being with and helping others goads her into action.

Nuptial Feast: Acceptance

Keeping the importance of the occasion in mind the brahmin women decide to attend the 'nuptial feast.' They have been placed in a conflicting situation, i.e., on one hand is their desire to go and welcome Moorthy, on the other is the solemn wedding. They feel that their presence is essential at the wedding for their absence would not only be inauspicious but would have graver consequences.

> "Why, you cannot refuse a nuptial feast. If there's no married woman to offer kumkum water to the wife and husband, well, to-

> morrow you may have your own daughter's marriage, and she may go unblessed." And they all say, "Of course! Of course!" (165)

The realities of the socio-cultural situation in which they have been placed, cannot be ignored, and therefore they accept the invitation of the wedding of the daughter of Venkamma.

The acceptance of the 'nuptial feast' against their wishes signifies the stronger bonds of communal feeling and deep religiosity which binds the people of the same community to one other. Knowing that refusal of the feast would not only be an act of sacrilege but also the repercussions would affect their own daughter's future, they accept it. Thus one sees that their existence has been controlled by greater traditional forces.

Moorthy's Confinement:
Fear and Doubt in the Mind of the Other

Moorthy's presence has horrified the other. Therefore, he is confined to Rangamma's house until the nuptial dinner is over at Venkamma's place. His confinement signifies the fear of rejection in the heart of the other i.e. Venkamma. Venkamma prefers to hold on to the old values. The two individuals are diametrically opposed to each other. On one side is Moorthy who transcends the limits of his Being and remains unchanged despite being in prison. (The author here has tried to project a conceptual contrast between the desire of the individuals). On the other side is Venkamma whose actions are motivated by petty hopes of accumulation of wealth, arranging of sons-in-law and complete annihilation of the forces which impede her progress. The disparity between the two not only reveals the differences in ideas but also in motives. In Venkamma we see the presence of the other who tries to find external justifications for the inner confusions, and therefore chooses to act in a self-centred way.

SECTION 13

Moorthy asks the people to come together and fight against the government. He informs the villagers that Gandhi has gone on a long pilgrimage with his eighty-two followers who wear Khadi and are teetotallers. Moorthy decides to pray collectively for Gandhi's success. He speaks to them of the oneness of being and asks them to be ready for action.

Moorthy tells the people about Gandhi and from the white paper he reads out the news of Gandhi's actions. Youngmen from the city visit Moorthy and after their departure Moorthy asks Seenu to ring the gong for the bhajan. He informs the villagers about the number of Patels who have resigned from their jobs and have become followers of Gandhi. Gandhi's Dandi march has created excitement in the hearts of the people. As the day draws nearer, they become more anxious. Unable to sleep at night they come to the riverside early in the morning and bathe. Priest Rangappa laughs at them and they know that he too, like Bhatta, is no more with them. After a wash they sit and meditate and later have special meals. Through white papers the next day, they are informed of Gandhi's success in manufacturing salt. More and more people begin coming to the seaside to make salt. They are beaten up and put into prison; yet the number of people who are joining the ranks of the Mahatma increases day by day.

People in Kanthapura become fearless and prepare themselves for action. Moorthy is waiting for the orders to come from the Karwar congress committee. Women begin practising the drills more often and are now less afraid of Badè Khan's lathi. Faith in the Mahatma has made them courageous. Nanjamma compares Mahatma to 'Sahyadri Mountains' whereas the people following him are the 'pilgrims of the Mountain. Moorthy is called 'The Small Mountain. The section ends on a note of hope where the people are still waiting for the call of 'The Big Mountain' (Mahatma).

CRITICAL ANALYSIS

The kernel situation in the given section expresses the hope, the fear, the anguish and the strength of the people of Kanthapura. Moorthy after having realized that a man could not succeed in attaining freedom alone asks the people to flight collectively against the oppressive forces. The following ensemble reveals the existential situation:

> A cock does not make a morning, nor a single man a revolution, but we'll build a thousand-pillared temple, a temple more firm than that hath yet been builded, and each one of you be ye pillars in it, and when the temple is built, stone by stone, and man by man, and the bell hung to the roof and the Eagle-tower shaped and planted, we shall invoke the Mother to reside with us in dream and in life. India then will live in a temple of our making. (170)

Realizing that the struggle could not be successful without coordination among the people, Moorthy tries to bring the people closer to each other. The signifying ensemble, 'the temple of our making,' reveals that the protagonist has a strong desire to be free within him. 'The temple' as a complete signifier stands for a holy place. It signifies the country which will be built and ruled by Indians. The possibility of being left alone is necessarily the most serious threat to Moorthy's existence. He therefore, asks people to unite and play for Gandhi's success.

Pilgrimage: Defiance and Rejection
Gandhi: Strength, Hope; Mahatma: Hope

Gandhi's pilgrimage to the Dandi beach signifies an act of defiance. Breaking the salt law is a symbolic act of protest. The people are anxiously waiting for Gandhi to realize his mission. The anxiety, the hope and the concern which the men and women of Kanthapura show towards Gandhi signifies not only their love but also their faith in him. The signifying ensembles reveal their state of minds and the faith they have bestowed on Gandhi:

> Oh no, the Mahatma need not go as far as the sea. Like Harishchandra before he finished his vow, the gods will come down and dissolve his vow, and the Britishers will leave India, and we shall be free, and we shall pay less taxes, and there will be no policemen. (172)

> It is not for nothing the Mahatma is a Mahatma and he would not be Mahatma if the gods were not with him. (172-73)

'Mahatma' as a complete signifier signifies indomitable courage and goodness. The faith which people have placed in him has made him a 'Mahatma'; an epitome of kindness and strength. People of Kanthapura realize the truth that Gandhi's guidance and perseverance alone could resolve their predicament.

'He says he likes our ancient ways, and like the ancients he will make the pilgrimage on foot.' (173) The proposition in comprehension shows that the figure of 'Gandhi' is a source of sustenance and he seems to have permeated their conscious selves. For in the figure of Gandhi it is not simply one individual protesting against the atrocities but we see even the simple illiterate people of Kanthapura identifying themselves with him. They are people living in a particular time-period, facing similar problems. As individuals, they may have different problems but seen from a broader perspective the most crucial situation they have been placed in is the same. All are living under British regime and undergoing suppression, estrangement and depression.

Britishers: We

The 'Britishers' in the present context signifies authority, wealth, domination and assertion. 'We' signifies the Indians who are working as slaves under the British regime and who stand for subservience, obedience and suffering.

It is their social being, their lives as slaves, which has awakened or rather determined their consciousness. They are hopeful that under the influence of Gandhi things would soon change. Rangamma's hopes are visible in the ensemble: 'Britishers will leave India, and we shall be free, and we shall pay less taxes, and there will be no policemen.' (172)

Her simple statement reveals her inner self where despite undergoing constant conflicts engendered by a specific historical situation, she still has faith in Gandhi. The Britishers signify the presence of the other—the other to whom the Indians have begun reacting violently.

Dore: Disillusionment and Loss of Hope

Dore's disillusionment is significant of the fact that he is not completely satisfied with the things as they are. There is a shift from an earlier enthusiastic stance to that of indifference beneath which lies the loss of hope. The following ensemble signifies the contingence of the character: "This is all *Ramayana* and *Mahabharata*; such things never happen in our times." (172) He has however, begun realizing that even after the attainment of freedom, life would not be happy. Rangamma's earlier statement that things would change soon has not been able to instil hope within his heart. His statement, 'I do not know,' signifies that he is in a constant state of uncertainty and despair. Dissatisfied with the situation he reflects on the ècart between the past, present and the future.

Salt: Defiance, Rejection, Independencc

Gandhi's success at the Dandi beach is a sign of protest. By breaking the salt law, not only is he able to voice his protest but he also successfully receives the support of his countrymen. The people in Kanthapura have become enthusiastic. Though the villagers have never confronted him personally, he has become the most potential force in their lives. The following ensemble reveals the success of the pilgrimage:

> And so day after day men go out to the sea to make salt, and day after day men are beaten back and put into prison, and yet village after village sends its women and men, and village after village grows empty, for the call of the Mahatma had sung in their hearts, and they were for the Mahatma and not for the Government. (175)

The code of action ranges from "go" to "make salt," "beaten back," "put into," "sends," "grows empty" to "had sung." The above ensemble carefully reveals the reaction of the people. They prepare themselves for the struggle and this preparation is political code which denotes their desire to fight for and claim their freedom. The women begin practising "the drill" and Rangamma is seen emerging as their leader. This awareness of the lack of freedom and constant suppression under British regime not only fills the women with a desire to struggle but also to reject the authority.

Gandhi: Sahyadri: Big Mountain
Moorthy: Small Mountain
People: Pilgrims of the Mountain

The 'call' is a potential signal for which the people are waiting anxiously. Gandhi to them stands for strength, firmness and stoicism. His being compared to Sahyadri is a cultural code: "No, sister, I do not imagine the Mahatma like a man or a god, but like the Sahyadri Mountains, blue, high, wide, and the rock of the evening that catches the light of the setting sun." (176) The narrator's comment reveals the same idea: "That's what he is. High and yet seeable, firm and yet blue with dusk." (176) Moorthy's being called "the Small Mountain" signifies the presence of source which derives its strength from a bigger source. The people of Kanthapura are strongly convinced that the 'Big Mountain' and the 'Small Mountain' are there to 'protect' them. This faith signifies their strong instinct for self-preservation. The presence of Gandhi and Moorthy not only provides them with strength but also makes them ready for action.

The 'Call' as a Code of Worth

Their waiting for the 'call' expresses their intense longing to struggle for and seek liberation. The predicament reveals to us the fact that after having realized the cause of their alienation, all the villagers are making a sustained effort to resolve the problems of their existence i.e. refusal to be treated as mere objects before the eye of the other. They wish to bring an end to the life of enslavement under the foreign rule which prevents them from realizing their lost identity.

Calling themselves 'pilgrims,' they associate themselves with Gandhi and Moorthy. Under the guidance and leadership of the two, they hope to attain freedom. Strong sustained optimism not only minimises their fear but also makes them reject the British authority.

SECTION 14

The people do not receive any call for action. The news of Mahatma's arrest creates a furore in the village. The villagers decide to fast and hold bhajans that evening. Men like Vasudev, from the Estate join hands with the people of Kanthapura. Moorthy asks them to begin the "Don't-touch-the-Government campaign" which includes picketing the toddy booths, establishment of parallel government, appointment of Rangè Gowda as Patel, and refusal to pay revenue dues to anyone but him. People's eyes are filled with tears for never before has any Harikatha touched them so deeply.

Two days later, women march on towards Boranna's toddy grove signing songs. One hundred and thirty nine men and women under the guidance of Moorthy refuse to bow down before the police and march forward amidst cries of 'Mahatma Gandhi ki jai.'

The police showers lathis on Pariah Rachanna as he runs to climb a toddy tree. The people remain undeterred by the blows falling on them. Finally the women are left on the roads looking for their husbands and children. Later, they are all taken to the Santur police outpost.

Pariah Rachanna, Lingayya and potter Siddayya are held while the rest are released. Left in the middle of the jungle, the women become scared and Rangamma pacifies them and asks them to march forward, singing. The cartmen agree to take them to Santhapura. They sleep in each other's arms on their way to Santhapura, where Rangamma's cousin gives them a warm welcome. With Imam Khan as their guide, they reach Kanthapura and feel as if they have returned from a pilgrimage.

The next morning, the women are filled with a sense of achievement. They plant their trophies, five twigs of toddy trees and a toddy pot before the temple. Venkamma remains as unrelenting as ever. Her mocking overtones, however, do not dampen their enthusiasm.

CRITICAL ANALYSIS

The kernel situation lies in the picketing scene which takes place at Boranna's toddy grove. "Don't-touch-the-Government" campaign is a political code of protest. Mahatma Gandhi's 'arrest' is the kernel semanteme around which the entire action of the people revolves. The people have decided to disobey the rules of the government. The following ensemble reveals the inner state of the mind of the protagonist Moorthy:

> Brothers and sisters, remember we are not out to fight the white man or the white man's slaves, the Police and the Revenue officials, but against the demoniac corruption that has entered their hearts, and the purer we are the greater will be our victory, for the victory we seek is the victory of the heart. Send out love where there is hatred, and a smile against brute force like unto the waters of the Himavathy that spread over boulder and sand and crematorium earth. (180-81)

'White man' signifies corruption and hatred. Moorthy asks the Indians to struggle and fight against hatred and win the heart of the other i.e. the British government through love. Moorthy propagates Gandhi's doctrine of 'revolution through change of heart.'

Moorthy, along with the villagers, decides to defy the policies of the government. Their deciding not to pay taxes to anyone but Rangè Gowda and making him the Patel are the significant codes of rebellion which reveal their desire to break away from the shackles of colonialism.

Moorthy: Pebble

Moorthy has become aware of his insecure existence:

> Brothers, remember, too, I am but a pebble among the pebbles of the river, and when the floods come, rock by rock may lie buried under, and yet there are some that stand out pointed and dry, and it is they that give you a hold for your slippery, seeking feet. (180)

'Pebble' as complete signifier not only signifies the insecure existence of Moorthy, but also reveals his sense of nothingness. The signifier 'buries,' in opposition with 'stand,' 'give' and 'hold' signifies the sense of estrangement. As a result of the ensuing struggle against the British, some people would be destroyed forever. The signifier 'buried' signifies the defeat of certain individuals and their passing into oblivion. On the other hand there would be some who would not only 'stand' but also 'give' and 'hold' the others. 'Slippery, seeking feet' signifies the uncertain existence of the others who need perpetual guidance and encouragement. A feeling of nothingness, emptiness, and desolation has made the protagonist, Moorthy, conscious of his temporary existence. His statement, 'my time too will come,' (181) reveals the self being torn between doubts and conflicts. On the other, he, as an individual, can be seen alienated from the rest of the village. His autonomy and existence are always in question. The proposition in comprehension reveals the protagonist as partially divorced from the company of others despite being physically with them.

Moorthy has a differential hierarchy of significance from that of the other people. He realizes that the villagers have put all their trust in him and is uncertain about the retention of this trust. Therefore, he says: "follow the one who follows me, for he is your chief and the Congress has made him your chief." (181)

The 'waters of Himavathy' as a complete signifier stands for purity and the source of sustenance, for not only does it represent the spirit of the lord but it also has the power to erase all the dirt and filth from this earth.

Picketing: Defiance, Rejection

As we see one hundred and thirty nine men, women and children marching toward Boranna's toddy grove, we realize the influence of Gandhi and Moorthy on them. They resist the 'attack' made on them by the police force:

> And we deafen ourselves before the onslaught, and we rush and we crawl, and swaying and bending and crouching and rising, we move on and on, and the lathis rain on us, and the cartmen have come back.

Signifiers 'deafen,' 'rush,' 'crawl,' 'swaying,' 'bending,' 'crawling,' 'rising' and 'rain on us' clearly signify their rejection of the British authority. Picketing Boranna's toddy booth is a major step towards one such rejection. It symbolises their refusal to be dehumanized further. Their 'shrieks' and 'shouts' and 'sobs' juxtaposed with their desire to 'move on' signify the unique predicament of these people. They have been suppressed for too long, and now, they simply refuse to walk back to where they came from. 'Picketing' as a code of action signifies their wish to give up whatever is harmful to their existence.

Trophies: Success, Satisfaction; Venkamma: Insecurity, Fear

Once the women return to Kanthapura they proudly display their trophies. The following ensemble reveals their pleasure and satisfaction that they had achieved: 'The next morning, with bell and camphor and trumpet we planted our trophies before the temple. Five twigs of toddy trees were there, and a toddy pot.' (191)

'Trophies' signify the sense of achievement which filled their hearts. 'We planted our trophies before the temple' (191) is a significant religious code. After having achieved success, the women go to the temple and place their trophies before the lord. A strong socio-religious code, this action of theirs signifies their deep faith in God without which they feel they could not have attained their goal. Their offering the best they could perform, to Kenchamma, expresses their desire to be in perfect communion with the Goddess. It also reveals their wish to solicit the sanction of the divine.

Venkamma's statement reveals her unconscious state of insecurity. She feels that the world, which she is living in, is in a perfect state of disharmony: "Look, look, a toddy god have they made of a Moon-crowned god." (191) Signifiers 'spat' and 'called' signify her predicament. The proposition in comprehension reveals that her hatred, her words full of vengeance express her desire to preserve her own existence. She has been noticing the changes coming over the village and herself, and being unable to identify with the changes, she discovers that she has been alienated from the entire milieu. Her getting into an argument with Rangamma or the others is a necessity, for without an argument she feels she would jeopardize her existence. Each change in society threatens her with a loss of identity and values.

The narrator's statement expresses her sense of satisfaction: 'Yes, yes, sister, we are toddy people!' But we don't marry our daughters to gap-toothed sons-in-law. Nor like Bhatta do we go on Kashi-pilgrimage with toddy contract money. Do we?' (191)

The marriage of Venkamma's daughter to a 'gap-toothed son-in-law' is made fun of. Bhatta's leaving the village on a pilgrimage, after making money, signifies his strong sense of guilt and insecurity which has forced him to leave his home and settle in alien lands. While in the company of the people of Kanthapura, he was painfully becoming aware of the fact that he would be soon rejected by the other. Unable to bear this harsh reality, he tries to escape. His pilgrimage signifies his strong desire to escape, and the inability to face the real world.

Thus, as the sections proceed, one notices the simple village folk becoming aware of their plight. They are devoting themselves whole-heartedly to the cause of freedom. The struggle gains momentum as we see them rejecting the opposing authoritative forces.

SECTION 15

The following Tuesday being a market day in Kanthapura, people get up early and finish their chores. They decide to go picketing toddy shop. On their way, several men and women greet them warmly. This is their first visit to the Coffee Estate and the place seems to have an aura of mystery around it.

As the men coming in carts hear what Moorthy intends to do, they laugh at him. Soon they see maistri coming out of the Estate and following him are the coolies. They are all being marched to Boranna's toddy grove and policemen are walking beside them. Moorthy signals his followers to squat on the ground before the booth.

With the rain, lathi blows too are showered on them. The policemen beat the coolies. Amidst loud cries of "Mahatma Gandhi ki jai" more men are heard arriving. Finally, the coolies join the people too and are beaten up by the policemen. As the women and men of Kanthapura plead with the coolies and ask them not to drink, the coolies promise in the name of Kenchamma that they will not. The 'rain still pours on.'

The last part of the section reveals how, except for Seenu, Vasudev, Rangè Gowda and Nanjamma's husband and Subbu who are taken to prison, the others are turned back home from the promontory. Moorthy is still with the people. Next morning over 'three and thirty' or more coolies leave the Estate and join the pariahs in Kanthapura. People pray to Siva to protect them. More and more people now join hands with the Mahatma.

CRITICAL ANALYSIS

Revenue Collector: Corruption, Cruelty

The existential predicament of the protagonist which makes him so unsure of himself is visible in the beginning of the section itself. The people begin to march on towards the toddy booth with a firm determination. As Moorthy and his followers head towards the Estate, they meet Betel Lakshamma. She asks them whether they are the soldiers of the Mahatma and Moorthy says, "Yes, mother." (192) Her agonising query in the following ensemble, reveals to us the exploitation and the violence inflicted on the common man by the other.

> "Then you'll free us from the Revenue Collector?" (192)
>
> "Why, Raghavayya, the one who takes bribes and beats his wife and sends his servants to beat us." (192)

Raghavayya, the revenue collector, signifies dishonesty and cruelty. His dishonesty manifests itself in his taking bribe from people while his cruelty is seen in his acts of beating his wife and sending his servants to beat the others. His actions signify his desperate need in the changing circumstances to dominate others. His resorting to violence reveals the fact that by no other means could he thus gratify himself. The being of the revenue-collector is manifest in his attitude towards the other.

Moorthy: Indecision, Sense of Failure

Moorthy's inability to offer full support to the suffering individuals like Lakshamma reveals his sense of failure and the realization of it. His "We are against all tyrants" (192) as an answer, in no way, reveals his strength. When Lakshamma says: "Why, then, come to our village, son, and free us from this childless monster," (192-93) here Raghavayya's being called a 'childless monster' not only classifies him as a heartless being but also suggests what he is from within. The given ensembles reflect Moorthy's weakness as an individual. He refuses to fight without the consent of the Congress: "I shall write to the Congress and if they say 'Yes,' I shall come." (193) His source of strength lies not in himself but is derived from the Congress. He seems to be moving in a particular direction where his own individuality would merge itself into a bigger reality i.e. the congress. His statement "we shall see" (134) is a confession of his own weakness to take an independent decision. It is also a confusion since it shows the protagonist being caught in a bog. Moorthy realizes that he is fighting a tough battle and it cannot be fought alone.

The socio-political context plays a vital role in the development of characters. In *Kanthapura*, we see Moorthy's unreflective consciousness moving into the reflective consciousness. One also notices that the historical macrocosm and the individual microcosm are dialectically related i.e. there is a constant interaction between the historical progression of socio-political structures and the life and ideas of Moorthy, the individual.

Coolies: Repression, Fear

The coolies coming out of the Estate and marching towards Boranna's toddy grove reveal the existential predicament of the labour class. Living in a state of terror, repression and constant fear, they have been completely desensitized:

> their faces dark as mops and their blue skin black under the clouded heavens, and perspiration flows down their bodies and their eyes seem fixed to the earth—one coolie and two coolies and three coolies and four and five come out, eyes fixed to the earth, their stomachs black and clammy and bulging, and they march towards the toddy booth; and then suddenly more coolies come out, more and more and more like clogged bulls clattering down the byre steps they come out, and the women come behind them, their

> sari fringes drawn over their faces and their eyes fixed on the earth, and policemen walk beside them, they walk beside the coolies with bulging stomachs and bamboo legs, coolies of the Godaveri banks, and they arc marched on to the toddy booth, to Boranna's toddy booth, to drink and to beat the drum and to clap hands and sing— they go, the coolies, their money tied to their waists and their eyes fixed on the earth. (196-97)

So terror-stricken have they become that their "eyes seem fixed to the earth." This statement and the repetition of the phrase "eyes fixed to the earth" reveals the gravity of the situation. For so long have these coolies, both men and women, been tortured and suppressed by the other i.e. the policemen and the Red-man's government that they have lost all desire to fight and protest against the atrocities perpetrated on them. They do not even possess the strength to look into the 'eyes of the other' for it has nothing but hatred and arrogance in them. The coolies have ceased to exist as human beings not only in the eyes of the other, but, also in their own eyes. Unable to assert their existence over the other they live a life of complete repression. So tired and exhausted has their work and life at the Estate made them that they appear completely dehumanized.

The proposition in extension reveals the alienation of the labour class. Fear, estrangement and ignorance have made the coolies unable to realize their worth. The impact of events at home and on the Estate has decomposed them both physically and mentally. They find they are unable to exert themselves to remedy the situation and modify their existence. A feeling of misery and dissatisfaction makes them feel homeless at work and therefore one sees them seeking satisfaction elsewhere. 'The toddy booth' signifies an escape from reality. It is a place where the collies go to drink, dance and sing and to forget for a while their wretched living hours. It also expresses their desperate need to be themselves. The coolies are being marched to the 'toddy booth' by the policemen. This time they are being compelled to go there. Thus one sees a strong contradiction between what they want and what they are forced to do. There is also an attempt at seeking some sort of relaxation. 'The toddy booth' remains a very complex sign. To the coolies, it is a place where they forget themselves and the drudgery of their work. To the maistri and the Red-men it aims at making the labourers weak, both physically and economically. Their spending the entire money at the booth not only restricts them from going home but also makes them impotent emotionally.

Squatting: Protest; Coolies: Resistance

The proposition in comprehension reveals the consequences of the action taken by Moorthy and his followers. Their squatting before the toddy booth is a most vital form of protest. The people bear the lathi blows and yet remain firm. Amidst cries of 'Vande Mataram' and 'Mahatma Gandhi ki jai' they march forward pleading to the coolies: "Oh, don't go, brother! Don't go, sister!—Oh, don't go, in the name of the Mahatma!" (198) "Do not drink, do not drink, in the name of the Mahatma." (200) Mahatma's name signifies the presence of that potential force which not only enlightens the hearts of men but also guides them in the moment of crisis. The coolies, on having realized the futility of their existence at the Estate, not only fight against the colonial forces but later on, quite a few of them, go and settle with pariahs in Kanthapura. Their taking the pledge not to drink is an act of protest: "By Kenchamma's name, we shall not." (200) We see the coolies exerting their consciousness against this fear of the ruler. Picketing is an event, a major step, which has changed them and made them realize their existence as passive beings on the Estate. The coolies, on having realized that to be something they would have to do something, join the followers of Moorthy and Mahatma against the police force. Picketing as an action not only activates their consciousness but also their thinking. They, therefore, decide to resist the colonial rule.

Their coming and settling in Kanthapura is an essential step towards their rehabilitation as human beings and not mere objects. This choice amounts to a decision to live consciously and struggle against the oppressive forces. They sequester themselves from the Estate in order to be a part of those forces that are trying to reassert themselves against the foreign rule.

Siva: Protection, Faith

The narrator ends the section by telling how the army of Mahatma is increasing in number day by day. Her asking 'Siva' to protect them from peril is a strong sign of faith in the powers of the divine: 'Siva is poison-throated, and yet He is the Three-eyed. May the Three-eyed Siva protect us.' (201) 'Siva' symbolizes the strength and permanence of the divine. It is this faith of the people in the supreme being, this realization of the supreme being i.e. Siva as a boundless space of consciousness. Indian religious ethos thus portrays a resolute will not only to know the truth but also to live up to the vision of truth.

SECTION 16

Gaining inspiration from the people of Kanthapura, the people in Rampur, Siddapur and Maddur too begin picketing their respective toddy booths. People sing songs declaring Mahatma as their king. People in Kanthapura wait anxiously for further action. Fasting has become a regular feature. Chandrayya tells them of his life in prison and the change it has brought about in him. He tells them of the city boy who had hoisted high the national flag and was later taken to a solitary cell and was never seen again. Despite being a brahmin, he ate with the non- brahmins and worked with them.

Seetharammu too narrates the tale of his woe in prison and the way he was ill-treated by the police despite being down with fever. They had to release him after his condition worsened. Moorthy, giving Seetharammu's example, asks people to fight courageously. Soon Boranna, Satanna and Madayya close their toddy shops. The blue paper mentions that 24 shops have been closed in Kanthapura. June tax assessments are likely to bring trouble and the people pray to Kenchamma to protect them.

People refuse to pay the revenue dues despite several threats from the police. The police begins beating the pariah women who protest. Except for a few men like Rangappa who also pays for Bhatta, Venkamma, Agent Nanjundia, postmaster Suryanarayana and shopkeeper Subha Chetty, 'terror stricken Devaru and concubine Chinna,' the others do not pay their taxes. People hide their jewels and rice thinking that the police force would come looking for them. One fine morning they find that all the roads to Kanthapura are barricaded and policemen are surrounding the entire village. A tall white man, the chief, stands with them.

That afternoon, amidst the beating of drums, a new beadle announces the imposition of one rupee and three pice as punitive tax on each man, woman and child above six, if the revenue dues are not paid. Warning is issued that the ones who create trouble for the government will be sent to prison. Rangamma, Ratna and Moorthy go from house to house at night asking the people to be prepared for the fight that will soon begin. People remain awake the whole night and with dawn comes the sleep.

CRITICAL ANALYSIS

Picketing: Non-Acceptance and Protest

Gandhian movement can be seen becoming a mass movement not only in Kanthapura but also in the nearby areas. People are picketing the toddy shops. Picketing is an elaborate action which people resort to in order to obtain a particular result. It appears as a sign of protest and non-acceptance. Here, 'call to the drinkers' (202) is a signal which pronounces the evils of drinking. The following is a statement in extension, defining the need for giving up drinking: "Oh, brothers, in the name of the Mahatma do not drink, for drinking is bad and the Government profits by your vice and the usurer profits by your debt and your wife goes unclothed and your children unfed and never again will you see a hut and hearth." (203) Here 'profits,' 'unclothed' and 'unfed' are significant codes of action which signify the evils of drinking. Thus the dialectical situation can be seen as questioning the old order and further making an effort to create a new one by asking people to give up drinking.

Songs: Collectivity

Singing songs is a symbolic ritual which signifies collectivity. People in their songs voice their protest and dissatisfaction.

They participate in this ritual not as 'individuals' but as a group signifying the coming togetherness of people who have common aspirations:

> The toddy tree is a crooked tree,
> And the toddy milk a scorpion milk,
> And who is it that uses the scorpion milk, sister?
> And who uses the scorpion milk, sister?
> Why, the wandering witches of the marshes, . . .
> O King, O King, why won't you come?" (202)

'Singing songs' is a ritual which signifies the need to commune. In the present context, its aim is to demonstrate the significance of purpose of the entire community. 'Toddy' as a complete signifier not only signifies drinking but also the evils attached to it. Picketing as the most significant code of action is an attempt to effect change in the society which has encouraged drinking. Each day is taken as a day of protest. Fasting too becomes a regular phenomenon.

Prison: Self-Realization

Many people disobey the government's orders and are taken to prison. Prison does not remain a symbol of fear any more but the people begin taking it as an experience. Inside the prison, men like Chandrayya, Seetharammu or the city boy remain undaunted by the brutal police force. This courageous stance instils strength in the people outside the prison. 'Prison' reveals an attempt of the colonialists to suppress the voice of the others. It also signifies their desire to estrange the strong opposing forces from the midst of the people. Men being put inside the prison is an act of seclusion which brings them closer to their own selves. It signifies self-realization of the being. In the worst moment of their existence, protagonists like Seetharammu and Chandrayya are forced to go in search of a justification which the world outside the prison cannot provide. They have now begun making a realistic appraisal of their actions and the liabilities of their personality. One can see them becoming aware of the dynamic potentialities of their existence and constructively developing them with a view to gaining freedom.

Revenue Dues: Refusal: Defiance; Sanctum Bell: Warning

People in Kanthapura refuse to pay the revenue dues and this refusal signifies defiance of the authority. Oppressed and alienated individuals of Kanthapura somehow realize that any reconciliation with the government will simply not be possible. 'But day after day, revenue notices fell yellow into our hands, and we said, "Let them do, what they will, we shall not pay our revenues."' (207) Their refusal to pay the revenue dues signifies the ineffectiveness of the threat. Their not paying heed to what the rulers threatened them with is a silent way of code which inevitably signifies not mere defiance but also voices the discontent, the anger and the rejection of one or the other. Men choose to defy the rules imposed by the government and this defiance is their refusal to accept things as they are under the British regime.

Ringing of the 'sanctum bell' is a codified ritual which not only issues warning to the others but also signifies the people's need to come closer to each other during any moment of crisis. It is also a code of action which prepares people for the struggle. It signifies growing awareness in the hearts of men and therefore reveals a strong desire to resist any kind of oppression.

Barricades: Suppression
White Man: Authority, Absolute Power

The entire village is barricaded one morning. The police force surrounding the village is an act of suppression of the individuals. By not allowing them to move out of the village, the colonial forces try to snap off their contact with the outside forces. An act of complete frustration, it signifies the fear of the Red-man's government and the power to assert itself amidst all odds. The given ensemble show the gravity of the situation: "Stones upon stones were piled on the road and tree upon tree was slain and laid beside them, and canal-banks were dug and the water let through, and thorns were laid where cactuses grew and earth was poured over it all, and one, two, three, four, five, six policemen stood behind them, bayonets and bugles in their hands, and for chief had they a tall white man." (208)

Signifiers 'piled,' 'slain,' 'laid,' 'dug,' 'let,' 'poured' and 'stood' significantly present the proairetic code. This is a code of action which is the outcome of a struggle begun by the others i.e. the Indians. The proposition in comprehension reveals the transfer of power from one to the other. Earlier Badè Khan and other Indians were leading the police force but now the presence of 'white man' as 'chief' shows who the true oppressor is. 'White man' symbolizes absolute power and authority. Barricading the village and levying of punitive tax on the people are attempts of the colonial forces to crush them.

The only quick and subtle effort expended in order to crush the movement is alienation of the defiant forces from the outer world. Indians now present themselves as a threat to Red-man's existence and identity. Therefore, feeling rather insecure amidst the rebellious spirits, the ruling forces attempt to curb their movement.

SECTION 17

The next morning people discover that the coolies who have joined the pariahs in Kanthapura, with their hands and arms tied, are forcibly marched back to the Estate. Except for the 'shrieking and weepings and bellowings' of the pariah women, nothing can be heard. They cry for Moorthy's support. But they also know that he cannot come for he has been arrested at night. Coolies are beaten up badly by the police. Rangappa is one of their victims.

The ones at the promontory could not bear the sight of torture any more and they curse the police. The policemen not only beat the women but also molest them physically. Puttamma becomes a victim of their lust. Seethamma too is beaten up. There is commotion everywhere as the men are nowhere in sight and the policemen resort to violence towards women. The entire village is full of shrieks coming from the Weavers' as well as the Brahmin Street. All their men had been taken away as prisoners while women were fast asleep at night. Amidst sheer confusion, Radhamma gives birth to a baby. Ratna escapes from the clutches of a policeman when the other women come to save her at the right moment. Ratna becomes the leader of the women and under her guidance they take refuge in the temple. Bhatta's house is set on fire by the pariahs.

Just as Ratna rushes to get a blanket from Seetharamma's place for Vedamma, who is down with fever, a policeman sees her. She rushes inside the temple and closer the door. After beating the door for some time, the policeman puts a lock outside and turns the key. The women begin feeling hungry after sometime. They still have hopes that men from other areas would come to free them. As it grows dark they light the camphor and sing Bhajans. Ratna tells them stories of the freedom struggle. Radhamma is protected against the chill by the other women, who stay close to her. They spend the night inside the temple and finally when the door opens they find Rachanna's wife Rachi at the threshold. She, on hearing their screams and moans at night, manages to get the key from the Patel's house. By jumping over Satamma's wall and Temple Rangappa's fence, she rushes and unlocks the temple door. As they go home, they find Karwar road empty and Batta's house burnt down.

That morning they hear of Puttamma's plight. She is now in bed and is wailing. Mere words cannot console her and she is repressed with feelings of guilt and wrong. Nanjamma then tells the other of the way Siddayya saved Puttamma from the policemen's clutches. At night women sleep confident that their men are wide awake and not far away from them.

CRITICAL ANALYSIS

Procession: Dominance and Assertion
Whip: Cruelty and Ruthlessness

A procession of coolies is taken out on the streets by the police. Coolies who had left the Estate and joined the pariahs in Kanthapura are, forcibly being taken back to the Estate. The following ensemble signifies their helplessness:

> the blue, pot-bellied, half-naked coolies, tied hand to hand and arm to arm—boys, old men, fathers, brothers, bridegrooms, coolies of the Skeffington Coffee Estate who had come to live with us and to work with us and to fight with us—they marched over the boul-

> dered streets, their blue bodies violet in the glittering sun, and with one policeman to every two men and one armed soldier at the back and one armed soldier at the front, they marched through the Brahmin Street and the Weavers' Street, and the Potters' Street . . . the coolies of the Skeffington Coffee Estate were marched bent-headed through our streets to show who our true masters were, and we knew . . . they would be pushed behind the gates, for the white master wanted them. (210)

The section in progression reveals the growing indignation towards the ruling forces. The code of action ranging from 'tied hand to hand,' to the more signifying action of their being 'marched over the bouldered streets' to a still more consequential action of their being 'marched bent headed through our streets' implies a definite attempt on the part of the rulers to suppress the identity of the coolies as human beings. Later on, their being 'pushed inside the gates' thematizes the connotative code of assertion. In order to remind them as to whose command they ought to follow, the colonial forces punish the coolies.

The signifiers 'true masters' and 'the white master' signify assertion and the strong desire to dominate. By forcing them out of the village, the rulers are trying to set a limit to what the coolies can become.

'Whip' as a complete signifier signifies the ruthlessness of the rulers. Their being whipped is a sign of cruelty. So averse to any kind of rebellion have these master become, that they use every possible means of repressing the action of the coolies.

The arrest of the men at night is a strong code of action which connotes the feelings of fear and insecurity which is growing in the hearts of the Red-men. In trying to escape from the Estate, the coolies not only try to seize their freedom but also refuse to be subservient. This refusal infuriates the Red-men, who, unable to bear defeat, first arrest the men of Kanthapura at night and the next morning physically force the coolies out of the village. 'Whip' appears as a tool in their hands with which they try and suppress the actions of the others.

Violence becomes an end in itself in the hands of the colonial forces. Through sheer force, one sees the other generating fear in the coolies. Coolies are being treated as slaves. There lies a conceptual opposition between the two forces posited by absolute power: complete equality; absolute independence: abject dependence. On one side are the rulers i.e. the white-man's government who desires complete surrender from the coolies and therefore forcibly tries to take them back to the Estate. On the other side are the coolies, who after having defied the rulers of the Estate had, in order to realize their desire to be free, joined the pariahs in Kanthapura and begun a life of their own.

There is a constant juxtaposition of conflicts and desire which gives rise to the development of tension in this particular section.

Women: Resistance

The arrest of men, beating up of coolies and the women results in a further serious action. Unable to bear the torture of their people any more, even the brahmin women join the pariah women in the struggle. Their accusing the police of being "Butchers, butchers, dung-eating curs," (212) signifies their wish to condemn all oppressive forces. The women actively fight against the external forces. Puttamma resists all attacks from the policemen i.e. the external force but is filled with an inner sense of guilt. The pain which she has been subjected to makes her weak.

The policemen, by inflicting physical wounds on the women, try to assert their superiority. Physical molestation of the young women takes place. Amidst this confusion, Radhamma gives birth to a child. Birth of the child is significant of the fact that the struggle would not end with these women but future generations are also being brought forth to carry the struggle later on in life.

Ratna escapes from the clutches of a policeman just in time. Her escape signifies not only the desire to carry the struggle further, but, also the emergence of Ratna as a leader of the women. She strikers us as someone who is too firm in her project and, by refusing to exist on terms dictated by the others, she asserts the individuality of the being.

Women later take shelter in the temple and are locked up inside the temple by the policemen. They, despite being in a state of absolute isolation, do not give up hope. Their lighting the sacred flame and singing bhajans is a ritual which signifies the strong religious bond which has brought them closer to each other. Their clapping and singing in a moment of complete seclusion and repression signifies their wish to be one with God. Singing of bhajans not only provides them with strength but also a hope that they would soon be freed. Their patience is rewarded and the next morning Rachanna's wife Rachi manages to get the key and sets them free from the temple.

The women in Kanthapura, collectively or individually, fight against a common enemy i.e. the British. They had earlier lived lives confined to their homes but soon we notice a change coming over them. On having realized their actual state of existence, they struggle to flight against the colonial forces. Absence of their men from the scene fills them with the desire to carry the struggle forward.

Puttamma: Anger, Guilt and Fear

Violence is inflicted on 'Puttamma.' Unable to overcome the feeling of guilt and fear which has gripped her, one sees her completely shattered.

> She had fits and fears and tearing angers. She asked for her child and pressed it to her heart and threw it over the bed, saying, "I am not your mother, the earth is your mother, your father is your father—I have sinned." (222-23)

This conviction that she has sinned fills her with remorse and guilt. The memory of the physical pain inflicted on her by the policeman is still fresh in her mind. The sinister consequences of her rape by the policeman leave her completely shaken and disillusioned with life. The struggle which she is undergoing within her inner self has not only torn her to pieces but also made her a sinner in her own eyes. So full of remorse has the individual become that no words console her. The trouble with Puttamma is that her consciousness has been full of contradictions. Her having been subjected to violence is a central cause of her frustration. Her feelings of guilt doom her to live with her fears and apprehensions. To her there seems to be no way out and she disowns her child.

The section ends on a note of faith which lets the women fall asleep: "And when the beds were laid and the eyelids wanted to shut, we said, 'Let them shut,' for we knew our men were not far and their eyelids did not shut." (223) The above ensemble expresses the faith women have in their men. This realization that they are not alone in their struggle for freedom keeps the will to fight in them alive and is enough to console their hearts.

SECTION 18

Three days later, policemen along with the white-men come to Kanthapura, and they begin to auction the lands of the farmers. Satamma blames Moorthy for creating problem in Kanthapura. Despite her reluctance she decides to go with the other women to Ratna's house. Ratna is now living at Sami's place. Rangamma's house has been locked and sealed. The women are confident that the city boys would be there to win back their houses. Their hearts are filled with joy as they reach home. The city boys too come to protest against the auctioning of lands. They speak of the way shops are closed. The Gandhian movement has spread all over India and the people are willing to accept only the Congress and the Mahatma as their ruler.

Slight resentment and loss of hope is visible in the people's attitude towards Satyanarayan Puja. But finally they ask the Mahatma and Moorthy to forgive them and prepare themselves for the fight. They prepare for the procession with gusto. There are several people of Kanthapura who come for the auction. As the land is sold off, people are gripped with a feeling of having lost something precious.

Ratna blows the conch and invites people for the Puja. They take out a procession singing songs, but are surrounded by policemen from all sides. Despite the lathi blows, they are undeterred. Finally they march towards the Skeffington barricades singing song and with flags in their hands. The entire crowd goes out of the police's control. They shoot in the air to frighten the people. Despite warnings, the people, along with the city boys, march on towards the Estate. Coolies keep on 'cutting the harvest' with their heads bent. All of a sudden, the coolies too join the movement and are seen running with flags in their hands towards the barricaded Estate. Skeffington coolies from the city also stop work and amidst 'yells and growls and gun shots' people march on. The tension has mounted to such an extent that it is difficult to cool down. People are scattered all over and can be seen looking for their kith and kin.

The next time the attack begins from the people's side and shots can be heard being fired at night. The boys refuse to bow down before the government flag and shout 'Inquilab Zindabad.' Several men are shot by the police. People of Kanthapura desperately keep on looking for Moorthy but he is nowhere to be seen. They reach the village gate moaning and weeping and find several others there. The entire village fields are set on fire by the women and they run away from the village and reach Maddur where people provide them with food and shelter. Leaving the wounded with the people of Maddur, they cross the Beda hills and the Ghats and settle down in Kanthapura.

CRITICAL ANALYSIS

The novel reaches its climax as we see the women along with the men of Kanthapura and city boys preparing for a procession. The auctioning of the lands by the white-men in Kanthapura signifies the assertion of power of the strong over the weak. The people of Kanthapura protest against the Red-man's government by refusing to pay the revenue dues to the new Patel. The Red-man's government punishes the people for this breach of law. Their lands are auctioned and the minds of the individuals and some of them start blaming Moorthy. Satamma's disgust is visible in her plans to go away from Kanthapura and settle in a town: "she said she had done nothing and she was not a Gandhi person and it was all this Moorthy, this Moorthy who had brought all this misery upon us." (225) The proposition in extension reveals that people are not holding themselves responsible for all the trouble which has been taking place in Kanthapura. The entire blame has been put on Moorthy and Gandhi. Satamma is caught in a dilemma. She wants to get away from trouble and has no faith in Ratna. On the other hand, one can see her reconciling to the situation. Earlier, she had refused to go to Ratna's house saying, "What, to that bangled widow? She will lead us all to prostitution, and I am not going to have my daughters violated." (225) 'Bangled widow' as a complete signifier signifies the status of a widow in society. Despite being a 'widow,' she wore 'bangles' which is a sign of breaking away from tradition. Finally Satamma agrees to go to her place: 'All right, I'll come.' (226) Her reconciling to the situation is a sign of acceptance despite her unwillingness. She accepts it not because she is willing but due to the fear of the police 'for she knew there were barricades and policeman at every footpath and cattle-path.' (226) The news of the city boys coming to help of the Gandhian movement having spread all over the country and the Indians being tortured and arrested by the police shakes them. Gandhi's magic has not worn out and they feel that one day they will be able to win over the enemy through their love and prayers.

Puja: Strength, Sustenance and Protest
Auctions: Estrangement

The people in Kanthapura pray regularly. 'Prayer' as a complete signifier stands for strength and sustenance and builds up courage in the hearts of the villagers. A disillusionment can be seen creeping in and they are observed struggling with their own selves. They are questioning their actions: "Of what use all this *Satyanarayana Puja*—and all these Moorthy's prayers—and that widowed Ratna's commands. Prayers never paid Revenue dues. Nor would the rice creep back to the granaries. Nor fire consume Bhatta's promissory notes. Mad we were, daughters, mad to follow Moorthy. When did Kenchamma ever refuse our three morsels of rice—or the Himavathy the ten handfuls of water?" (230)

This doubt and the fear of leaving their homes makes them realize the futility of their past actions: "we are not cattle to leave our homes and our fires and the sacred banks of the Himavathy."

(230) The fear of being rendered homeless has become too strong in them. But so committed are they to Gandhian ideology that backing out of it would be a sign of betrayal.

> But some strange fever rushed up from the feet, it rushed up and with it our hair stood on end and our ears grew hot and something powerful shook us from head to foot, like Shamoo when the goddess had taken hold of him; . . . such a terror took hold of us, that we put the water-jugs on our hips, and we rushed back home, trembling and gasping with the anger of the gods. . . . Moorthy forgive us. . . . We shall go. Oh, we shall go to the end of the pilgrimage like the two hundred and fifty thousand women of Bombay. We will go like them, we will go. . . !. Men will come from the city, after all, to protect us! We will go." (230-31)

This realization that they are not alone in the struggle for freedom, but several women from other areas too are fighting for their rights, instils courage in them. They seek forgiveness from Goddess Kenchamma. As a symbolic act it reveals the trust which they have bestowed on their deity. They derive strength from the fact that men from the city would come to protect them.

The women prepare for the 'Satyanarayan Puja.' 'Satyanarayan Puja' as a complete signifier stands for protest. Men from the city had started coming for the auction. The predicament of the people has placed them in a dilemma. So deeply attached are they to their lands that the thought of separation is unbearable to them. The proposition in extension reveals that they have come to accept the painful truth. They know that their lands will be taken away from them soon and they will have no claim over their property.

The farmers to whom the land belonged have not been able to claim the land as their own because of their refusal to pay the revenue dues to the government. Absolute power lies in the hands of the government. It exercises this power by auctioning the lands without consulting its owners. The real owners of the land are not the people but the state i.e. the government. Freedom from the oppression of the state is possible only when the British rule is over.

To these simple village folks, 'land' is not only a symbol of 'Lakshmi' i.e. wealth, but also prosperity and well-being. To an Indian farmer, land is a sacred ancestral heritage, which passes on from generation to generation. Giving up land is not only an act of sacrilege but also a sign of being rendered homeless. The villagers who have joined hands with Gandhian movement say: "What is lost is lost, and we shall never again look upon our fields and harvests." (232) By dint of sheer courage, in spite of a deep-seated feeling of resentment towards the British, they accept. One can see a real conflict going on in the minds of the villagers. On one hand, they regret having lost their lands and on the other, they try to overpower their love for the land by showing a greater love for the nation. They are filled with remorse for those who have joined hands with the British and come for the 'auction.'

There is another set of people in Kanthapura who do not join the movement but live secluded lives. To them the extension of property is the only form of prestige. Their desire for material gains drives them to participate in the auctions. This becomes, in a sense, a betrayal of the masses by them. The ruling class has successfully lured them with promises of material gains. The dominant interest of a few members like Bhatta, Rangappa, Agent Nanjundia appears to be profit and expansion of power while that of the pariahs working in the fields is a better treatment and adequate, timely wages.

Slogans, Song: Protest and Hope

A procession is taken out by the enthusiastic people in Kanthapura. The religious procession signifies the Indian reality. It reveals the way religion becomes a potential force in their lives through which they try and achieve freedom. The 'religious procession taken out in the name of 'Satya Narain Maharaj' signifies protest, resentment, faith and hope of the people. In a village where few own and rule, while the rest are owned and ruled, the struggle becomes intense. The 'police,' being a representative of absolute power, does not allow them to move further. Religious fervour changes and is transformed into the present reality. Instead of chanting God's name, 'Vande Mataram, and 'Mahatma Gandhi ki jai' are the main slogans. The city boys too join the procession: "city boys with floating shirts and Gandhi caps, and they swarmed around us like veritable mother elephants round their young." (236) The villagers feel protected in the company of the city boys. There is a bond of mutual interest, an affirmation that empowers and enhances their existence. Cries of 'Mahatma Gandhi ki jai,' 'Vande Mataram' and 'Inquilab Zindabad' fill the air and the people march forward towards Skeffington Coffee Estate which has been barricaded. Such cries create a complex sign situation. It leads people towards one goal i.e. the attainment of freedom. As a communicative sign, it indicates that some kind of action is required. As a moralizing agent, this tool i.e. national songs gives rise to shared meanings and it serves common values. Such cries are necessary for they define and give direction to the villager's actions. The policemen stand blocking their way and despite having been given a warning, the people march forward fearlessly. The women are beaten up and bruised in a scuffle: "We whirl in shrieks and shouts and yells, and we leap into the harvests. And a first shot is shot into the air." (239) Violence means conflict. As we see the proposition in comprehension, we can notice the way violence takes place in Kanthapura. The villagers are not allowed to march across the fields for they are no more their owners. As the boys protested, "the fields are ours," and the soldiers said, "The fields are bought, you pigs," a farmer's voice says: "It's we who have put the plough to the earth and fed her with water." (240) The entire crowd marches forward and refuses to disperse. Thus we can see that the conflict leads to struggle. Passing from Bhatta's fields they march towards the Estate, confident that "The Skeffington coolies will not let us down." (241-42) The struggle becomes violent as the city coolies stop their work, and the Skeffington coolies march forward with flags in their hands. Braving the attack, the Skeffington coolies join the struggle collectively because they have been thwarted for long by the government and now their only objective is to fight for liberation. The women march forward too and are badly wounded. They all march with flags in their hands. There is utter chaos and commotion as shots are fired in the air. The people have all dispersed. Moorthy, Ratna and others are nowhere to be seen. 'There seems to be not a beating pulse in all Kanthapura' (247) suggests the fact that the village is now completely surrounded by the police and white-men.

The attack begins from both sides. The men's refusal to accept the British rule instigates the latter to resort to violence. The Indians refuse to bow down before the "Union Jack." Instead, several of them try to hoist their national flag. This violation of law results in violence:

> And men are kicked and, legs tied to hands and hands tied to legs, are they rolled into the canal, and the waters splash and yells rise up, "Help, Help, Ammayya" . . . and a bayonet is thrust at one and he falls, and again through the night rises the lamentation "Ammayya—he's gone—he's gone—he's gone, he's gone. Moorthappa." (250)

The women along with the men creep out through the village and at the village gate several others join them. Thus we can see that the entire struggle is rooted in the disposition of men to affirm their individuality and cooperative powers in their common interests and their hope for a better future i.e. Swaraj. The struggle is not only for the present but also for the future. We can see the oppressed men, women and coolies unite to remove power from the hands of foreigners, the undertaking to guard and preserve the roots of human morality.

The predicament reveals the fact that the villagers know that they have been uprooted from their lands. "Who will ever set foot again in this village?" (250) reveals the existential predicament. Their refusal to bow down has led to violence and conflict: "Even if you want to, the police are not your uncle's sons, are they? For every house and byre is now attached." (250) The entire village is guarded by the police.

Fire: Extinction

As more and more wounded are brought out, the people start moving out of the village. Rachanna's wife Rachi's reaction reveals her anguish and anger:

> she spits once, twice, thrice towards the Bebbur Mound, and once, twice, thrice at the village gate, and she rushes towards the pariah lines and Lingamma and Madamma and Boramma and Siddamma follow her, crying, "To the ashes, you wretch of a village!" and they throw their bodices and their sari-fringes on the earth and they raise a bonfire beneath the tamarind tree, and they light this thatch and that thatch, and we cry out, "Our houses, Our houses," and they say, "Go, ye widows, don't ye see the dead and the dying?" and more and more men and women go this side and that and say, "If the rice is to be lost let it be lost in the ashes, and granary and byre and haylofts are lighted." (251)

This action reveals the fact that violence and conflict lead to total disgust. This wish for the extinction of the village and crops signifies the desire of the people to destroy what is no more their own. As a sign of protest, it reveals their pain, their sense of having lost what they had produced.

This alienation of life is painfully felt. People like Rachi feel estranged from their own product i.e. the rice crops. Setting the houses and the crops on 'fire' signifies their total disillusionment with the entire ruling class. They feel that no one else should benefit from their toil. They are filled with a sense of satisfaction as they see that what could not belong to them would also not be consumed by the others. It also reveals the powerlessness, the sense of being uprooted and disoriented from their own land and village.

'The shots are fired in the air.' Both the 'burning fire' and the 'gun shorts' as signifiers stand for complete extinction. The desire of one to destroy the other is inherent in their actions. Groups of men, women and children march on from Kanthapura to Maddur. After having left the wounded there, they proceed from Maddur to the Ghats:

> we walked down to the banks of the Cauvery. 'Across it was the Mysore State, and as dawn broke over the hissing river and the jungles and the mountains, we dipped in the holy river and rose, and men came to greet us with trumpet and bell and conch. . . . They hung garlands on our necks, and called us the pilgrims of the

> Mahatma. Then we ate and we slept, and we spake and we slept, and when they said "Stay here, sisters," we said "we'll stay, sisters," and we settled down in Kashipura. (253)

The section thus ends on a note of stability. The narrator Achakka along with same others has settled down in Kashipura. Thus we can see the people are collectively opposed to what hinders and destroy them.

The police and the Red-man's government are bent on annihilation of all those who stand against them. The people of Kanthapura are aroused and awakened to a new critical consciousness and practical activity by the fetters of their oppression. They struggle to destroy the crippling and dehumanizing contradictions in their lives. They are driven by an instinctive and socially produced desire to be free from the British and thus realize themselves as individuals capable of independent thought and action.

SECTION 19

The coming Dasara will make it a year and two months since all this happened and yet, things here are as they were in Kanthapura. The section opens giving the time which has passed ever since the movement took place in Kanthapura. Some people have shifted from the village to Kashipura. Seethamma and her daughter Nanja live at Shanbhog Chikkanna's house and Chikkanna is searching a Mysore B.A. groom for Nanja. Najamma is staying alone in temple Vishveshvarayya's house. Pariah Rachanna's wife Rachi is staying at Patel Chandrayya's house. The narrator Achakka and Timmamma are living in Jodidar Seetharamaiah's house and are treated warmly. Timmamma prepares pancakes for the children whereas Achakka tells stories to them.

In the afternoons, Temple Vishwanath's son Shamu reads out the Upanishads. Rangamma is to be released soon. Seenu has been sent to another jail. Ratna received a year's imprisonment. Moorthy's letter to Ratna reveals his loss of hope. His faith has been restored in Nehru. Ratna leaves for Bombay after her release from the prison. All the women are for the Mahatma and have faith in him.

Only Rangè Gowda had gone back to Kanthapura and one day he comes to meet them in Kashipura. He speaks of the way the entire village has been destroyed. New houses are being constructed by the men from Bombay. Bhatta has sold his lands and left for Kashi. He says that he had sought the blessings of Kenchamma and asked her to protect all of them: 'But to tell you the truth, mother my heart it beat like a drum.'

CRITICAL ANALYSIS

Dasara: Victory

The concluding section narrates the way people leave Kanthapura and settle in other areas. The movement's aftermath has left not a soul in Kanthapura. It has been a year and two months since the trouble began. 'Dasara' has come. 'Dasara,' one of the most important festivals celebrated in India, is symbolic of the victory of Rama over Ravana i.e. good over evil. Some people from Kanthapura have settled in Kashipura. Nanjamma is staying alone at temple Vishveshvarayya's house and the narrator is confident that even now she has not been able to give up her old devious ways. Pariah Rachanna's wife Rachi has settled at Patel Chandrayya's house. Her daughter's marriage to Kotwal Kirita's son would take place as soon as the girl's father is out of prison. The narrator, along with Timmamma, is staying at Jodidar Seetharamiah's house. The proposition in extension reveals that people have adjusted well outside Kanthapura. But the oppression has not ended since their men are still in jail.

Their religious fervour prevails in a new form even in Kashipura. Women hear the 'Upanishads' from Temple Vishwanath's son, although he is not as good as Ramakrishnayya. Listening to 'Upanishads' signifies that women's interest in Indian philosophy is still alive. They are trying to retain the best traditions of Kanthapura. Rangamma is to be released soon. The narrator Achakka's son had fought vehemently against the oppression by going on hunger strikes and raising cries of 'Vande

Mataram.' Therefore he is sent to a northern jail and his term is extended for another six months.

Jail: Oppression and Denial; Truce: Submission

'Hunger strike' and 'Vande Mataram' are not just tools in Seenu's hands but they signify a certain purpose and direction in life. Thus the Gandhian movement emerges as a movement of the common man and his wish to abolish the present state of things. An extension of Seenu's punishment for another six months is a sign of oppression. Seenu is sent to a northern jail. 'Northern jail' stands for attempt on the part of their government to suppress the voice of Seenu.

The British government denies him freedom, self expression and a right to exist as an independent being. They are afraid of his strength and power. Therefore he is sent to a 'jail.' 'Jail' signifies repression and a desire of one to control and overpower the other. Not only Seenu but Rangamma, Ratna, Moorthy and the others who fought for their rights are put into prison. Ratna after being released from the prison comes back and narrates tales of torture. The opposition here signifies the acceptance of British rule versus the rejection, or the acceptance of authority versus the defiance of authority. Inside the prison, they are beaten up and forced to 'Salute the Union Jack.' (255) This reveals the proliferation of crimes inside the jail. The Red-man's government has failed in its efforts to achieve the people's confidence and therefore has to take recourse to fighting out the differences with physical force. Beating the people signifies an attempt to deny and destroy the power to protest in man. Mahatma Gandhi has finally made a 'truce' with the Viceroy according to which the peasants would pay back their revenues and the young men would not boycott the toddy shops.

"Truce' signifies as attempt to establish peace and order in society. As we examine the proposition in comprehension, we find that 'truce' is not merely an attempt on the part of Gandhi to maintain peace but is an act of submission. Earlier their refusal to pay revenue dues and picketing the toddy shops had been a sign of resentment, an attempt to destroy the prevailing order which had led to the suppression of the other beings. Submission here sets in a vague defiance as everything, they say, will be as before. "No sister, no, nothing can ever by the same again. You will say we have lost this, you will say we have lost that." (255)

Not even the signing of the pact with the Viceroy could resolve the predicament. People have become more alive and conscious of their surroundings after the movement. Their way of thinking and reasoning out has undergone a complete transformation. The women of Kanthapura are no more confined to the kitchen but have started reflecting on what should be and what is. This newly developed consciousness has made them realize the fact that things could never be the same. Even the Mahatma's assurance could not stem the tide. The following statement reveals their sense of achievement:

> Kenchamma forgive us, but there is something that has entered our hearts, an abundance like the Himavathy on Gauri's night, when lights come floating down from Rampur and Maddur and Tippur, lights lit on the betel leaves, and with flower and kumkum and song we let them go, and they will go down the Ghats to the morning of the sea, the lights on the betel leaves, and the Mahatma will gather it all, he will gather it by the sea, and he will bless us. They have burnt our dead, too, by the Himavathy, and their ashes too have gone out to the sea. (255)

A sense of achievement combined with an awareness of their present state of repression and the faith in Kenchamma has given them hope and generated their trust in the Mahatma: "but there is something that has entered our hearts. . . . They have burnt our dead too, by the Himavathy, and their ashes too have gone out to the sea." (180) The above ensemble signifies the Hindu tradition after death so that all that which is temporary is destroyed forever. The soul passes out from the body into the realms of eternity. 'Ashes' here signify the impermanence and the illusory reality of human life.

'Sea' as a complete signifier stands for permanence, vastness, open-heartedness and purity. The 'sea' accepts everything which comes to it and is eternal. Even the 'ashes' of the dead 'have gone out to the sea' and merged into the unknown.

Moorthy: Disillusionment and Despair
Masters: Oppression and Dominance

Moorthy is one of the prisoners released after the pact with the Viceroy has been signed. "You know, sister, Moorthy is no more with us" (180) reveals that he has gone far away from his own people. His letter to Ratna reveals his existential predicament. Moorthy's disillusionment, his anguish, loss of hope and despair are visible in his words:

> they all say the Mahatma is a noble person, a saint, but the English will know how to cheat him, and he will let himself be cheated. Have faith in your enemy, he says, have faith in him and convert him. But the world of men is hard to move, and once in motion it is wrong to stop till the goal is reached. (256)

His faith in Gandhian idealism somehow seems crushed for he has realized that the authorities are ruthless and cunning. 'But the English will know how to cheat him, and he will let himself be cheated.' (256) The opposition between the Mahatma and the English signifies the ècart between innocence and wickedness. It is manifest in the way English have successfully tried to cheat Gandhi and he has allowed himself to be cheated by them

Acceptance and rejection are the two opposing forces. Moorthy has started analysing Gandhi's idealism and he feels that "the world of men is hard to move, and once in motion it is wrong to stop till the goal is reached." (256)

These signifying ensembles reveal his reflections on freedom: "and yet what is the goal? Independence? Swaraj? Is there not Swaraj in our States, and is there not misery and corruption and cruelty there." (256) The protagonist realizes that the entire system of living has to change. The 'goal' here signifies the aim in life. The struggle which has ensued is not merely a struggle for freedom or Swaraj, but has a deeper connotation. He sees the socio-historical contradictions which are responsible for man's oppression even in states where Indians are the rulers. He has realized that mere attainment of Independence from the British rule would not solve their predicament. Misery, corruption and cruelty have always been there, in the lives of ordinary people.

But as long as oppression exists in one form or the other, absolute freedom would remain a dream.

The protagonist's statement reveals the conditions responsible for such a state of existence: "Oh no, Ratna, it is the way of the masters that is wrong. And I have come to realize bit by bit, when I was in prison, that as long as there will be iron gates and barbed wires round the Skeffington Coffee Estate, and city cars that can roll up the Bebbur Mound, and gas-lights and coolie cars, there will always be pariahs and poverty." (256)

Moorthy's stay in prison has given a new dimension to his thinking. This is already revealed in his earlier statement. 'Prison' not only has stood for oppression but has created a new consciousness and an awareness.

There is a strong defiance directed towards the 'masters.' This realization that 'it is the way of the masters' (256) which is responsible for misery and corruption on earth comes forth as a shock. Coolies living on the Estate are surrounded by 'barbed wires.' They have not been able to live and act according to their wishes. Their very existence is controlled by the other, thus leading to an estrangement. There exists an ècart between their lives and the lives of men controlling their existence.

City Cars: Coolie Cars

'City cars' signify the authoritative and dominating attitude of the masters, coming from cities, to rule the coolies. 'Coolie cars' signify the oppressed class who has lived under the domination of its masters. The 'pariahs and 'poverty' signify the weak and oppressed. The pariahs and poverty would exist in society as long as there is a disparity between the ruler and the ruled.

Nehru: Equality and Change

The protagonist's loss of hope is not complete. There is a ray of hope in what he says later: "Ratna, things must change. . . . Jawaharlal will change it. You know Jawaharlal is like a Bharatha to the Mahatma, and he, too, is for non-violence and he, too, is a Satyagrahi, but he says in Swaraj there shall be neither the rich nor the poor." (256-57)

Moorthy has taken it for granted that change alone would free them. He feels that Jawaharlal would be capable of bringing in such a change. 'Change' here signifies the breaking away from old shackles of oppression and leading one towards new horizons. 'Jawaharlal' as a potential force stands for strength, tenacity and equality. He is a symbol of all that is lacking in others. A representative of India, he has been compared to 'Bharatha' in the freedom movement. For, like 'Bharatha' who ruled Ayodhya during the absence of Rama, Nehru would guide the people, following the footsteps of Mahatma Gandhi. The protagonist Moorthy feels that until there was an equal distribution of wealth between the rich and the poor, things would remain as bad as ever. Thus one can see him trying to trace the root cause of all misery and poverty. The predicament can be related to Marx's concept of "alienated labour" where he says in the Economic and Philosophic Manuscripts of 1844: "If the product of labour does not belong to the worker, if it confronts him as an alien power, then this can only be because it belongs to some other man than the worker. If the worker's activity is a torment to him, to another it must give satisfaction and pleasure not the gods, not nature, but only man himself can be this alien power over man."

Thus we see that the problem has been created by man and only a collective effort on their part would resolve their predicament. 'Nehru' becomes his leader and Moorthy's hopes are pinned on him.

Soon Ratna leaves for Bombay. Rangamma is yet to be released from the prison. The narrator's statement: 'we are all for the Mahatma' (257) reveals her confidence in Gandhi. The ensembles expresses the confidence of people in Gandhi.

> He will bring us swaraj, the Mahatma. And we shall all be happy. And Rama will come back from exile, and Sita will be with him, for Ravana will be slain and Sita freed, and he will come back with Sita on his right in a chariot of the air, and brother Bharatha will go to meet them with the worshipped sandal of the Master on his head. And as they enter Ayodhya there will be a rain of flowers. (257)

Like Bharatha, worshipping the sandals of the brother saint, the narrator along with the others has confidence in Gandhi. Despite the destruction and the tensions which result due to the Gandhian movement in Kanthapura, one sees that a ray of hope for a better future is still burning bright.

Gandhi' has been compared to 'Rama' the Hindu God who had freed his wife Sita from the demon 'Ravana.' 'Sita' stand for purity and innocence. 'Sita' here symbolizes the motherland i.e. India. The demon who has captured Sita or the motherland is signified by the British. The British stand for suppression and evil. The village women have faith that, like Rama, the figure of Gandhi would save them from evil and a day would come when they would all be free. 'Swaraj' signifies the rule of the people and not of an individual. 'Chariot' signifies the seat of victory on which Gandhi would reside with his country. Bharatha would welcome him. 'Bharatha' signifies the presence of a young ruler who would take care of the people. 'Ayodhya' stands for the motherland 'and then there will be a rain of flowers.' (257)

'Rain of flowers' here signifies the welcoming hands of people who would greet the victorious Gandhi. 'Flowers' are a sign of life, contentment and happiness. 'Rain of flowers' symbolizes the hope for a betterment of future once freedom is attained.

Kanthapura: Desertion and Destruction

Rangè Gowda is the only one who goes back to Kanthapura. The village has been completely deserted by the people. His wife Lakshmi too has come to Kashipura and is now staying with Patel Chenna Gowda's family: "You are one of our community, come in and stay with us all this life and all the lives to come, sister!" (257) The statement reveals the brotherly feeling that the Indians have for the people of their own community and it enables them to help each other in times of distress. Rangè Gowda's arrival at Kashipura takes place one evening. "There's a tall man at the door, and he's frightening to look at," (258) said the children. His physical appearance reveals his inner state of mind and is manifested by a signifying ensemble: 'and he was now lean as an areca nut tree' (258) His statement after he comes back from Kanthapura, "Couldn't leave . . . till I had drunk three handfuls of Himavathy water," (258) reveals his faith in God. Himavathy is a symbol of purity and strength to the people of Kanthapura. Two contradictory situations emerge as we read the narrator's statement, "but he had gone to tell you the truth, to dig out his jewels." (258) This statement betrays Rangè Gowda's love for money and wealth. The signifier 'his jewels' signifies the wealth which Rangè Gowda had accumulated as a Patel and found difficult to part with. The narrator's comment reveals the real motive behind his visit to Kanthapura. Rangè Gowda further describes how the corner-house had fallen and several other people's houses were destroyed.

> "All said in a knot," he concluded, "there's neither man nor mosquito in Kanthapura." (258)

Man and mosquito signify life and action which are absent in Kanthapura. The entire village has been deserted by its people. The whole place is now empty, permeated with a sense of loneliness.

Bhatta: Escape; Kashi: Holiness and Money

The people from Bombay have come over to nearby areas like Bebbur Mound and are building houses like the ones in the city. It is made clear that the owners of the land, after having been estranged from their property, are uprooted whereas infiltration of the foreigners, that is, men from city has begun. Men like Bhatta and Maddur Chenayya have sold their lands. Bhatta leaves Kanthapura and settles in Kashi. 'In Kashi, for every hymn and hiccup you get a rupee.' (258) Bhatta, being a moneylender thought always in terms of profit. His settling in Kashi is symbolic of his desire to hide from his people. He is gripped with complexes and therefore does not support his own people and prefers settling in an alien land. 'Kashi,' a religious city, is a symbol of holiness, purity and redemption.

The opposition is signified by the fact that while on one hand Kashi is a place of holiness where people go to purify their souls, on the other its being a religious centre also makes it a money-minting place where priests are paid heavily by pilgrims. Bhatta's motive is therefore two-sided—both purification and material gains. Venkamma settling at her son-in-law's house is another form of escape. Concubine Chinna is the only one left in Kanthapura. 'To lift her leg to her new customers' (258) shows her low status in society.

Heart: Drum: Life and Action

Rangè Gowda's seeking Kenchamma's blessings is symbolic of his faith in God which has remained alive. His spitting 'three times to the west and three times to the east' (258) signifies the Indian way of expressing disgust. 'But to tell you the truth, mother, my heart it beat like a drum.' (258)

The last sentence in the novel which is spoken by Range Gowda reveals the existential predicament. The struggle which had begun against the oppressors still continues. Despite the fact that the village has been deserted and destroyed completely, one can see that the desire to struggle is still alive in the characters of the novel. "My heart it beat like a drum," (258) signifies the presence of hope, action and the strength to fight in Rangè Gowda. Though Rangè Gowda has been left homeless like the other Kanthapurians in his struggle for freedom yet he is full of hope and courage. This confrontation between the being and the other has resulted in alienation. The alienation has not only left him weak but has also awakened him to the reality of his individual existence. The self has started realizing its insignificance in an alien rule of the British and therefore it believes in liberating itself by rejecting the authority. Beating of the heart like a drum signifies the confrontation of life with action. 'Drum' is therefore a powerful force which stands not for emptiness but action in life. Life without struggle is meaningless. The self has realized the importance of struggle. As a choosing, creative moral individual, he ought to rise up and realize his being.

Kanthapura: The Gandhian Purana

PREMA NANDAKUMAR
Tiruchirapalli

Ever since K.R. Srinivasa Iyengar gave individual chapters to Mulk Raj Anand, R.K. Narayan and Raja Rao in his *Indian Writing in English (*1963), these novelists have been referred to as the 'Big Three' in Indian-English literature. And yet, it was close to a chance encounter that Raja Rao gained a whole chapter for himself in Iyengar's book. After writing the chapters on Mulk Raj Anand and R.K. Narayan, Iyengar had begun a chapter that was planned to accommodate Raja Rao, Bhabani Bhattacharya and Manohar Malgonkar. Raja Rao was to be given the pride of place as *Kanthapura* had already formed a significant niche for itself in Indian fiction written in English.

While writing the chapter, Iyengar received the novel *The Serpent and the Rope* which had been just published. The novel had a tremendous impact upon the critic, for the promise of *Kanthapura* seemed to have been fully justified in this sumptuous production. Readers had waited for twenty years after *Kanthapura* and "reading it *[The Serpent and the Rope]* one felt that one had not waited so long in vain." Iyengar then devoted a whole chapter to Raja Rao and wrote: "At the very least, *The Serpent and the Rope* is an ambitious and meritorious effort at achieving a total projection of India in vivid fictional terms, and, perhaps, it is the most impressive novel yet written by an Indian in English."[1]

However, the subsequent writings of Raja Rao have not enhanced these first impressions of an earlier generation. My own review of his *The Chessmaster and His Moves* in *The Hindu* of 23 August 1988 was unflattering. Shyamala Narayan felt that I was not unjustified in asking, "Is he [Raja Rao] a Vedantic philosopher or an insufferable poseur?" and said: "It is difficult to see any structure in the book; endless discussions are just strung together anyhow. . . . One of the first reviews of the novel to appear in print is by Prema Nandakumar, the well-known Indian-English critic. She finds the tedium of the discussions 'often unbearable.' Nor is she happy with the large number of quotations; according to her, transliterated chunks from various languages are strewn around like undigested pieces of food in a gourmet's innards, and Raja Rao goes on and on mesmerised by his own voice.' One has to agree that the book would have profited from editing."[2]

Though the other works of Raja Rao do abide the question, *Kanthapura* remains a classic of modern India. Novelist and short story writer, Raja's Rao's novels are: *Kanthapura* (1938), *The Serpent and the Rope* (1960), *The Cat and Shakespeare* (1965), *Comrade Kirillov* (1976) and *The Chessmaster and His Moves* (1988); his story-collections are *The Cow of the Barricades* (1947), *The Policeman and the Rose* (1978) and *On the Ganga Ghat* (1989). He has received several awards including the Sahitya Akademi Award and the Neustadt International Prize.

Of the works of Raja Rao published so far, *Kanthapura* and *The Cow of the Barricades* are one in style, vision and evocation of the Karnataka milieu. The short stories are treasure-houses of unforgettable characters who are literally the salt of the earth. Poverty and social tyranny never dried up the springs of love in these people. Javni the domestic servant; Akkayya the ancient aunt, "an obscure but heroic figure, all the more heroic because her heroism is so little openly acknowledged"[3]; Narsinga the shepherd boy absorbing the Gandhian advent in his own way; and even Gauri the Cow who becomes an offering of self-sacrifice in the non-co-operation movement of the Mahatma, falling down with a tear in her eye "clear as a drop of the Ganges," felled by a shot from the British policeman.

Language plays a very important part in the success of these two volumes, for it is a language deliberately forged by Raja Rao to convey best the Indian experience. In the remarkable introduction to *Kanthapura,* he writes:

> One has to convey in a language that is not one's own the thought that is one's own. One has to convey the various shades and omissions of a certain thought-movement that looks maltreated in an alien language. I use the word 'alien' yet English is not really an alien language to us. It is the language of our intellectual make-up—like Sanskrit or Persian was before—but not of our emotional make-up. We are all instinctively bilingual, many of us writing in own language and in English. We cannot write like the English. We should not. We cannot write only as Indians. We have grown to look at the large world as part of us. Our method of expression therefore has to be a dialect which will some day prove to be as distinctive and colourful as the Irish or the American. Time alone will justify it.[4]

There is then, the style. Raja Rao adopts the puranic style which associates the place with gods where there is no control over time in its Einsteinian relativity, and the telling is seamless: "We have neither punctuation nor the treacherous 'ats' and 'ons' to bother us—we tell one interminable tale. Episode follows episode, and when our thoughts stop our breath stops, and we move on to another thought. This was and still is the ordinary style of our story-telling."[5]

As it is when Narsinga the shepherd boy constructs his own Gandhi-Ramayana, "The Mahatma is going in the air, with his wife Sita, and in a flower-chariot drawn by sixteen steeds, each one more beautiful than the other. And they will fly through the air and the heavens will let fall a rain of flowers. The Mahatma will have the Mother on his right, and our Master at his foot, and they will go across the clouds and the stars."[6]

The same Narsinga style permeates the novel, *Kanthapura*. The novel is not constructed in the formal pattern. It is a continuous remembrance of things past as a pulsating present by a brahmin widow. As Raja Rao admits in the foreword: "It may have been told of an evening, when as the dusk falls, and through the sudden quiet, lights leap up in house after house, and stretching her bedding on the veranda, a grandmother might have told you, newcomer, the sad tale of her village." (ii)

Kanthapura is a prototype of an Indian village, situated in the Malabar coast. It is a well-endowed village with all classes and castes living in happy togetherness. Minor jealousies and irritations are there but these are negligible. There are streets, lanes, a pond, hills, and the bounteous Himavathy river. The area is presided over by Goddess Kenchamma. Traditional beliefs handed down from generation to generation permeate the air and a crystalline faith in the Goddess protects their everyday life:

> O Kenchamma! Protect us always like this through famine and disease, death and despair. O most high and bounteous! We shall offer you our first rice and our first fruit, and we shall offer you saris and bodice-cloth for every birth and marriage, we shall wake thinking of you, sleep prostrating before you, Kenchamma, and through the harvest night shall we dance before you, the fire in the middle and the horns about us, we shall sing and sing and sing. (3-4)

Kanthapura is a village of 24 houses and the characters leap to life with their sobriquets: *Postmaster* Suryanarayana, *Patwari* Nanjundia, *Waterfall* Venkamma, *Front-House* Akkanna, *Corner-House* Narasamma, *Nose-Scratching* Nanjamma. There is a Brahmin quarter, a Sudra quarter, a Potters' quarter, a Pariah quarter and so on, and the village has more huts as well. Among the people there are all shades of liberalism, obscurantism, tradition and spirituality. The new element that comes in is Gandhism and this re-arranges the time-honoured casteism. Gandhism has its enthusiasts as well as detractors. There is the famous Harikatha exponent Jayaramachar who expounds a Harikatha on the life of Gandhi and his message:

> Fight, says he, but harm no soul. Love all, says he, Hindu, Mohammedan, Christian or Pariah, for all are equal before God. Don't be attached to riches, says he, for riches create passions, and passions create attachment and attachment hides the face of Truth. Truth must you tell, he says, for truth is God, and verily, it is the only God I know. And he says too, spin every day. (16)

But there are others who do not like the young men going after Gandhi: "When there are boys like Moorthy, who should safely get married and settle down, they begin this Gandhi business. What is this Gandhi business? Nothing but weaving coarse hand-made cloth not fit for a mop, and bellowing out bhajans and bhajans, and mixing with the pariahs. Pariahs now come to the temple door and tomorrow they would be in the heart of it." (36-37)

The whole of India seems to be in this village and there are good and bad characters among brahmins, caste Hindus and the pariahs. Close by is the ten-year-old Skeffington Estate, a living hell for labourers, infested with snakes, malaria, greed, avarice and lust. The entry of Gandhism brings into sharp focus two major evils that beset the rural community: untouchability and the drink habit. This is the village scenario when the novel opens. Jayaramachar's kalakshepam on Gandhi has its effect on the British bureaucracy: "But hardly had he [Jayaramachar] finished the Harikatha and was just about to light the camphor to the god, than the Sankur Police Jamadar is there. Moorthy goes to him and they talk between themselves, and then they talk to Jayaramachar, and Jayaramachar looks just as though he were going to spit out, and we never saw him again. . . . Two days later, Policeman Badè Khan came to live with us in Kanthapura." (17)

Moorthy, Seenu and others who had been talking about Gandhism till now, become Gandhian workers. Moorthy undergoes a self-purifying fast and presently the Kanthapura Congress Group is in action with the clearly enunciated rules: Speak Truth, Wear Khadi, Practice Ahimsa and Spin Khadi. Moorthy starts a night school in the Pariah quarter, and his mother dies when she hears they would be excommunicated by the Shankaracharya. Moorthy is arrested along with sixteen workers for spreading disaffection against the government by preaching the 'Don't-touch-the-Government campaign.' He is sentenced to three months' rigorous imprisonment. The cause is kept alive by the Sevika Sangha of Rangamma. In this masterly thesis, we are given a very clear picture of how women joined the Gandhian movement in large numbers and transformed the village that had been tradition-bound for centuries, and how literacy brought illumination and self-awareness into their lives: "But how can we be like we used to be? Now we hear this story and that story, and we say we too shall organize a foreign-cloth boycott like at Sholapur, we too, shall go picketing cigarette shops and toddy shops, and we say our Kanthapura, too, shall fight for the Mother, and we always see the picture of Rani Lakshmi Bai that Rangamma has on the veranda wall, a queen sweet and young and bejewelled, riding a white horse, and looking out across the narrow river and the hills to where the English armies stand." (146-47)

When Moorthy comes back after his release, he gives the call for action. The Mahatma has left Sabarmati for the Dandi beach for manufacturing salt. The Mahatma is arrested and the Kanthapura Congress Group readies itself for action, having been lectured to by Moorthy on the need for non-violence in their struggle. The evil of untouchability is for once eradicated (at least among these idealists) and they march forward together to eradicate the other evil from their midst. Horanna's toddy shop is now the target: "Two days later, our sari fringes tied tight to our waists, our jewels hid deep beneath the earth, with men on the right and children beside us, with drum and horn and trumpet and a cart before us all adorned with lotuses and chaṁpaks and mango twigs in which are seated Moorthy and Rangamma and Rangè Gowda and even Pariah Rachanna, we march on and on, and when we come to the village gate Seenu sounds the conch from the top of the Promontory, and Vasudev, with his twenty-three pariahs from the Skeffington Coffee Estate, breaks a coconut before us." (176)

July 1930. One hundred and thirty-nine satyagrahis in all and they are the winners of the day. "The next morning, with bell and camphor and trumpet we planted our trophies before the temple. Five twigs of toddy trees were there, and a toddy-pot." The joy is short-lived. On the second day's picketing, the Skeffington Coffee Estate coolies and soldiers are ordered to walk over the satyagrahis but they join the satyagrahis and all of them are felled by the brute force of the police. The No Tax campaign means further repression and the city people join the village people and there is police firing and it is as if the whole of India has walked into these pages of *Kanthapura* to defy the government. The straggly survivors of Kanthapura go across the bonier to the Mysore State and settle in Kashipura waiting for the return of their neighbours and relations who have been imprisoned.

September 1931. The political picture has changed, Gandhi has made peace with the Viceroy, the peasants will pay taxes henceforth and there will be no further boycott of toddy shops: "everything they say, will be as before. Was then the movement a failure? Was all this idealism and suffering in vain? Was the exile from one's beloved native Kanthapura a senseless sacrifice? The aged narrator, Seenu's mother, speaks with her characteristic rustic common sense, ageless in its spiritual comprehension of the evolutionary destiny:

> No, sister, no, nothing can ever be the same again. You will say we have lost this, you will say we have lost that. Kenchamma forgive us, but there is something that has entered our hearts, an abundance like the Himavathy on Gauri's night, when lights come floating down the Rampur Corner, lights come floating down from Rampur and Maddur and Tippur, lights lit on the betel leaves, and with flower and kumkum and song we let them go, and they will go down the Ghats to the morning of the sea, the lights on the betel leaves, and the Mahatma will gather it all, he will gather it by the sea, and he will bless us. (249-50)

Though the novel closes with Moorthy moving a little away from the Gandhian viewpoint to that of Jawaharlal Nehru's socialism, *Kanthapura* does not stress upon the future possibilities with any definite force. Suffice it to the day which is for the Mahatma alone. He is the Rama to whom Jawaharlal will be a Bharata. The Mahatma is the reality for these village innocents abroad as they wait for independence, much in the same way as the shepherd boy, Narsinga:

> He will bring us Swaraj, the Mahatma, And we shall all be happy. And Rama will come back with Sita on his right in a chariot of the air, and brother Bharata will go to meet them with the worshipped sandal of the Master on his head. And as they enter Ayodhya there

> will be a rain of flowers. Like Bharata we worship the sandals of the Brother saint. (251)

With its English style often rising to sheer poetic heights, *Kanthapura* remains unsurpassed in its handling of the Indian-English idiom and as an evocation of the Gandhian inspiration in India's social transformation. To conclude in the words of Srinivasa Iyengar: "*Kanthapura* is a veritable grammar of the Gandhian Myth—the myth that is but a poetic translation of the reality. It will always have a central place in Gandhi literature." (396)

NOTES

1. K.R. Srinivasa Iyengar, *Indian Writing in English* (1983), p. 407
2. Shyamala Narayan, *Raja Rao: The Man and His Works (*1988), p. 131.
3. Iyengar, p. 387.
4. Raja Rao, *Kanthapura* (1947), p. 1.
5. Qtd. Iyengar, p. 388.
6. *Loc. cit.*

Moorthy and the Influence of the Vision of Gandhi

RANU UNIYAL
University of Lucknow

The present chapter deals with the protagonist Moorthy's dilemma. Exposed to the evils present in the society, he revolts against them. The most crucial incident in his life is the vision of Mahatma Gandhi in his dreams. Gandhi becomes the major influence in his life. As we delve deep into his character, we find him protesting vehemently against the growing disparity between the rich and the poor and the unending hatred of brahmins towards the pariahs. We see the protagonist pondering over issues like 'how is one an outcaste?' The main source of Moorthy's alienation is the gap he sees between his concept of liberty and the liberty which others are striving for. Moorthy's final realization that the basic contradictions in life cannot be resolved completely by ousting the British from India forms the central core of the existential predicament. The major cause of estrangement is purely socio-economic. He feels it is rooted in and dependent on oppression. Within the existing caste structure, freedom would remain an illusion. An effort is made to study the fundamental conflicts which force Moorthy to fight against the entire system created by the ruling class.

This theme clearly deals with the rapid influence of Gandhi on Moorthy, the young protagonist. Gandhi, as a political signifier, has been capable of influencing the Indian masses by delicately handling their conscious selves. Moorthy was one such individual of Kanthapura who had come to the city for higher education. He left his studies incomplete and joined the struggle for freedom along with Gandhi. Gandhi stands not only for struggle but also for change and it is the potential weapon of

Ahimsa, which enables him to hold sway over the people. Moorthy once had a vision of Gandhi in his dreams, which invoked him to join the struggle:

> For, as everybody knew, one day he had seen a vision, a vision of the Mahatma, mighty and God-beaming, and stealing between the Volunteers Moorthy had got onto the platform, and he stood by the Mahatma, and the very skin of the Mahatma seemed to send out a mellowed force and love, and he stood by one of the fanners and whispered, "Brother, the next is me." And the fanner fanned on and the Mahatma spoke on, and Moorthy looked from the audience to the Mahatma and from the Mahatma to the audience, and he said to himself, "There is in it something of the silent communion of the ancient books" and he turned again to the fanner and said, "Brother, only when you are tired?" And the fanner said, "Take it, brother," and Moorthy stood by the Mahatma and the fan went once this side and once that, and beneath the fan came a voice deep and stirring that went out to the hearts of those men and women and came streaming back through the thrumming air, and went through the fan and the hair and the nails of Moorthy into the very limbs, and Moorthy shivered and then there came flooding up in rings and ripples, "Gandhi Mahatma ki jai!" "Jai Mahatma!" (52)

The above ensemble reveals that the visionary contact with Gandhi has not only brought Moorthy closer to the Mahatma but has also made him choose a particular destiny. The power that the 'vision' filled him with invokes him to take a decision. Mahatma Gandhi's vision as a powerful signifier not only guides his later actions but also invokes him to decide for himself what he wants in life. The protagonist, after having realized that he has been thrown into a world where liberty and individuality are curbed by alien forces and man harassed by strong colonial forces, elects to respond to his environment by acting upon it. His decision to act and the choices he makes are to some extent influenced by Gandhi.

Growing Consciousness and the Persisting Dilemma

Moorthy's throwing his foreign clothes and his foreign books into the bonfire and walking out as a Gandhi's man all are the actions expressing his disgust with the present set of circumstances. From indifference, he awakens to a state of rejection. 'Bonfire' suggests complete destruction of all that is evil and harmful to existence. This single step of Moorthy makes way for several other actions. Earlier he had once seen a linga and said, "why not unearth it and wash it and consecrate it?"

'Linga' signifies the presence of absolute power and is a symbol of Siva. A pervasive religio-cultural symbol throughout all phases of Hindu life, it stands for continuity of life. 'Unearth,' 'wash' and 'consecrate' reveal the desire of the protagonist to revive and bring back to life which has been left hidden from the ordinary eye.

Moorthy, the protagonist, becomes the centre of the novel not simply because it is principally concerned with him but also because it is his wish to provoke change in the world in which he exists. Moorthy's trying to revive the old Hindu traditions through Harikathas and celebrating festivals is a cultural code which helps in uniting the people of the village. His refusal to get married to Venkamma's second daughter not only infuriates her but also makes her antagonistic towards him. Venkamma holds Moorthy responsible for breeding trouble in Kanthapura. Moorthy asks people to spin and thus be self-reliant. Spinning is not an indifferent act. He tells the village women of the ways in which the foreigners have been exploiting the Indians. He asks them to be independent and self-sufficient. 'Spinning' as a code of action would not only make the people self-reliant but would also do away with despotism and the ever-growing colonialism under which the masses are being trapped.

Moorthy voices Gandhi's opinions and whatever Gandhi says or does is sacred to him: "The Mahatma, sister? Why, every morning he spins for two hours immediately after his prayers. He says spinning is as purifying as praying." (32)

Moorthy's refusal to marry is a polysemic code. When Narsamma said, "You are a grown-up boy, Moorthy, and if you don't marry now, you will take to evil ways." (54) Moorthy's refusal is a sign. Behind that sign is the significant act which produces the sign. Moorthy's statement is also a promise. "No, mother. I swear upon my holy thread I shall keep pure and noble and will bring no evil to my ancestors." (54-55)

'Holy thread' as a religious code signifies the superior status of a brahmin in Hindu society. Moorthy's wearing a 'holy thread' and swearing upon it are both codes of action whereby Moorthy seeks to protect himself from the consequences of his own acts. Later on, as he entered the Pariah Rachanna's house his hands steal mechanically to the holy thread, and holding it, he feels he would like to say, "Hari-Om, Hari-Om." (105)

'Hands steal mechanically,' 'holding it' are all signs of the strong bond which he and the holy thread have with each other. 'Holy thread' not only stands for purity but also one sees him immobilized as he enters the Pariah's house. Moorthy wants to bring in a change in society. He appreciates the importance of changing social conditions; he believes in the need to be involved in action which will bring reform and freedom. Yet one sees the protagonist in a dilemma as he is being put into the most trying situations. His entering the Pariah-house for the first time is one such situation: "Moorthy thinks this is something new, and with one foot to the back and one foot to the fore, he stands trembling and undecided, and then suddenly hurries up the steps and crosses the threshold and squats on the earthen floor." (104)

The protagonist 'thinks,' 'stands trembling,' 'undecided,' 'hurries,' 'crosses' and 'squats'—all these codes of actions reveal his inner state of mind, his confusion and indecisiveness. Rachanna's wife offers him 'milk' and it is this offer from a Pariah which creates fear in the brahmin's heart: "Moorthy, with many a trembling prayer, touches the tumbler and brings it to his lips, and taking one sip, lays it aside." (105)

'Trembling,' 'touches,' 'brings,' 'taking,' all these significant codes of actions reveal the existential predicament of the being. He still feels committed to the brahminical fold and therefore drinking what has been offered to him by a Pariah is unthinkable. Yet we see that where he wishes not to function, he cannot escape. His action of acceptance activates not only his consciousness but also his thinking. His old 'samskaras,' though put to critical question, have not been totally dispelled with. He is after all Moorthy, and his being brought up as a brahmin is a fact which cannot be totally dismissed.

His inability to influence the pariah women to spin makes him restless and sad. Later on, his going to the backyard of Rangamma's house and taking a bath and purifying himself with Ganges water signify his inability to give up his religious fears. In his refusal to change the 'holy thread,' "Now that I must go there everyday, I cannot change my holy thread everyday, can I?" (107) one sees that Moorthy still knows fear and it is against this fear that he now tries to exert his consciousness. He knows that to be something, he will have to do something and this something is his decision to go to the homes of Pariahs everyday.

Moorthy: The Individual Estranged

In his attempts to be himself we have seen that Moorthy has already been alienated from his mother, and the brahmin Bhatta along with the Swami has excommunicated him. Moorthy has refused to marry and this has created fear in his mother's mind. His constant mixing with the Pariahs disturb her. Her greatest fear is that of excommunication. The fear of his being excommunicated is in Sartrean terms her 'anguish in the face of the future' (Sartre 69). Moorthy's mother seems to have a synthetic apprehension of the situation, therefore she forbids him to mix with the Pariahs. But Moorthy as a being has already started doubting and thinking. He consciously makes a choice by refusing to adhere to his mother's requests, as a result of which communication between mother and son is snapped. This breaking up of relationship between the two signifies the gravity of the situation. Each believes what he or she did was right. Both are conscious in their own ways. The choice of Moorthy's mother is identical with the self-consciousness which she has. To her being a brahmin and living like one is a primary need whereas Moorthy feels that by mixing with the Pariahs one need not lose his identity as a brahmin. Thus perpetually threatened by the nihilation of her son's existence as a brahmin, she severs all communication with him. The news of Moorthy's 'excommunication' brings a complete separation between the two. His mother's death again signifies her choice. In her choosing death, she seeks freedom. There seems to be no reason to live with others, since the others can do nothing to help her.

Thus we see that Moorthy, who has abandoned almost every idea which he regarded worthless, is himself being abandoned by those around him. He has been sequestered by the others like his own mother, Bhatta and the orthodox brahmins. Severance of his relationship with others is because of his mixing with the company he wants.

Moorthy consciously tries to give up age-old values of the society which had been proving a hindrance to freedom. He holds himself responsible for the violence which broke out inside the Estate. He cannot cease being an individual; he justifies his entering the Estate and says to Badè Khan:

> "Coolies are men, Police Sahib. And according to the laws of your own Government, and that of Mr. Skeffington no man can own another. I have every right to go in. They have every right to speak to me."
>
> "You will not cross this gate."
>
> "I shall." (87)

Moorthy's forcing himself inside the Estate demonstrates in a memorable way that he has a strong will to act. He acts when it is necessary for him to do so. His refusal to be cowed down by the policeman shows his inner strength. As we go about judging him methodically, we discover that this strength has been inculcated in him by Gandhi. 'Gandhi' to Moorthy has become one chief force without whose assistance no struggle can go ahead.

Moorthy: Growing Influence of Ratna

Moorthy's fasting for the violence which occurred inside the Estate is his conscious attempt to redeem himself. 'Fasting' as a tool appears to Moorthy as one socio-religious code which not only purifies the heart but also the soul. Three days of fasting had left him free as a bird. Though Raja Rao has not developed the relationship between Ratna and Moorthy, yet as we read the pages of the novel the truth emerges that both Ratna and Moorthy are deeply attached to one another.

Earlier he had gone looking for Ratna as he came to the village 'with a bundle of khadi on his back and a bundle of books in his arms.' (61) "Maybe Ratna would be at the well, he thought." (61) His search for her signifies his need to communicate and thus be close to her. But later on, as a result of fasting, we find a change in his attitude to her:

> That was why, when Ratna came to see him, he felt there was something different in his feelings towards her. Her smile did not seem to touch his heart with delicate satisfaction as it did before. She seemed something so feminine and soft and distant, and the idea that he could ever think of her other than as a sister shocked him and sent a shiver down his spine. (94-95)

'Something different' signifies that what he is feeling for Ratna at present was not what he felt before. He had looked upon her as a man looks upon a woman. That she was not just a friend to him but he had desired her presence is evident from his earlier attitude to her. Her smile had once filled him with 'delicate satisfaction.' He had considered her as someone other than a sister. Ratna had reciprocated his feelings for she considered him as her master and accepted his decision. This too is visible in her actions while she promises to do whatever he wants. He discovers the other to be 'feminine,' 'soft' and 'distant.' In his confrontation with the other, he rejects the other and thus tries to be for itself. The idea that he could think of her as any one but a sister shocks him. In this admission that he thought of her as someone other than a sister, he admits his weakness for her. It is quite evident that Moorthy was attracted to Ratna. He rejects her as a woman and accepts her as a 'sister,' thus trying to fight against the forces which would impede him from becoming a true Gandhi man. What he is afraid of is his becoming an objcct, and therefore he alienates himself from her. The truth has dawned upon him that the fusion between himself and the other will not be possible. Therefore he slowly solves the difficulty by asking her to pray: "Pray with me that the sins of others may be purified with our prayers." (95) In Sartrean terms one can say that unable to comprehend the mystery of the other, for he finds her distant, he turns her into a 'sister': "The objectivation of the Other . . . is a defence on the part of my being which, precisely by conferring on the other a being for-me, frees me from my being—for the others." (Sartre 359).

In asking her to pray with him, he also asks her implicitly to pray for him so that sins of others may be purified. Through prayer and fasting, the two socio-religious codes, Moorthy tries to equip himself against all the threats from the others.

What he experiences is 'shock' when Moorthy discovers that Ratna exercises a kind of superiority over him. He feels a need to estrange himself from her, yet, in some ways, feels close to her. By asking her to 'pray,' he is in one way trying to exert his power over her: "She could hardly grasp his idea. She was but fifteen. Praying seemed merely to fall flat before the gods in worship." (95)

Ratna's inability to 'grasp his idea,' in totality reflects her innocence. In brief, by agreeing to his wishes, she tries to identify herself with Moorthy. In order to satisfy the needs of their own subjectivity, both Moorthy and Ratna want to possess each other but in different ways.

Raja Rao has not developed the relationship between the two any further. We see Ratna emerging as a powerful influence with the absence of Moorthy from Kanthapura.

The Journey Ahead

Moorthy's forming a Congress Committee in Kanthapura is an act showing the people that only Congress can bring back their freedom to them. "One cannot become a member of the Congress if one will not promise to practise ahimsa, and to speak truth and to spin at least two thousand yards of yarn per year." (102) Here 'promise,' 'practice,' 'speak,' and 'spin' are pre-eminently signifying the presence of 'ahimsa,' 'truth' and 'yarn' as political signifiers. 'Truth,' 'Ahimsa' and 'Khadi' are the tools in the hands of the protagonist through which he hopes to overcome the other. Rangè Gowda's statement shows his disapproval:

> Learned master, at this rate I should have to go and bow down to every pariah and butcher and, instead of giving them a nice licking with my lantana switch, I should offer flowers and coconuts and betel leaves in respect and say, 'Pray plough this field this-wise, Maharaja! pray plough this field that-wise Maharaja! . . . No learned master, that is not just. (102-3)

He believes that mere submission would not solve the problem. Rangè Gowda knows that submission gives birth to frustrations. He therefore refuses to accept Moorthy's logic. But later on, one sees him accepting the superiority of the other, i.e., Moorthy. He knows that common action alone can bring a change for the better: "If you want me to be a slave, I shall be your slave. All I know is that what you told me about the Mahatma is very fine, and the Mahatma is a holy man, and if the Mahatma says what you say, let the Mahatma's word be the word of God." (103)

Moorthy knows that unless he seeks the help of the other people he will not be able to achieve success and therefore he approaches Rangè Gowda. Joint action can lead to fruition and without the cooperation of others all roads to freedom seem blocked. As a result Moorthy forms a Congress group in Kanthapura. Rangè Gowda's submission to him and his willingness to do what Moorthy asks for suggests that Moorthy has been accepted as a leader by him. 'Gandhi' has not only entered his consciousness, but has also become a part of him. 'Gandhi' therefore becomes a symbol for Moorthy with which he tries to exert his influence over the people. His perception of life has changed and one sees Moorthy replacing Gandhi by becoming him. People say 'He is our Gandhi.' Moorthy becomes an ideal for them. In so doing not only does he lose his own self but consciously imitates Gandhi.

One with Truth

After his arrest, which takes place in Rangamma's house, Moorthy is sent to Karwar. His refusal to accept the assistance of an advocate is an indication of the fact that he wants to merge his identity with that of an ordinary man and be what Gandhi had wanted his followers to be.

When Rangamma says to him: "Judges are not for Truth, but for Law, and the English are not for the brown skin but for the white, and the Government is not with the people but with the police," (125) one notices a fundamental ècart between the two signs of identity 'brown' and 'white.' 'Brown' signifies the Indian whom the 'white,' that is, the English regard as inferior to themselves. It also signifies the distance—psychological and physiological—which has been responsible for this ècart between the two. It also brings out the tendency of the English to oppress the Indians and thus assert their being. Moorthy's refusal to have an advocate is also an aesthetic code through which he tries to overcome the other: "But if Truth needs a defence, God Himself would need one, for as the Mahatma says, Truth is God, and I want no soul to come between me and Truth." (126)

Moorthy as one can see in his fight against the Other, makes his choice dependent on Gandhi. By doing what Gandhi prefers not only does he succumb to another powerful force but also reveals his desire to be in sole communion with God. 'Truth' as a political signifier is one such force which can lead him to God and he admits it frankly: "I want no soul to come between me and Truth." (126) Using truth as his weapon, Moorthy wants to direct the other so that ultimately the Other would respond to his needs. How deeply is he influenced by Gandhi can be seen from the similarity between his and Gandhi's ideas. As Gandhi once said: "When you want to find truth as God, the only inevitable means is love, is non-violence. And since I believe that ultimately means and ends are convertible terms, I should not hesitate to say that God is love" (Gandhi in Kumarappa 41).

Moorthy in his attempt to be a true Satyagrahi refuses the help of advocates and is later given a rigorous imprisonment of three months. His 'imprisonment' signifies the impending war. It also indicates that the path of escape for the protagonist is a narrow one.

Moorthy's physical absence from the village has in no way diminished his psychological presence. He has embedded himself in the consciousness of the people of Kanthapura. 'Our

Moorthy is like gold—the more you heat it the purer it comes from the crucible." (136)

The use of the term 'gold' exemplifies a particularly well-structured and coherent code. Moorthy's being compared to 'gold' signifies his purity and malleability. Like 'gold' alone has he retained his purity even after mixing with the Pariahs. The news of his release from the prison creates a happy atmosphere in Kanthapura. Venkamma connives with the priest Rangappa and fixes the date for her daughter's wedding on the same day: 'Well, choose between a brahminic feast and a feast for a polluted pig." (164)

To Venkamma, Moorthy signifies nothing but pollution and dirt. For her Moorthy is the other which cannot be dismissed or avoided. Her daughter's marriage is the test through which she wishes to find out whether people would come for her daughter's wedding or go to receive Moorthy. She deliberately chooses the same date in order to humiliate the Other.

Moorthy comes having undergone a major transformation in the prison. He has realized the futility of one man's struggle against the British who are well equipped: "A cock does not make a morning, nor a single man a revolution, but we'll build a thousand-pillared temple, a temple more firm than any that hath yet been builded, and each one of you be ye pillars in it, and when the temple is built, stone by stone, and man by man, and the bell hung to the roof and the Eagle-tower shaped and planted, we shall invoke the Mother to reside with us in dream and in life." (170)

Moorthy has discovered that without any collective action of some kind, freedom will not be achieved by them. He tells the people about the pilgrimage of the Mahatma to the Dandi Beach to manufacture salt. The people collectively participate in prayers. Seenu rings the 'gong' for the bhajan. The villagers listen to Moorthy. 'Holding of bhajan' is a ritual to commune. It demonstrates the bonding of the individual to national and religious sentiments. Thus we see that holding of 'bhajans,' the ringing of 'gong,' dipping in the 'river' and the eating of 'paysam and chittranna' for the mid-day meal are highly conventionalized signs which establish a link between the villagers and Gandhi. It signifies the hope, the wish and the desires of the people.

Moorthy had never taken a decision to march on his own. After having led people to heights of frenzy, he leaves them there waiting for the orders to come from the Karwar Congress Committee: "'but I am a small man in the Congress, and I wait for the orders,' says he." (175) The code 'small' signifies the inability of the being to lead the others. He has discovered the smallness of his being. He cannot by himself create circumstances which will carry the movement forward but waits for the 'orders.'

People refer to the 'Mahatma' as a 'Big Mountain' which not only guides but also protects the ones under him. They call Moorthy 'The Small Mountain.' Here again the use of the significant political signifier 'The Small Mountain' in contrast with a 'small man' reveals the predicament of Moorthy. Moorthy had all this time been aware of his limitations and the smallness of his existence. Next only to Gandhi, Moorthy to them appears as a symbol of strength and solidity.

He leads the "Don't-touch-theGovernment" campaign in Kanthapura and propagates the famous Gandhian doctrine of 'revolution through change of heart': "the purer we are the greater will be our victory, for the victory we seek is the victory of the heart." (180) Moorthy's words echo Gandhi's thoughts: "And remember always, the path we follow is the path of the Spirit, and with truth and non-violence and love shall we add to the harmony of the world." (181)

Gandhi's originality lies in his effort to extend the scope of suffering to mass political action. Moorthy too in his speech and actions seems to be echoing Gandhi. Gandhi had said, "The conviction has been growing upon me, that things of fundamental importance to the people are not secured by reason alone but have to be purchased with their suffering . . . suffering is infinitely more powerful than the law of the jungle for converting the opponent and opening his ears which are otherwise shut to the voice of reason. The appeal of reason is more to the head, but the penetration of the heart comes from suffering. It opens up the inner understanding in man. Suffering not the sword is the badge of the human race." (Gandhi in Kumarappa 67)

Through Gandhian thoughts, Moorthy is capable of motivating people to act. Picketing at Boranna's toddy grove and the collective march to the Estate are significant acts of protest.

Conflict Unresolved and the Struggling Souls

As we delve deeply into the character of Moorthy, we discover him as a complex being. One sees that people have put all their trust in him but Moorthy, after having discovered his inability to do anything alone against the tyrannical Other, follows the path of Gandhi. He knows that he cannot let people live in a world of illusions. Therefore, when Betel Lakshamma asks him to come and save them from Raghavayya, "the one who takes bribes and beats his wife and sends his servants to beat us," (192) Moorthy does not know what to answer and he says. "We are against all tyrants." (192) He evades her request by a simple "we shall see" and when she says "we ask you to come," Moorthy's answer "I shall write to the Congress and if they say 'Yes,' I shall come" (193) shows his uncertainty. After having been exposed to such fundamental questions as 'how is one an outcaste?' (117) the protagonist finds himself left with no answer to these questions. It is obvious that in his efforts he has had some success, yet he has made no real gains. What he is left with after all this contemplation is a series of questions with no answers.

Moorthy's growth represents his growing sense of estrangement which even Gandhi has not been able to dissolve. The proletariat at the end of the novel realizes that mere protests against the bourgeoisie world of the Other cannot lead to freedom and even if it does, the freedom attained would not be a freedom as long as there was a big ècart between the rich and the poor.

As the action progresses in the novel, Moorthy recedes into the background. The entire village suffers as a result of this struggle. Moorthy is blamed for the destruction of the village. The reactions of the Kanthapura people vary. People like Satamma and Venkamma feel it to be a futile act fighting against the Other who has more power to defeat them. They blame

Moorthy for bringing trouble for they know that defeat would mean annihilation. Satamma had already begun feeling insecure and plans to go away to the town. She feels that "it was all this Moorthy, this Moorthy who had brought all this misery upon us." (225)

Her trying to escape in the midst of the struggle turns her against Moorthy as well as Gandhi. Terror forces her to take such a decision. But then we see her joining the other women and seeking escape we discover that it is fear, which motivates her to act as she does. She knows that for her, escape would be impossible and therefore she is forced to cooperate with the women: "she knew there were barricades and policemen at every footpath and cattle-path." (226) Her blaming Moorthy for the trouble signifies her fear of the struggle and its aftermath.

The struggle against the Other results in a complete destruction of the village. People had to flee from the place and settle in other areas. Kanthapura no more remains their own village after the Gandhian movement. Forced to leave the place, they seek refuge elsewhere. Many men and women are imprisoned and some settle in Kashipura and other neighbouring areas. Life is no more the same for them. Everything has altered considerably. After a year and two months since all the trouble began, much remains to be achieved. Women who had settled in Kashipura have not given up their old ways. Reading of Upanishads and old texts is being done by Temple Vishwanatha's son each afternoon. Rangamma is to be released soon. Ratna was released after a year from the prison and she came to visit the people in Kashipura and then left for Bombay. Her leaving for Bombay signifies her strong desire to fight against the Other. Moorthy has been writing letters to her. Narrator Achakka's statement, "Moorthy is no more with us," (256) reveals her sense of loneliness. Her own son Seenu's term in the prison is extended. Mahatma Gandhi's signing the pact with the Viceroy is a compromise. The pact symbolizes the intention of the Other to reduce his opponents to inaction. Several prisoners are freed once the pact is signed. Moorthy is one such prisoner. In his letter to Ratna, Moorthy voices his disgust at the way things have been proceeding. His anguish and despair lead him to think about the usefulness of freedom. He has realized the futility of being simple and saintly. His experiences have made him discover the fact that the Other is hard to move:

> Since I am out of prison, I met this Satyagrahi and that, and we discussed many a problem, and they all say the Mahatma is a noble person, a saint, but the English will know how to cheat him, and he will let himself be cheated. Have faith in your enemy, he says, have faith in him and convert him. But the world of men is hard to move, and once in motion it is wrong to stop till the goal is reached. (256)

The simplicity and nobility of Gandhi would not be powerful enough to drive the enemy away. Moorthy has begun contemplating the actions of his leaders. He knows that the enemy is not a weak force and cannot be won by simple means. The protagonist feels that going back to where one came from, before the goal is achieved, is not only a sign of defeat but also an act of cowardice. He refuses to accept defeat. The question that haunts him has a deeper dimension. He has realized that mere attainment of freedom by driving the British away from the country will not bring an end to conflicts. Moorthy has begun to discover the questions posed by freedom. In his letter to Ratna, he asks himself: "And yet, what is the goal? Independence? Swaraj? Is there not Swaraj in our States, and is there not misery and corruption and cruelty there?" Moorthy's introspection leads him to a state of disgust and dissatisfaction. The self seems to be asking itself what exactly is the aim of all this struggle. The protagonist has become aware of the social forces which influence and shape man's life. It is his confrontation with the environment which is responsible for the vacillations within him. He, after having discovered that misery and corruption are also present in states ruled by Indians, realizes the futility of his actions. Not only does he begin analyzing his actions but he also tries to find out the root cause of all conflicts:

> Oh no, Ratna, it is the way of the masters that is wrong. And I have come to realize bit by bit, and bit by bit, when I was in prison, that

> as long as there will be iron gates and barbed wires round the Skeffington Coffee Estate, and city cars that can roll up the Bebbur Mound, and gas-lights and coolie cars, there will always be pariahs and poverty. (256)

His stay in 'prison' proves to be a blessing in disguise for Moorthy has once again been made aware of his state of existence. He has realized that so long there is oppression in any form being practised by the rulers, there would be poverty and presence of the Pariahs. Unlike the others who feel that the horizon would be beautiful to look at once freedom is achieved, Moorthy has begun realizing that they are living in a false world. Their moral optimism would soon be eroded by the continuous economic disparity which exists among individuals. There is a subsequent alienation of the Being from the masters. Moorthy feels that rulers would frustrate the freedom achieved. The proletariat seems to be making protests against the presence of the bourgeoisie world which has been responsible for economic disparity among the masses.

'Iron gates' and 'barbed wires' as logical codes signify the desire of the one to rule the other. The 'city cars' and 'coolie cars' and presence of 'gas lights' indicate the presence of 'Pariahs' and poverty. 'Pariahs' signify the socio-cultural codes. 'Pariahs' are the suppressed and the neglected members of society who have lived in sheer poverty as mere objects. Moorthy, on having realized that economic disparity is the main cause of all problems, thinks of ways to get away from it. Moorthy begins focusing his attention on the barriers which exist as a result of an ècart between the ruler and the ruled. His attitude indicates that his consciousness has given him a better understanding of the existing problems. He craves for change in society. The protagonist has realized that mere attainment of freedom by driving the British away would not satisfy human needs at all levels. The protagonist Moorthy repudiates, authoritarianism of any kind.

"In economic terms one could classify it as capitalism; in political terms, fascism; in social terms, class oppression; and in human terms, exploitation" (Parsons, 275). He feels that driving the red-men away from India would only be a temporary attempt to free oneself from the tyrannies of the rulers. The demand for freedom is followed by a call for equality, for to be equal men have to be freed from a system imposing inequality on them. The struggle against poverty, exploitation, apathy, hopelessness, authoritarian attitudes, alienation, dehumanization would always continue as long as the evils remained in society. Moorthy regarded the treatment of the Pariahs by others as the gravest evil in society. Like Gandhi, he in his letter to Ratna gives a clarion call to rebel against untouchability.

An Intricate Web: From Despair to Hope

Despite having been disillusioned by the presence of 'Pariahs' and 'poverty' in the country, Moorthy tries to assure himself that things will change. His last words to Ratna in his letter indicate that the flame of hope has not been extinguished in him. He feels that there is a way out and the struggle has just begun. Moorthy realizes the necessity of change and we can see him placing his faith in Jawaharlal Nehru:

> Ratna, things must change. Jawaharlal will change it. You know Jawaharlal is like a Bharata to the Mahatma, and he, too, is for non-violence and he, too, is a Satyagrahi, but he says in Swaraj there shall be neither the rich nor the poor. And he calls himself an 'equal-distributionist,' and I am with him and his men. We shall speak of it when you are here. (256-57)

Jawaharlal's comparison to Bharata is a symbol of duty and devotion. Like Bharata was to Rama, Jawaharlal is devoted to Gandhi and committed to social change. Like Prometheus, Moorthy takes Nehru as his hero. He has placed his trust in Nehru for he feels that he has the courage to fight against oppression of any kind:

> To defy power, which seems omnipotent;
> To love, and bear; to hope till Hope creates;
> From its own wreck the thing it contemplates. (Shelley 268)

Moorthy, the protagonist has discovered the main cause of estrangement. His discovery that the struggle has just begun and will continue much further leads him to unknown paths. The protagonist like the world seems to be moving in circles and returns always to where it started to conflict.

Like Moorthy, the faith of others has also not been killed. Their hopes are alive and they do have confidence, that Mahatma would bring them 'Swaraj.' Despite their being uprooted from their homes, their estrangement from their kith and kin, their loss of property, there is this wish in them to struggle and fight which means the presence of the hostile other. Under the presence of external threat, not only have they been dislocated from their families but also their homes. Unlike Moorthy who has discovered the presence of several other conflicts within the main one, the simple people of Kanthapura still dream of the arrival of 'Ramarajya' once the Britishers are totally ousted from India. Beating of narrator's 'heart' as a 'drum' is a logical code. It signifies the presence of hope, a desire to struggle and overpower the Other. It also reveals that the predicament of the protagonist has not yet been resolved. Amidst fear and confusion and insecurity there still burns bright the flame of hope.

Works Cited

Thomas Hutchinson, ed., *Shelley: Poetical Works* (London: Oxford University Press, 1967).

Bharatan Kumarappa, ed., *M.K. Gandhi—My Religion* (Ahmedabad: Navajiwan Publishing House, 1955).

Howard L. Parsons, *Humanism and Marx's Thought* (Illinois: Charles C. Thomas Publishers, 1971).

Raja Rao, Kanthapura. (New York: New Directions Paperback, 1967).

Jean-Pauk Sartre, *Being and Nothingness* (New York: Washington Square Press Pocket Books, 1966).

Kanthapura: Glorious Struggle of a Village

SATISH BARBUDDHE
Achalpur City

India has always been the land of imagination and inspiration, the region of fantasy and sensibility. The equilibrium between tradition and individual talent is being practised in Indian literature. The greatness as well as success of any literature rests wholly upon the aesthetic pleasure. Raja Rao's first novel *Kanthapura* gives the readers not only the aesthetic pleasure, but it stimulates their interest further in Indian English literature. Raja Rao has rightly described the various interesting modes in the peasants' lives. He has given us a balanced and interesting view of Kanthapura in a lyrical language which mesmerizes the readers from the very beginning.

The novel begins by portraying the geographical state of the village:

> Our village—I don't think you have ever heard about it—Kanthapura is its name, and it is in the province of Kara.
>
> High on the Ghats is it, high up the steep mountains that face the cool Arabian seas, up the Malabar coast is it, up Mangalore and Puttur and many a centre of cardamom and coffee, rice and sugarcane. Roads, narrow, dusty, rut-covered roads, wind through the forests of teak and of jack, of sandal and of sal, and hanging over bellowing gorges and leaping over elephant-haunted valleys, they turn now to the left and now to the right and bring you through the Alambè and Champa and Mena and Kola passes into the great granaries of trade. There, on the blue waters, they say, our carted cardamoms and coffee get into the ships the Red-men bring, and, so they say, they go across the seven oceans into the countries where our rulers live.[1]

Every detail is narrated in a spectacular manner. The village Kanthapura has separate quarters for brahmins, pariahs, potters and others. There is a temple of goddess Kenchamma on the hill. It is the village deity and the villagers believe that she killed a demon long, long ago, who demanded their young sons as food. It is believed that she came from the Heavens. Kanthapura is a typical village which has twenty-four houses. There is a double-storied house of Postmaster Suryanarayana by the temple corner. The beauty of rural landscape is brilliantly portrayed by the novelist. It is the vivid Indian style of narration which is exceptionally touching and remarkable. The village Kanthapura seems to be itself the main character of the novel. Raja Rao's profound knowledge of Indian life, India's rich cultural, and spiritual heritage have got expression in this inspiring, entertaining novel. The political, the religious and the social experiences strengthen the novel.

The story of the novel is narrated by an elderly woman, Thalamma, who is an active rebel against the British rulers. Moorthy is a young man of the village under whose leadership the people of Kanthapura unite together to fight against the British rulers. The tumultuous course of the lives of the people of Kanthapura, their passion for freedom, the graceful narration of their struggle are some of the fascinating features of this towering novel. Moorthy is the Gandhi's man of the village and the early days of Mahatma are described in the following words:

> And lo! when the Sage was still partaking of the pleasures Brahma offered him in hospitality, there was born in a family in Gujerat a son such as the world has never beheld. As soon as he came forth, the four wide walls began to shine like the Kingdom of the Sun, and hardly was he in the cradle than he began to lisp the language of wisdom. You remember how Krishna, when he was but a babe of four, had begun to fight against demons and had killed the serpent Kali. So too our Mohandas began to fight against the enemies of the country. (22)

Raja Rao was greatly influenced by the Gandhian thought and ideology. This is the reason, why he presents Gandhi as an incarnation of Krishna. For Gandhi Truth is the only God he knows. His message is, 'spin and weave everyday.' We must weave as our poor Mother needs clothes. Gandhi is a true saint for Raja Rao. It is Gandhi, who inspires Moorthy. He throws his foreign clothes and his foreign books into the bonfire. This incident in a vision changes his normal life. He becomes true follower of Gandhi. There are thousands of young men like Moorthy, who want to join the freedom struggle. *Kanthapura* opens up before the reader a dramatic and inspiring story of numberless freedom fighters whose only aim was the liberation of their motherland. The novel is a narrative of a remarkable journey of the people of Kanthapura.

The purely Indian rural world of *Kanthapura* is the result of Raja Rao's keen observation of the village community and his predominant interest in nature. The clear weather is described as "the sky became blue as a marriage shawl." (78) A commonly used critical tool divides possible conflicts into several basic categories: man against man, man against nature, man against society, man against machine, man against God, man against himself. In *Kanthapura*, man is not against Nature, but there is a matchless empathy between Man and external Nature. Here the 'ungrudging rains pours' making men, women and children happy. But the Nature's fury shatters everything:

> But the south-west rain went flying away, and then came the north-east wind and it blew and blew until the thatches were torn away and the walls felled; and then it dripped, fine, endless, unflooding rain, whilst the fevers still came and went. Then Madanna's second child died, too, and two days later Sidda's father Ramayya, and Venka's old mother—and just as children began to fall out of their mothers' wombs, children, men and women were going away and were buried or burnt on the banks of the Himavathy. (80)

This straightforward and fast-moving novel has a closely-knit plot too. It is argued by A.N. Dwivedi that in other novels this structure of action grows thinner and thinner: "Although in all the novels events are chronologically connected and their relationship with the character is consistently developed, yet in *Kanthapura* the elements of casualty and mystery, relating to the impact of freedom movement on the village life, are happily balanced than in other novels in which the structure of action grows thinner and thinner."[2]

The impact of freedom struggle on the village is so distinctive that the story soon turns out to be a saga of the eternal war between good and evil. Men and women of all castes join the movement. Politics and religion combine together for noble cause. Religious processions become political and instead of 'Satyanarayan Maharaj Ki Jai,' people shout 'Mahatma Gandhi Ki Jai.' There is a tremendous impact of Gandhi's 'Free India' movement on the people of Kanthapura. Moorthy fights against the cruelty, injustice and men like Bhatta who exploit the poor. He fights against the casteism and narrow-minded attitude. Jagdish Prasad comments: "Moorthy is not just a young man who gives up his studies after he has seen the Mahatma in a vision, and by his own fearlessness and love for the country inspires the people of Kanthapura to scale lofty heights of sacrifice and fills their soul with nobility which none could consider them capable of; he is actually, an embodiment of the dreams and aspirations of the Kanthapurians."[3]

The credit for bringing Gandhism to Kanthapura goes to Moorthy. He carries on his fight along with the villagers against the British rule. Though he is conservative, his ideas and actions are revolutionary. He sees no wrong in entering the house of a pariah. He accepts, though reluctantly, a tumbler of milk given by Rachanna's wife. She requests Moorthy to touch the tumbler.

> and Moorthy says, 'I've just taken coffee, Lingamma . . .' but she interrupts him and says, 'Touch it, Moorthappa, touch it only as though it were offered to the gods, and we shall be sanctified,'; and Moorthy, with many a trembling prayer, touches the tumbler and brings it to his lips, and taking one sip, lays it aside. (105)

Moorthy feels the fear of excommunication in accepting what is offered by the pariahs, at the same time he is deeply attached to the Gandhian philosophy of universal brotherhood. But Moorthy, 'the Small Mountain' is firm in his decisions. He has a special power to move the people in the right direction and the people of the village follow him without any grudge. Jagdish Prasad comments: "There were, in Kanthapura, some people who, for reasons of their own, opposed the freedom movement, and the novel acquaints the reader also with the changes which took place in their character under the impact of the movement. Each one of them has his or her own peculiarity; but the most noteworthy thing about their character is obsession with either money or power or with both, and though their conduct may be guided on different occasions by different motives, the driving force is the same. Such persons are, basically, cowards; they cannot rise against people in power because they know that it will harm their interests."[4] These characters help the rulers in ruling the country. They harm their own countrymen, but they are least bothered about them. Their chief motive is to earn more and more money and stick to the foreign rulers. They hate the 'Swadeshi' movement and they live in their own world. These men strongly oppose Moorthy's campaigns. These 'evil spirits' are found everywhere. The cruel nature of the landgrabber Bhatta is described in the following words:

> Bhatta now owned thirty-seven acres of wet land and ninety acres of dry land in all the villages—in Kanthapura and Santur and Puttur and Honnalli. And there was not a pariah or a brahmin that did not owe him something. But nobody would say anything against him. He was so smiling and so good. Never had he charged us more interest than Subba Chetty or Rama Chetty. These two brothers were the ruin of our village. (40)

Bhatta has a great passion for money. He belongs to one of the best brahmin families of the village. He knows how to perform 'Puja' at various occasions such as birth, marriage and death. He is a well-known priest in the village. He never forgets to collect the fees. Very soon he becomes a landowner. The journey from a brahmin to a moneylender and landowner gradually weakens his interest in working as a priest. As Bhatta becomes richer and richer, he loses interests in rituals. When the village is destroyed, his house is also burnt. He spends his last days in Kashi. Though he has a strong obsession for money, the narrator says, "he was not a bad man, was Bhatta." His isolation from the villagers is sorrowful; his last days he spends in Kashi, where he struggles for a hand-to-mouth existence.

The people in Kanthapura know that their fight against the British rulers is not an easy one. They do not care about the hardships, as something has entered their souls which encourages them to work for the freedom of their motherland. The names of the villagers are made descriptive in nature. It gives the special rural touch to the novel. For example: Nose-scratching Nanjamma, Temple Rangappa, Waterfall Venkamma, Cold-bangle Somanna, Nine-beamed House Rangè Gowda, Front-house Akkamma and Corner-house Moorthy. Then there are simply Corn-people, puffed-rice and Bengal-gram people, bangle-sellers, buttermilk and betel-leaf people. Again, he gives a variety of names to the people and their appealing nature, for example: One-eyed Nanjayya, Jack free Tippa, Gap-tooth Siddayya, Bend-legged Chandrayya, Husking Rangi and Left-handed Madanna's son.

The village is calm and serene. R.K. Srivastava writes about the Indian village: "The absence of machines and motorised transport makes an Indian village insulated, idyllic, calm and serene, like the still water of a lake well surrounded by mountains. An outsized stone dropped into it could create sounds and ripples disturbing its peace and serenity as the setting up of tannery does in a village in Markandaya's *Nectar in a Sieve* and the visit of a police inspector in *Kanthapura*."[5]

Raja Rao's deep knowledge of Indian traditions is depicted in the description of the small South Indian village of Kanthapura. Festivals are celebrated with lot of enthusiasm and fun. The oft-quoted description of the month of Kartik refreshes the readers:

> Kartik has come to Kanthapura, sisters—Kartik has come with the glow of lights and the unpressed footsteps of the wandering gods; white lights from cloy-trays and red lights from copper-stands, and diamond lights that glow from the bowers of entrance-leaves. (118)

K.R. Srinivasa Iyengar calls the description of the Kartik month 'a brilliantly sustained piece of rhythmic prose.'[6]

Age-old tradition of story-telling is revived by Raja Rao in the novel. The language of the novel is richly poetic. The incidents in the novel are narrated with unusual realism. The novel can be called an epic of noble sacrifice. It is a novel of rural life, depicting the glorious struggle of the ordinary people of the country.

NOTES

1. Raja Rao, *Kanthapura* (New Delhi: Orient Paperbacks, 1992), p. 7.
2. A.N. Dwivedi, *Studies in Contemporary Indian Fiction in English* (Allahabad: Kitab Mahal, 1987), pp. 187-88.
3. Jagdish Prasad Singh, *The Fictional World of Raja Rao* (Ludhiana: Kalyani, 1998), p. 12.
4. *Ibid.*, p. 22.
5. R.K. Srivastava, "Raja Rao's *Kanthapura*; A Village Revitalized," *Commonwealth Fiction*, ed. Dr. R. K.. Dhawan (New Delhi, Classical, 1988), Vol. I, p. 124.
6. K.R. Srinivasa Iyengar, *Indian Writing in English* (New Delhi: Sterling, 1984), p. 395.

Kanthapura: A Realistic Novel of Village Life

G.L. GAUTAM
Lajpat Rai College, Sahibabad, Ghaziabad

In introduction to *Kanthapura* of Raja Rao, the noted critic C.D. Narasimhaiah aptly questions as to why our villages remained unrecorded in creative works: "To what extent then, have our writers depicted village life. But the writers are, by and large, of the two and the city which absorb all attention, or is it that life in the villages is eventless and so our villages remain unsung and unknown to the rest of the world."[1] Both the factors recounted by C.D. Narasimhaiah contributed to the neglect of villages from figuring in creative imagination until the modern mode of production substituted the previous one based on feudalism. The deeply entrenched feudal relations favoured the continuance of status quo, so village life from outside presented idyllic, monotonous, static and uneventful view. But this so-called idyllic static reality experienced fissures when the modern capitalist mode of production was brought in the Indian life purely out of colonial interests in mind: to ensure the smooth rolling on the wheels of the British Indian administration and to exploit the already bled white Indian economy. This had been done under the veneer of civilizing the backward, static, feudal Indian life. Nevertheless, in whatever lop-sided and half-hearted way the capitalist mode of production was introduced into Indian life, it sooner than later had to bring about transformation of feudal thinking, redefining the relations inherited from the past, but the new system's fundamental exploitation and colonial character alarmed the intellectuals and national leadership.

So the winds of awareness of the alien, colonial character of British rule that had begun blowing half a century before were hastened to assume stormy speed in the first quarter of the twentieth century. The dynamic and prophetic vision Gandhi provided to the Congress enthused a section of intellectuals to cherish a fond hope to see India free from the colonial masters. However, it needs to be stressed that Indian political scene when Gandhi exercised tremendous influence had not been monolithical in ideological connotation but represented dialectical conflicts of ideologies, because thinkers with socialist hope had been fired by the revolutionary restructuring of the exploiting relationships. At that time Nehru had socialist hopes.

The changes of far-reaching significance occurring at the national level must inevitably affect the each part of the nation's body. How could then the villages remain static as they were earlier? They too must undergo the process of flux, since the cities, the upper part of nation's body, having experienced the value-shaking wafts, had undergone profound transformation. For that matter, how could the creative minds remain unshaken in their beliefs about the villages? So, there appeared on the literary firmament a generation of writers to whom the village was no longer remote; in fact, many of them were proud of their being village-born. The greatest among the fiction writers of Hindi, Prem Chand (1880-1936) remained grounded in his native village Lamahi in Eastern Uttar Pradesh. Needless to add, Prem Chand in his classic work *Godan*, which was also his last one, recreates the village life as an epic of struggle between the landlord with his cronies and the peasants fired by the consciousness of change.

Similarly, Thakazhi Sivasankar Pillai (1912-1999) who hailed from Kerala had used his native village name Thakazhi along with his real name. Thakazhi would always be proud that he was born on a sheaf of corn. As a student, he was introduced to European realists: Zola, Balzac, Flaubert, Maupassant, Chekhov, Tolstoy. The renowned critic and poet K. Sachidanand remarks how Thakazhi was intimate with village life: "His own social background as the son of a landed farmer from the low lying and water logged countryside with oppressive aspects of the uneven rural economy helped him grasp the class struggle in the village community instinctively even before he had read his

Marx or Lenin."[2] Thakazhi's love for village-legends finds its tragic poetic expression in *Chemeen* (1956). However, Thakazhi in the 1940s had written realist works such as *The Scavenger's Son (*1947) and *Two Measures of Paddy* (1948). These novels established him as a powerful social realist as they were product of progressive realism, which was a dominant literary trend in the 1930s and 1940s in India. As a novel of progressive realism, Tarashankar Bannerjee's *Ganadevata* deserves special mention, as it may be put alongside Premchand's *Godan* (1935). Mulk Raj Anand (1905-2004) acknowledged Premchand, especially his *Godan*, and Tarasankar as the great writers in the tradition of social realism.

Mulk Raj Anand, who regarded Raja Rao as an anti-novel novelist, had rated *Kanthapura* as a great novel. *Kanthapura* evokes an Indian village's reality at many levels: social, religious, economic and political, though the novel is set in South India. Kamala Markandaya's *Nectar in a Sieve* too, has a Keralite village in South India for its setting. Mulk Raj Anand, who was an internationally known writer along with Raja Rao had the creative sensibility to create rural characters of abiding interest. His famous novel about village life entitled *The Village*, graphically describes the village peasantry's ardour to live, to struggle against their exploiters and oppressors. If we include Bhabani Bhattacharya's *So Many Hungers* while thinking of village life in Indian literature, though this novel, like *Kanthapura* vividly portrays Gandhian characters, we will notice that one cannot think of village-oriented work without the inevitability of struggle between the masters of land and the workers on land. Even if an individual peasant woman does fight for survival as happens in Kamala Markandaya's *Nectar in a Sieve*, a sensitive reader will see in the individual will for survival a whole humanity pitted against the social power bent upon ruining it. This will to live, though life has taught many bitter lessons, constitutes the novelty of a village life. Rukmani, the woman protagonist of *Nectar in Sieve*, has lost husband, has mourned the death of a young son, met with frustration at the hands of an indifferent daughter-in-law, but still she finds hope in a boy who is not her own, who has no fingers, only stubs. Rukmani finds comfort in Puli, "the child I clung to who was not mine, and he no longer a child. Puli is with me because I tempted him, out of my desperation I lured him away from his soil to mine."[3]

In a realist work the writer has to create credible characters with their strengths and weaknesses brought into sharp focus. Hori, the protagonist in *Godan*, dies a peasant's death; till he breathes his last he works for his family. Thus he dies a Karamyogi in the true sense of the term. He had no Gandhi in his life to have strength from. Similarly, Aniruddha in Tarashankar Banerjee's *Ganadevata* finds himself grilled by the social power-wielding people. Though made to suffer one torment after another, yet the spirit of survival never deserts him. In *Kanthapura* we have Aniruddha's counterpart in Rangè Gowda. Nihal Singh in Mulk Raj Anand's *The Village* demonstrates no less exemplary courage in facing landlord Harnam Singh than either Hori or Aniruddha.

In the execution of clandestine designs, Harnam Singh's parallel in *Kanthapura* is landlord Bhatta who is responsible for the tragic death of Moorthy's mother Narasamma by having Moorthy's family excommunicated. Moorthy's profound commitment to Gandhian philosophy is as moving as Devesh Basu is an every inch Gandhian in *So Many Hungers* by Bhabani Bhattacharya. Devesh Basu is called by the villagers of Baruni as "Devta, a celestial being." In *Kanthapura*, the narrator Achakka, out of respect for Moorthy, calls him "Corner-House Moorthy, who had gone through life like a noble cow, quiet, generous, serene, deferent and brahmanic, à very prince."[4] Moorthy, having come under Gandhian philosophy, has given up his studies, has brought Gandhian principles to his native village from where he had gone to city for higher education. But is it really so easy a thing to model on Gandhian principles a feudal village organised around watertight compartment of caste? Kanthapura, like any Indian village, is divided into quarters such as Brahmin quarter, Pariah quarter, Potters' quarter and Weavers' quarters. Moorthy, freely moving about the houses of pariahs does an ennobling deed for those who have lived an ignoble existence under the feudal caste divided social setup. So naturally Moorthy's followers will be those who have been denied to live a dignified existence. Apart from the outcast people, Rangamma, her niece Ratna, Patel Rangè Gowda are Gandhian Moorthy's followers in the village.

The Gandhian agenda of village self-reliance is linked up with the Karwar City Congress. At Kanthapura, Gandhian Rangamma's house becomes the hub of activities, no less than an office, where piles of books and spinning wheels have come from the city. The transformation of Kanthapura from a primitive feudal village into a Gandhian one takes place in a well-worked out way. After dealing with the breakup of the people into castes, Raja Rao with personal interest in the religious life of people brings home how the people have enjoyed the religious festivals. A temple has been recently constructed, the construction of which coincided with the celebration of *Sankara-jayanthi*. That was followed by the recitation of Harikatha for the organization of which funds were raised from all and sundry. Among the donors we have two sections: the rich and middle class; the former do not have to think twice for giving as has been shown in the example of Bhatta and others, and the latter who have to think and calculate many times over as the narrator herself, not being so rich. For example, she calculates that a rupee is a significant amount for her: "It was a twenty-fifth of my revenue, and tell me, when did we ever pay it in time? But the rupee is for the gods. And it is Moorthy that asks for it. We always bless him." (19) Moorthy has been collecting money for the religious festivals. Thus he is creating political consciousness by way of religious festivals, treating all castes equally. Finding Moorthy in the pariah quarter, the narrator being a brahmin widow is shocked: "and I closed my ears when I heard he went to the Pariah quarter. We said to ourselves, he is one of those Gandhi men, who say there is neither caste nor clan nor family, and yet they pray like us and they live like us. Only they say, too, one should not marry early, one should allow widows to take husbands and a brahmin might marry a pariah and a pariah a brahmin." (19) This radical ideology is not welcomed by the conservative people, including the narrator who is an old widow.

Moorthy has a tough task ahead of him. Thanks to his single-minded and whole-hearted devotion as a Gandhian and the religious fervour with which he is working, he wins many people over for his cause. Being educated, he has power of argument. The Congress programme of village reconstruction through spinning wheel takes up all his energy. The work of spinning, argues Moorthy, will ensure work to the jobless and make the lazy active. As a true follower of Gandhi, Moorthy believes in the dignity of labour and self-help. By meeting the needs of cloth spun and woven on our own, we can stop the draining away of our money to foreign country. In Gandhian spirit he calls the spinning "as purifying as praying." Moorthy is also against the idea that the paddy produced in Kanthapura should be sold to the Bombay traders who after husking and washing send it back to the village, the middleman earning profit in the process. He feels that the paddy should be husked in the village itself to exclude the profiteers like Subba Chetty from defrauding the producers of paddy. That these liberal political ideas should win followers is no surprise.

However, there are some who oppose this ideology because it adversely affects them. Bhatta, the owner of half of Kanthapura's land who also acts as a moneylender, an agent of the city advocate and a friend of city swami, must count his supporters to stop the dissemination of Moorthy's radical ideas. So Bhatta takes an account of his friends who will stand by him against Moorthy's pariah business: "'Well, well, every squirrel will have his day,' repeated Bhatta to himself. But Temple Rangappa is still with me, and Patwari Nanjundia and schoolmaster Devarayya, and of course, Rama Chetty and Subba Chetty. And they all with me and the Swami, and against all this pariah business." (112-13) As a landlord and a moneylender rolled into his person, Bhatta thinks of teaching a lesson to outcastes who are Congress members. Not a pice less would he charge than 20 percent interest on their mortgages. Nor would he allow a week's time as grace period for enabling a pariah to pay up the loan. Bhatta plans to work with vengeance like a typical landlord:

> Pariah Lingayya has his Big-bund field in mortgage, and if he does not pay up this harvest-time, he will not have a rag-wide left. And there will be no accepting, 'Just a week, master. Just a week more, say ten days, and this gold-flower in guarantee. . . .' None of this any more. (113)

Bhatta thinks of the city Swami as his pillar of support against what he calls the pariah business. The Swami-landlord collusion in settling village affairs, whereby one favours another against the peasantry, is not limited to Raja Rao's *Kanthapura*. Such connivance between the landlord and the religious authority is fundamental to understand the complex matrix of the oppression and exploitation the economically underprivileged have been subjected to not only under the feudal set up but also under the modern dispensation. Pandit Datadin and Jhungeri Singh in Premchand's *Godan* and landlord Harbans Singh and Sikh Mahant Nandgiri in Mulk Raj Anand's *The Village* are examples of secret agreement operating between the centres of power. The landlord in committing wrong would fear no authority outside village after garnering up the support of the ochre-coloured temporal authority. In Kanthapura, which has come under the Gandhian movement, the Hindu fundamentalist Swami emits his venom not only against the pariahs but against the Muslims, purely on religious grounds. This Hindu-Fascist brand sadhu is not physically present as are other characters in the novel. Yet his shadow looms large on the village as he keeps issuing dictats from the city, threatening them through Bhatta. Bhatta has been creating Swami's terror by quoting his words: "We must stop this. The Swami says he will outcaste every brahmin who has touched a pariah." And again "Today it will be the pariah, tomorrow it will be the Mohammedans, and the day after the Europeans." (45)

Raja Rao has demonstrated a profound vision for probing human nature and a deep awareness of the class behaviour pattern in the portrayal of Bhatta's character. He has shown how Bhatta has graduated to the present status of Zamindar of Kanthapura from the earlier phases during which he had been an obsequial dinner-eater brahmin and then an ordinary money-lender.

In these roles as well, Rao brings out the essential traits of Bhatta's character, acting as a priest and a moneylender. In his role as a brahmin invited to obsequial dinners, Bhatta has been as greedy and gluttonous as any person of this sort. When he goes to such a dinner for pleasing the manes, he finishes over the ritual ceremony in the winking of an eye so that he may eat as much as was available:

> Then the real obsequial dinner begins, with fresh honey and solid curds, and Bhatta's beloved Bengal-gram *khir*. "Take it, Bhattarè, only one cup more, just one? Let us not dissatisfy our manes." The children are playing in the shadow, by the byre, and the elderly people are all in the side room, waiting for the holy brahmins to finish their meal. But Bhatta goes on munching and belching, drinking water and then munching again. "Rama-Rama. Rama-Rama." One does not have an obsequial dinner every day. And then, once the holy meal is over, there is the coconut and the two rupees, and if it is the That-House people it is five, and the Post-Office-House people two-eight. That is the rule. (36)

The money Bhatta receives in charity contributes immensely to his rise as a moneylender. This way he has accumulated a capital amount of Rs. 350. This amount may not look impressive by today's standards, but just think of the 1930s when Rampur Mada comes over Bhatta to raise a loan of ten rupees for nuptial ceremony. Similarly, Lingayya's revenue is not paid. If Lingayya fails to pay up the loan of twenty-one rupees eight annas by the harvest, he will have to pay ten percent interest. Then the Potters' street Kanthama has to go to Bhatta for one hundred and twenty rupees. But some paper agreement is to be concluded with her. After these small loans to the poor, Bhatta lends out for litigations to the farmers, locked in legal squabbles on the issues of the boundaries of the fields. Now the money is loaned out in lieu of mortgages of fields. Thus Bhatta has a meteoric rise as a man of riches. We can form an idea of his riches from the assets in land and money due from others:

> Bhatta now owned thirty-seven acres of wet land and ninety acres of dry land in all the villages—in Kanthapura and Santur and Puttur and Honnalli. And there was not a pariah or a brahmin that did

> not owe him something. But nobody would say anything against him. He was so smiling and so good. (40)

The proverb 'One may smile and smile and yet be a villain' could be applied to Bhatta's character as a typical landlord. Bhatta need not look back his lowly status of a pontifical brahmin. With the money he has on him, he can have connections in the city which houses lawyer Seenappa and religious fundamentalist Swami. It is not at all difficult to identify such characters imbued with fascist ideology in the cultural turbulence we have had in the recent past in India. They launched a diatribe against Gandhi and his ideology, as does the Swami in *Kanthapura*. Bhatta now can boast of his connections with big people in the city because with money he can buy every thing. He has married a second time, the girl being only twelve-and-half years of age; the marriage has also fetched him a handsome dowry. But how can he be at peace with himself unless the Gandhi business is sabotaged? Coward by temperament, he cannot come face to face with the members of the Congress. Insidious and scheming, he thinks of provoking the Waterfall Venkamma against these pariah lovers who, he argues with himself, are degrading the moral standards in Kanthapura. And we have already noted how he would take those members of the Congress to task who owe him money. He is not an inch different from Srihari in *Ganadevata* in causing harm to his adversary. Similarly, in *Godan*, Jhungeri Singh and others of his company plan against Hori whose son dared to defy the village morality by marrying a widow. We can know how insidious in nature Bhatta is:

> "And there is Venkamma too!" And at the thought of Venkamma an idea came into his head like a cart-light in the dark, an auspicious, happy idea, and he said, "I shall find a bridegroom for her daughter, and she will be always with us, and what with her tongue and her tail, she will set fire where we want." (113)

Moreover, Bhatta settles the cases in Kanthapura since he has come in contact with the lawyers in the city. For settling the cases, he charges money which people give without nursing a grudge against him. Hence, Bhatta has come to be acknowledged as a lawyer: "There's no use going to the city for a lawyer. We've one in Kanthapura." (40)

At the local level, Waterfall Venkamma will work according to the clandestine design of Bhatta. At the national level, the cronies of Swami organize a hate campaign against the Gandhians to disrupt their meetings held to propagate Gandhian ideals like abolition of untouchability and promotion of Hindu-Muslim unity. Swami's men have the backing of the Government. The Mohammedan rule preceding the British taking over India has been projected as inefficient, anarchic and disorderly. An agent of Swami has seen every good in British rule:

> "What did we have, pray, before the British came—disorder, corruption, and egoism, I say—" he continued, though there were many shouts and hootings against him—"and the British came and they came to protect us, our bones and our dharma." (128)

It is no wonder that the Swami is bounteously rewarded by the British Government. The Swami's agent proudly says: "the Swami has just received twelve hundred acres of wet land from the Government." (129) And also not surprisingly enough, the Swami has been received by the governor. So, through the Swami, Bhatta has connections to the corridor of the British power as contemporary history bears it out that big zamindars, the Rajas and Jagirdars were the protégés of the British in India.

Meanwhile the Gandhian Movement has progressed immensely in Kanthapura. Bhatta is quite powerful, but to counter him amongst the Gandhians is Rangè Gowda whose character is reminiscent of Aniruddha in *Ganadevata* as both do not feel cowed down by the landlord. Aniruddha walks out of the village Panchayat convened to call his explanation as to why he has shifted his forge to the market place. So does Rangè Gowda growl at the landlord Bhatta. He does not have a fear to call Bhatta's anti-Gandhian party as a group of jackals. How Rangè Gowda reacts angrily is explicit here:

> And when Bhatta's name is mentioned, Rangè Gowda's neck stiffens and spitting across the veranda to the gutter he says, 'yes, he had come to see me too!' (100)

Patel Rangè Gowda, however, believes that Bhatta is as coward as a jackal. He comments on his character: "yes, learned Moorthappa. He had, of course, come to see me—he wanted me to be his dog's tail. But I said to him, the Mahatma is a holy man, and I was not with the jackals but with the deer" (100-1) Patel Rangè Gowda's character is evocative of a tough healthy village man who is not only distinguishable from other village characters but also captures the reader's imagination with his distinctive mien that sets him apart from others. That he should impress us with his strong built and his humanity has been his creator's motive: "He was a fat, sturdy fellow, a veritable tiger amongst us . . . his words were law in our village. . . . He is an honest man and has helped many a poor peasant. And heavens! What a terror he was to the authorities." (14) The representative of government authority Badè Khan, who succeeds in brow-beating other simple village folks, behaves sheepishly in the presence of Rangè Gowda. Unlike Moorthy, who has had wide exposure under Gandhi and is a city-educated youth, Rangè Gowda owes his rustic wisdom to what he has experienced as a sturdy farmer. He hardly believes that Gandhian ideal of loving one's enemy will be workable in Kanthapura. He would innocently argue with Moorthy on this ideal: "That's for the Mahatma and you, Moorthappa—not for us poor folk." (102) Such responses from the characters who are down to earth with regard to ideals lend authenticity to characters where characters have not been shown getting transformed by the magic wand of Gandhi.

Another such instance is when Moorthy decides to fast on the outbreak of violence at Skeffington Coffee Estate. Moorthy goes on a three-day fast for self-purification as preached by Gandhi. However, Rangamma dissuades Moorthy from doing so, arguing: "Moorthy, this is all very well for the Mahatma, but not for us the poor creature." (91) Similarly, Nanjamma, whom Moorthy persuades to take to spinning, argues: "My son, we have weavers in the village. There is Chennayya and Rangayya." How can the pariah woman grasp the significance of the Gandhian ideal, under which the Panchayat is founded to promote spinning, practising ahimsa and speaking the truth? The pariah women talk indifferently to Moorthy on spinning a hundred yards of yarn per day. 'I'm going to have a child' and Satana's wife says, 'I'm going for my brother's marriage,' and her sister says, 'I'll spin if it will bring money. I don't want cloth like Timmayya and Mandayya get with all their turning of the wheel.'" (106)

Rangè Gowda, too, fails to live up to the Gandhian ideals. As per directive from the Karwar Congress, every Gandhian will have to practise ahimsa which is most fundamental to the ideals Gandhi loved. But a thoughtless impulsive man Rangè Gowda retaliates when he sees Moorthy being taken by the Police under framed charges of having organized an assault on the police in Skeffington Coffee Estate. For Rangè Gowda, to come to terms with this situation is impossible; hence, he assaults the policeman. Rangè Gowda acquiesces to become a member of the Congress, but not without expressing his inability to live up to the Gandhian high standards. He believes that Moorthy who belongs to Kanthapura will stand by him in true faith. On hearing of the ideal of ahimsa, he bursts into laughter telling Moorthy: "Then I too will have one day to sit and meditate, taking three cups of salted water per day." (103)

However, Moorthy has, before he is sent behind the bars, looked after the pariah night school held in the Panchayat hall. Thus the Gandhian action programme embraces all in its orbit. Women are also taken in the Congress Committee:

> 'We need a woman in the Committee for the Congress is for the weak and the lowly'; and then everybody says, 'Rangamma, say yes!' and Rangamma says 'Yes.' And Moorthy then turns towards the pariah and says, 'One among you!' and then there is such a silence that a moving ant could be heard, and then Moorthy says, 'Come, Rachanna.' (110-11)

After the exit of Moorthy from the scene, for he has been sentenced to three months' rigorous imprisonment, Raja Rao focuses attention on two more characters who are true followers of Gandhi; they are Rangamma whom Moorthy counted among his ardent supporters, and Sankar who is a reputed lawyer based in Karwar. Rangamma, in the words of the narrator, "had enough money." And further, she, being educated, reads every day such significant newspapers as *Tai-nadu*, *Vishwakarnataka*, *Deshbhandu* and *Jayabharatha* and she would keep the village women abreast of what was happening outside India, especially Russia, the land of socialism: "Oh, she told us so many interesting things—and all came from these white and blue papers, sister!" (48) remarks the narrator. Unfortunately, she is a widow, and her niece Ratna, too, is a widow. So another widow Waterfall Venkamma would be busy casting aspersions on their character: that Rangamma goes to Karwar to enjoy the pleasures of men and that Moorthy and Ratna liaison, which is unfortunate, but this is how things are. Raja Rao defends Rangamma against the allegations hurled at her and calls her as tame as cow wholly committed to Gandhian ways of passive resistance; she prepares the home-loving women for Satyagraha. As a member of the Congress committee, she organizes Kanthapura women in an organization called Sevika Sangha and instructs them how to keep unprovoked in the face of an assault by the police, how to keep healthy by taking yogic exercises. In fact, she makes the women take interest in politics by being useful for their health needs. The women enrolled in Sevika Sangha would naturally be at discord with their husbands who have feudal mindset and one of them is beaten up in the process. But Rangamma helps them divide their time between politics and home. She tells them: "In the city there are groups and groups of young women, girls, married women, and widows who have joined together and have become Volunteers—Volunteers they call them—and they practise exercises like the Police, and when meetings are held they all get together and maintain order." (149) She tries to convince them to become volunteers. She narrates gripping accounts of Rani Lakshmi Bai and the Mutiny of 1857 to fire their imagination so that they devote themselves to the nationalist cause. She tells them that the nationalist women idols like Kamaladevi, and Saroijni Naidu and Annie Besant are the finest products of the Congress who need to be followed by all women. Her niece Ratna feels quite enthused: "I shall part my hair to the left, and wear just a tiny kumkum mark and wear the sari till it reaches the toes and it will float and flutter so well.' (151) These village women are being prepared for the movement to be launched by Gandhi in 1930 that came to be known as Salt Satyagraha, or Civil Disobedience Movement. Among Gandhian women characters, Ratna is a modern girl who as a young widow wants to live with the freedom the city women enjoy, instead of living like a morose widow in a corner of the house.

When Moorthy is in prison, another Gandhian devoted to the Congress, who is a true ascetic, takes over. Advocate Sankar, as Secretary of Karwar Congress, holds a meeting in Gandhi Maidan to promote the Gandhian beliefs. This meeting is sought to be sabotaged by the Swami's man, which, of course, deserves condemnation in fiercest terms. To this meeting has been invited Rangamma who brings home to the audience gathered there the nefarious work the British Government-paid Swami is doing: "And therefore, brothers, know for sure what religion is wearing behind its saffron robes. Choose between a saint like Mahatma Gandhi who has given up land and lust and honours and comfort and has dedicated his life to the country, and these fattened brahmins who want to frighten us with their excommunications, once the Government has paid them well." (132) Rangamma helps Sankar with the correspondence work of the Congress. Sankar, though an advocate like Seenappa, presents a contrast to the latter. A brilliant man well-versed in law, he would rather defend those who cannot afford a lawyer than make money by this profession. Nor would he marry a second time, though he is a young widower. He loves Gandhi's ideal of simple living, wearing Khadi and speaking Hindi.

Rangamma, Sanker and Moorthy are rooted in great ideals Gandhi practised all through his life. When a man or society or a nation struggles for its existence, it has to call up superhuman strength. At such critical moments, there emerge committed men and women making highest sacrifices for the cause dear to them. Moorthy is dear to all because he is true follower of Mahatma. When the mighty British government puts him in prison, people feel rudderless without him. The people of Kanthapura feel vanquished, desperate and helpless. They can do nothing but pray to Kenchamma: "Rangamma vowed she would offer a Kanchi sari to Kenchamma if he were released, and Ratna said she would have a thousand-and-eight flames ceremony performed, and Nanjamma said she would give the Goddess a silver belt, and Pariah Rachanna said he would walk the holy fire, and said, 'The Goddess will never fail us—she will free him from the clutches of the Red-man.'" (134)

Moorthy comes out from the prison: his release from the prison coincides with launching of the Salt Satyagraha by Mahatma Gandhi. So Moorthy would like the congressmen to adhere to Gandhi's ideals like speaking the truth, spinning daily one hundred yards, and practising equality in social relationships. He apprises the congress members of Kanthapura how Gandhi with his eighty-two followers has gone to the Dandi to manufacture salt. To the mass of people through the press, Gandhi asked people to disobey the British laws, which in the opinion of Gandhi were unjust. In *Kanthapura* this political movement has been named as "Don't-touch-the-Government Campaign." Moorthy explains to the Congress activists of Kanthapura the main points of this programme: "he talks of the taxes that are not to be paid, 'even if the Government attaches the lands,' and of the toddy booths that are to be picketed, 'for toddy trees are Government trees, and toddy booths are there to exploit the poor and the unhappy,' and he continues, his voice rising higher, 'And we shall establish a parallel Government, and it is this Government that will rule.'" (179-80)

Ratna and many other activists had been put behind the bars for following Gandhi. When Ratna comes out on parole, she reads a letter Moorthy had written to her from prison: "The youths here say they will change it. Jawaharlal will change it. You know Jawaharlal is like a Bharatha to the Mahatma, and he, too, is for non-violence and he, too, is a Satyagrahi, but he says in Swaraj there shall be neither the rich nor the poor. And he calls himself an 'equal-distributionist' and I am with him and his men. We shall speak of it when you are here." (256-57)

This however, does not mean that the Satyagraha Movement failed without yielding any positive outcome. The most single contribution of Satyagraha movement lay in the fact that it went a long way in linking up the women with active politics, a fact focussed in the narrative of *Kanthapura*. As many as twenty-two women picketed toddy trees, which filled them with confidence and hence they showed the same endurance as men do during the passive resistance. They are kicked, beaten, wounded, abused and arrested by the police during the picketing. The toddy booths are places where the poor coolies of Skeffington Coffee Estate drink toddy. But the coolies too participate in passive resistance when it is driven home to them how they throw away their hard-earned money by way of drinking toddy at Government-run toddy booths. Thus the coolies are also made a part of Gandhi's Satyagraha Movement. The peasants, the low castes and the coolies—all get united against the alien Government. This should be considered as significant as the Salt Satyagraha.

The Congress activists learn from the city Congress that Gandhi has been arrested by the British Government, which fuels the fire of people's anger. The movement launched by the Gandhimen of Kanthapura has been shown as having failed because of the outbreak of violence. All the Gandhimen are arrested by police, many poor coolies are shot dead. And Moorthy, too, feels drawn to socialism because Nehru was socialist in his political beliefs in the 1930s.

NOTES

1. C.D. Narasimhaiah, *Raja Rao* (New Delhi: Doaba, 2000), p. 42.
2. K. Sachidanandan, "The End of An Era: Thakazhi Sivasankar Pillai (1912-1999) The Historian of Instincts," *The Book Review*, volume XXIII, number 7.
3. Kamala Markandaya, *Nectar in a Sieve* (New Delhi: Sagar, 1968), p. 9.
4. Raja Rao, *Kanthapura* (New Delhi: Orient Paperbacks, 1971), p. 6.

The Struggle of Coolies from Bondage to Freedom

RANU UNIYAL
University of Lucknow

The present chapter describes the way coolies are lured from different areas to the Estate. They become mere tools in the hands of the colonial forces. When the coolies discover that the ruling class is interested in its own apotheosis rather than in the welfare conditions of the workers, there appears a direct confrontation with the other. From an earlier state of apathy and indifference, one sees the coolies raising voices of protest. They demand the amelioration of their existing conditions. Along with the people of Kanthapura, they make a call for freedom.

Trapped in a cage, the coolies inside the Estate present another form of estrangement. The Skeffington Coffee Estate is the cage to which the coolies are lured by the hunter. The Red-man's government tries to capture and to cage the very life of the coolies. Once in a cage, they are unable to free themselves and live in perpetual imprisonment. Maistri lures them to the place by promising them better wages and better prospects for life. The description of the Estate by the narrator has an aura of mystery around it:

> Nobody knows how large it is or when it was founded; but they all say it is at least ten thousand acres wide, and some people in Kanthapura can still remember having heard of the Hunter Sahib who used his hunter and his hand to reap the first fruits of his plantation. (67)

> More and more coolies came—coolies from below the Ghats that talked Tamil or Telugu and who brought with them their old men and their children and their widowed women—armies of coolies

> marched past the Kenchamma temple, half-naked, starving, spitting, weeping, vomiting, coughing, shivering, squeaking, shouting, moaning coolies—coolie after coolie passed by the Kenchamma temple, the maistri before them, while the children clung to their mothers' breasts, the old men to their son's arms, and bundles hung over shoulder and arm and arm and shoulder and head; and they marched on past the Kenchamma Temple and up to the Skeffington Coffee Estate—coolies from below the Ghats, coolies, young men, old men, old women, children, baskets, bundles, pots, coolies passed on—and winding through the twists of the Estate path. (67-68)

The Estate becomes a place where conflicts multiply because of the hostilities which develop between maistri and labourer, between master and servant. The estate appears as a battleground where coolies fight against the demands of social realities. Maistri had promised them 'two Anna bit for each woman and four Anna bit for each man hand' but as he approaches the Estate along with the coolies a gradual change comes in his behaviour: "and the nearer they came, the harder became the road and the stiffer the maistri." (69) Coolies had been uprooted from their homes, they had come from far off places expecting a better life in the Estate. Maistri tries to convince them by saying, "there is nothing but rice around us." (68) He creates strong hopes in them. Mothers promise their children: "I'll take you over the mountains where you can have milk like water—just like water." (69)

The Estate has been projected to them as a place where there would be less work and more to eat. Disillusionment creeps in slowly as the master tries to assert his supremacy over them. "The sahib says that if you work well you will get sweets and if you work badly you will get beaten—that is the law of the place." (70) Next day the coolies begin their work and there is no respite for them. Maistri appears as a symbol of tyranny as he beats them asking them to work without any rest. The presence of the snakes in the Estate is a sign of the presence of the other which moves around fearlessly creating fear in the coolies. The cobra is not only a symbol of absolute power but also of pity. It has never harmed an innocent person. The hot blazing sun and the hard work tire them soon. The arrival of rains heralds the coming of disaster in the Estate. There is fever and death all over the Estate. Coolies find themselves menaced by problems from without as well as from within. Their arrival inside the Estate has plunged them into a situation from which there is no escape. The master has invaded their lives. In one way or the other, they have to face the coming problems. Their praying to Kenchamma reveals their unflinching faith in the supernatural. Having always thought that mother Kenchamma would look after their welfare, they persistently refuse to take the pills. Despite all these problems, hopes within their hearts have not been crushed. Coolies feel that soon they will return to their homes with lots of money. This fact, that their dreams could never materialize, is known to Siddayya. Pariah Rangayya says: "We'll make three hundred rupees in all—three hundred rupees each, and we shall take our money and scuttle down the passes like kitchen bandicoots." (80)

They have realized the danger within the Estate and seek, by all means, to free themselves from the Estate. They do not know that setting themselves free from the Estate is not an easy task. Siddayya knows that once inside the Estate they are all tempted to the toddy booths and will spend whatever they earn on 'deaths and festivals and caste-dinners.' Siddayya has stayed here for ten years and knows it all. Their escape becomes a dream unrealized; to attain it they can apparently do nothing.

A Desire to Escape Leads towards Resistance

A change in Sahibs takes place but the exploitation of the coolies continues in one form or the other. If the earlier sahib assaulted them with sticks, the new one would physically assault the women on the Estate. Thus we can see that a change in sahibs has brought no change in the plight of the coolies. Violence is inflicted on them and the rape of their wishes takes place intermittently. Another strong form of oppression is the sahib shooting Seetharam, when he refuses to give up his daughter to him. The death of Seetharam becomes a protest against the atrocious attitude of the master. His giving up his life to save the honour of his girl implies that the daughter is worth such a sacrifice. "I'm a brahmin. I would rather die than sell my daughter," (83) says he.

Seetharam's death is an act of revenge. His death appears purposeful for we can see that no brahmin's daughter was ever touched by the sahib, 'And when a pariah says, "No," he hardly ever sends the maistri to drag her up at night.' (83)

Though the sahib is set free by the Red-man's court, we see that Seetharam's resistance has created fear in him. Death as a point of departure reveals the success of the coolies. It offers a justification and as a strong symbol of protest is a refusal to succumb.

Life inside the Estate is however dominated by the master and his maistri. By refusing to bow down to his master's wishes Seetharam reveals his wish to be himself. His desire to be free results in his death. Labour of the coolies is no longer a free activity. They have been estranged from it because it's not they, but the owners of production, who decide what and how they have to work and produce. Coolies are unable to realize themselves through their work and therefore this desire in them to escape becomes stronger.

Moorthy's arrival inside the Estate is stopped by Badè Khan. Badè Khan as a badge of authority dominates the existence of the coolies. His statement reveals the coolies' state of existence:

> Free man you may be in your palace. But this is the Skeffington Coffee Estate. And these are Skeffington Estate coolies. You'd better take care of your legs. I've orders. (87)

It is quite apparent that the colonial rule has spread its tentacles too far. Stark distinctions have been drawn between those who decide and the ones who obey. The owners and the masters who are also the few, control and determine the policies and lives of the many men working for them. Coolies, once having entered the Estate, have given themselves and the fruit of their labour to their masters. They are being used by the Red-man's government, and exploitation continues to oppress the people. Some have offered themselves to be treated as objects (for example,

Siddayya) whereas men like Seetharam and Rachanna refuse to be reduced to objects and thus protest.

Rachanna's expulsion from the Estate along with his family and then later on his settling in Kanthapura is an act of defiance. His confrontation with the other is watched silently by his friends and they raise no voice at his expulsion. Expulsion is an act which seeks to reveal the desire of the Other to curb whatever dominant force is present in the coolies. It is a reflection of one's desire to oppress and rule the others. Rachanna's refusal to be dictated is an indicator of the fact that despite being a coolie he wishes to be free. He is accepted by the people of Kanthapura and this creates a new consciousness in him.

The picketing of Boranna's toddy booth by enthusiastic followers of Moorthy and the participation of coolies in this act is symbolic of their desire to struggle. The Estate has an unknown and fearful appearance to the outsiders. Therefore, while women along with men were marching towards it, their hearts were filled with fear. The coolies, once out from the Estate with 'their eyes fixed on the earth' and 'money tied to their waists,' they marched on to the toddy booth 'to drink and to beat the drum and to clap hands and sing.' (196-97)

As the men squat on the floor, the coolies refuse to walk over them. They are beaten up by the police in return. They promise not to drink in the name of Kenchamma. The simmering discontent and disgust at the behaviour of the Other has surfaced and is symptomatic of a new perception.

Suppression of the Being through Force and Violence

As the novel proceeds we see the coolies caged inside the Estate. A large section of this oppressed class throws off its old role and begins to assume the role of free men by determining a course of action for itself and by moving out from the Estate. These coolies, who had left the Estate and settled in Kanthapura, were one morning forcibly marched towards the Estate. The narrator's statement reveals her state of helplessness as well as those of others around her:

> Coolies of the Skeffington Coffee Estate who had come to live with us and to work with us and to fight with us—they marched over the bouldered streets . . . the coolies of the Skeffington coffee Estate were marched bent-headed through our streets to show who our true masters were, and we knew they would be driven over the Bebbur Mound and the Bear's Hill and the Tippur Stream, and two by two they would be pushed behind the gates, for the white master wanted them. (210)

The domination of the English over the Indian labourers by means of brutal force, simply for the sake of satisfying its own desires, without any regard for the wishes of the others, is a most significant form of colonial oppression. Raja Rao focuses on this exploitation of one man by the other. He has tried to bring to light those vitiating forces which are responsible for creating unrest in the minds of the working class.

Coolies, who knew that they were being exploited by the bourgeoisie, had tried to break away from its tyrannical clutches but were forcefully driven back to the Estate. But as we see later, the Estate is unable to hold them any longer and they pine for freedom. They join the struggle with men and women of Kanthapura and are further subjected to pain and torture.

Coolies from the city come and start reaping at the Estate. Their arrival signifies the fact that once slavery is established inside the Estate, it is maintained by conscription. The coolies who had run away from the Estate and revolted are forcibly brought back to the Estate. The police employed by the Red-man's government uses force on the disrupters of the law and order. Underlying the struggle is an intense desire for freedom. The coolies realize that they are being treated as means by the other. This increases their suffering and oppression. It creates in them a hatred for the colonial rule.

Gandhi: A Symbol of Non-Violence
Coolies: The Lost Identity

Gandhi, on the other hand, becomes a symbol of intense struggle. He has become a part of people's consciousness. Though the coolies have never met him personally, yet like the people of Kanthapura, they join hands and collectively seek to attain their ideal. Gandhi believed non-violence to be the only possible form of resistance to the colonial-racialist oppression. The coolies had resorted to violence, when once, Moorthy was not allowed to enter the Estate and was beaten up by the police. Their resorting to violence at that time is a crucial action which is responsible for Moorthy's arrest and Rachanna's expulsion.

If we look deeply into the cause of unrest within the Estate we find that certain conditions were responsible for the agitation. Economically deprived due to poor wages, physically exploited and mentally tortured, the coolies had earlier been living a totally suppressed existence. The arrival of Moorthy inside the Estate, and their constant mixing with Gandhi's men makes them conscious of their plight. After having been stripped of all identity, history, family and human rights by the Other, they realize the futility of their existence. Through the ideals of Gandhi and under the guidance of Moorthy, the coolies strive hard for emancipation. In seeking refuge at Kanthapura, the coolies have sought to avoid a destruction of their identity. The coolies are illiterate and ignorant at the time of oppression. A gradual change comes over them as they begin mixing with the people of Kanthapura.

Their refusal to walk over the people who had squatted on the floor and then going to Boranna's toddy grove is a sign of their growing awareness of the problems present in the country. Later on, as they cry 'Mahatma Gandhi ki Jai' and promise never to drink in the name of 'Kenchamma,' we can see an essential step being taken in the positive direction.

The coolies had walked 'bent headed' from Kanthapura back to the Estate. They have refused to bow down before their masters. 'Their eyes fixed on the earth'—repetition of this psychological code signifies the state of repression the coolies have been forced to live in. Later on, their 'escape' from the Estate signifies the desire to live and be themselves. The coolies being forcibly taken back to the Estate is another significant political code which brings to light the existential predicament. On the one hand are the coolies who after having realized their predicament refuse to accept the situation where they find themselves trapped by the other. The desire in them to get out, to say 'no' and still survive creates a fear in the mind of the Other. On the other we find the existence of the Other who has dehumanized the being i.e. the coolies. What results is rebellion. Unable to bear the oppression any longer, the coolies seek to become individuals and not mere objects. By trying to defy the norms and rules set by the Other, coolies like Vasudev, Rachanna and Madanna have realized the importance of their being. After having become aware of the raison d'être they seek to bridge the ècart, which lies between the subject and the object.

The project of living under the Other has promised nothing but disillusionment. Earlier they had been lured to the Estate by the maistri who promised them good money, and better treatment with less work. But soon they realize that Gandhi alone can fulfill their dreams. This discovery sets them on a very different path. In agreeing to be with Gandhi, the coolies come into conflict with the Red-men.

The coolies have become aware of the existence of the Other who treats them as mere means. The Other is the cause of fear and proves to be a menace in the life of the coolies. The coolies collectively cooperate with men and women of Kanthapura in opposing the organized force of the Other who is regarded as enemy. This sort of a situation is revealed in the picketing scene where coolies refuse to walk over the men and women who have squatted on the floor. Later on, as they bravely face the shots fired at them and cry 'Mahatma Gandhi ki Jai,' one feels that they have begun to identify themselves with Gandhi.

'"Stop, or we shoot," says a voice to which "Shoot!" answers one of the coolies, and a shot bursts straight at him.' In this direct confrontation between the being and the Other is visible a change in the attitude—from that of servility to a state of defiance. This defiance and refusal to be cowed down by the Other appears as a most significant action on the part of the being.

The forceful removal of men from Kanthapura and then their being taken to the Estate, in brief, signifies the fact that the other needs the being. Without the coolies they would not have been able to fulfill their wishes and thus attain material gains. This forcible taking away of the coolies from Kanthapura also strengthens the belief that the Other, i.e. Red-man cannot exist without the support of the being i.e. the coolies.

Towards Self-Realization:
Struggle for Fulfillment of One's needs

Thus we can see that Raja Rao has successfully tried to portray the predicament of the coolies inside the Estate. From a state of complete acceptance of conditions they had been placed in, we see a gradual change as the coolies, after having been subconsciously motivated by Gandhian ideology, begin acting as individuals by insisting that their wages be paid and they be allowed to remain free.

What saves them from oppression both physical and psychological, inside the Estate, is their own decision to escape from the place. The coolies have no choice but to defend themselves against those who have trapped them inside the cage i.e. the 'Estate.'

Their struggle against colonial rule forms the basis of the novel. Though the movement led by Moorthy has no immediate positive recourse in sight, the impetus behind the struggle proves to be a source of optimism.

Kanthapura: India in Miniature

JAYA SRIVASTAVA
Mahila Vidyalaya P.G. College, Lucknow

Raja Rao's profound and philosophical knowledge of Indian life, passionate attachment with the Indian National movement and his literary quest to search a soothing and inspiring language for delineating his thought have got expression in his debut novel *Kanthapura*. This is perhaps the finest evocation of the Gandhian age in Indian English fiction. It is the story of a small South Indian village caught in the maelstrom of the freedom struggle of the nineteen thirties and transformed so completely in the end that 'there's neither man nor mosquito' left in it. There is no central character (other than the village, what happens to it, what it becomes). Village life is certainly more closely at the heart of the novel than any of the other works, in spite of the fact that Raja Rao describes the movement of the village from solidarity to complete and utter annihilation. There are at least three strands of experience in the novel; the political—a struggle for securing freedom of the country, the religious—a life that highlights Indian life and the third the social concerns. All the three are woven inextricably into the one complex story of Kanthapura.

The village Kanthapura is like any other village in India with its own culture and history. Much of the early part of the book is spent developing a sense of the village, establishing its ambience. In the first para Achakka informs us of its geographical location: "Our village—I don't think you have ever heard about it—Kanthapura is its name and it is in the province of Kara."[1]

Nestling among the Blue Mountains up in the western ghats "it lies curled up like a child on its mother's lap. Like Hardy's Edgon Heath, Kanthapura has remained in isolation for ages cut off from the rest of the world, far from the madding crowd's ignoble strife. It has nevertheless its own stable social structure, a culture and an unchanging pattern of life blessed by the life-giving waters of the Himavathy and no doubt by the ever-bountiful goddess Kenchamma who has protected them through the ages against many a natural calamity. There is a folk song which evokes in us images and attitudes as to what Kenchamma means to the people of Kanthapura:

> Kenchamma, Kenchamma
> Goddess benign and bounteous,
> Mother of earth, blood of life,
> Harvest queen, rain-crowned,
> Kenchamma, Kenchamma.
> Goddess benign and bounteous. (4)

There may be small pox or influenza around, but you make a vow to the goddess, the next morning you wake up and you find the fever has left you.

If Kanthapura has been steeped in darkness and ignorance and has accepted its obscure destiny without question, it has also kept alive the flame of religion and spirituality through its rituals, poojas, Harikathas and cycles of festivals and the lighting of Kartik lamps is but one of the symbolic acts by which Kanthapura society reassures itself time and again of the presence of an eternal light which, through Avatars and incarnations, would save them and save the world from the darker powers. It is this firm faith in an inner stability and strength and it is to this faith that Moorthy appeals when he makes them see the advent of Mahatma Gandhi on the Indian political scene not as a political event but as a religious experience right in the tradition of the Hindu Avatars. Herein lies the key to one's understanding of India. As Sri Aurobindo has pointed out in his "The Renaissance In India,"[2] all movements in this country whether political or social begin only as religious or spiritual movement and as Narasimhaiah has argued out the point with reference to Raja Rao's debt to Ignatio Silone's Fontmara, "Religion becomes the nucleus of social regeneration in Kanthapura in the true tradition of India where social reformers have been profoundly religious men."[3]

When Moorthy threw out a hint that 'Somebody will offer a dinner for each day of the month,' there was a spontaneous response from everyone and this is not stated by the novelist but comes home to us through the characters themselves: "'Let the first be mine,' said Bhatta, 'the second mine,' said agent Nanjundiah,' 'the third must be mine,' insisted Pandit Kenkateshiah." (10) The verb 'insisted' suggests both a willing co-operation in team work and the issues of social prestige in a small community—for the individual has no existence apart from the village. Soon they observed *Sankara-jayanthi*, the Rama festival, the Krishna festival and the Ganesh festival. When Moorthy collects money, they have Harikathas and readings from the epics and the puranas. The novelist captures in the Harikatha-man's performance the whole of the Indian tradition brought-up-to-date as he hears it rendered in the villager's own idiom. It is worthwhile to suggest that the Dandi March has been portrayed as a pilgrimage. From this point of view, one may say that Kanthapura is India.

While Kanthapura is India in this large sense, it is India in miniature in another sense. As a typical Indian village, it has a physiographical, civic and socio-economic structure which makes it an allegorical version of a larger India. The structure of social living and social relationship in this village is firm and well-knit and caste system and untouchability are part of these structures. There is a Brahmin quarter, Potters' quarter, Weavers' quarter and the Sudra quarter. There was Bhatta, a priest-turned-moneylender and Zamindar, Postmaster Suryanarayana, Snuff Shastri, Pandit Venkateshia, Old Ramakrishnayya better than whom nobody could read the *Sankara-Vijaya* and Corner House Moorthy. They were all brahmins, the dominating sections of the society. Then there are the potters Lingayya, Ramayya, Subbayya and Chandrayya, weavers Chennayya, Rangayya, Beadle Thimayya, Patwari Nanjundia and Ramanna, businessman Rama Chetty and Patel Rangè Gowda—the most powerful man in Kanthapura. "If the Patel says it, even a coconut leaf roof will become a gold roof." (9)

Thus there is a pervasive veil of caste hierarchy. Every caste has its own space of living. Of all the castes, brahmins are the supreme inhabitants of the village. Achakka's brahmin status, as a narrator, at first poses some problem. She has been taught in her childhood to uphold the caste system. When she describes the outcaste quarter early in the narrative, she comments: "of course your wouldn't expect me to go to the Pariah quarter." (7)

When Moorthy returns to Kanthapura and begins to associate with the artisans, Achakka comments again mirroring the rigid and claustrophobic caste system in the village: "He even goes to the Potters' quarter and the Weavers' quarter and the Sudra quarter, and I closed my ears when I heard he went to the Pariah quarter. We said to ourselves, he is one of these Gandhi-men who say there is neither caste nor clan nor family, and yet they pray like us." (19)

Gandhi rejected the tenet of Hindu caste system. The opening of the temples to the pariahs whom Gandhiji called Harijan is an event of historical importance in the novel. Untouchability was considered to be a scar on the face of the society. But Moorthy, being free from caste prejudices, starts eradicating untouchability. Like Gandhi, he understands it is man who created caste and for human welfare it should be eradicated. So Moorthy's work for improving the lives of Harijans progresses without any fear of excommunication by the authoritative Swami. The chants of 'Satya Narayan Maharaj Ki Jai' changes into the shouts of 'Inquilab Zindabad' and Gandhi mahatma has come on this earth 'to slay the serpent of the foreign rule.' Apart from this, poverty is the Keynote of life in Kanthapura and it is this eternal poverty which has helped usurers like Bhatta, Rama Chetti and Linga Chetti prosper and grow richer through the years. Bhatta seems to walk out of the novelist's pages into the larger world with his 'Oily calendar' and 'learned calculations on his agile fingers. He 'began life with a loincloth at his waist and a copper pot in his hand,' and went on adding 'several acres of the peasants' lands' to his own domain. He turns usurer and charges ten percent interest. He later raises this to twenty percent. The novelist who has a higher conception of the avocation of the brahmin, the type of whom he sees in men like Ramakrishnayya of the older generation and Moorthy of the coming generation, now witnesses his degradation in Bhatta, and yet he is the first brahmin of Kanthapura, for with increasing prosperity Bhatta loses interest in his priesthood. "It was so difficult to get him for an obsequial dinner or marriage ceremony." (30)

The evil of exploitation is, however, presented in grimmer proportions in the depiction of life as in the ghats, in the Skeffington Coffee Estate, the symbol of the impact of industrialization on the traditional community life of Kanthapura. While the coffee plantation is physically encircled by a fence and gate keeping both the coolies in and the others out, the village is represented as closed and exclusive social order keeping the agents of the colonial matrix out. Hence, Badè Khan, the policeman as a figure of colonial authority is not offered a home in Kanthapura and instead finds himself quarters in the Coffee Estate. While the tyranny of the European planters assisted by shameless panderers like Badè Khan projects a realistic vision of India under the British which was a hotbed of extreme tyranny on the one hand and extreme servility on the other, Moorthy's heroic efforts to fight these evils in that little world is symbolic of the fact that it is these little Gandhis of the countless villages in the country who made the advent of the Mahatma a reality. The Gandhian movement spreads in Kanthapura and the village becomes a part of All India Panchayat, a territory to be ruled by a parallel government. The inspired women sing:

> There's one Government, sister,
> There's one Government, sister,
> And that is the Government of the Mahatma. (207)

The inhabitants of Kanthapura willingly pledge to spin yarn, maintain non-violence (ahimsa) and speak 'Truth.' But the walls of orthodoxy are breached suddenly; revolution comes as a flood and carries all before it. The villagers comprising the men and women of all castes and professions and labourers of Coffee Estate readily meet the onslaught of bureaucracy. An unequal fight it inevitably proves to be, for the Satyagrahis are maimed, broken and scattered and a remnant reaches after sore trails and vicissitudes—another village Kashipur, beyond the border where they settle down. Our villages provide a basic pattern easily discernible all over India. As Meenakshi Mukherjee observes: "It is because often in the rural context that the regional reality and the Indian reality more or less merge."[4]

Kanthapura is India in microcosm. What happened there is what happened in many places during India's fight for freedom. What happens in Kanthapura is by no means a unique exception, but the telling of the story gives the whole affairs,[5] an ithihasic, at least a puranic, dignity. Raja Rao has presented the story in the puranic "Akhyan style'"[6] which he terms in the 'Foreword' as *sthala-purana* in which 'the past mingles with the present and the gods mingle with the men, reliving and mingling the contemporaneous socio-political history with the rich and religious mythology. It is a breathless tale from the beginning to the end and beautifully narrated by a typical Indian grandmother—Achakka with her own idiosyncratic norm. The narrative is hardly very straightforward: there are involution and digressions, there are meaningful backward glances, there are rhythmic chains of proper names (Rachanna and Chandranna and Madanna, Sampanna and Vaidyanna), there are hypnotic repetitions and refrains and there are also sheer poetic iridescences. A village, a picturesque region, an epoch of social and political change, a whole complex of character and motive, reason and superstition, idealism and cold calculation, all spring up before our eyes demanding recognition and acceptance, it is almost a tour de force.

For the first time in contemporary India, the novel in Raja Rao's hands has become a mature means of enlarging the frontiers of human consciousness. It is interesting that global consciousness should come to Kanthapura through the 'blue paper' and the 'white paper' of course with the novelist's shattering irony. Rangamma's sources of this global consciousness are the Tainadu, Vishwakarnataka Deshbandhu and Jayabharata, all of them snobbishly dismissed by big people during the period in question as three piece tags.

Kanthapura is thus a miniature version of resurgent Bharat in which we see the pilgrim's progress of a great nation marching towards the promised land of freedom carrying on its shoulders the burden of poverty and hunger. In the final analysis, it is a poignant vision of the human predicament as poignant as that of Piers, the plowman and it is this dimension of the novel which raises it above the level of a regional novel and makes it much more than an Indian novel.

Works Cited

1. Raja Rao, *Kanthapura* (Madras: Oxford University Press, 1974), p. 1.
2. Sri Aurobindo, *The Renaissance in India* (Pondicherry: Sri Aurobindo Ashram, 1973), p. 30.
3. C.D. Narasimhaiah, *Raja Rao* (New Delhi: Arnold-Heinemann India), p. 49.
4. Meenakshi Mukherjee, *The Twice-Born Fiction: Themes and Techniques of the Indian Novel in English* (New Delhi: Arnold Heinemann, 1971), p. 213.
5. K.R.S. Iyengar, *Indian Writing in English* (New Delhi, 1962), p. 392.
6. K.R. Rao, *The Fiction of Raja Rao* (Aurangabad, 1980), p. 60.

Raja Rao's All-Pervasive Indian Sensibility in *Kanthapura*

VANDANA SINGH
Women's College, Patna

Raja Rao's thoughts and temperament were moulded by several external influences. Originally belonging to a brahmin family of South India, he was exposed to different influences. He was educated in different parts of India and later on went to France. His doctorate on "The Influence of Indian Thoughts on the Mysticism of the West" paved the way to the search for the unknown. Marriage to a French school teacher further moulded his way of thinking and on his wife's advice reverted to his writing in Kannada. Instead of writing in English which was a blend of stylistic influences of McCauley, W.B. Yeats and Rabindra Nath Tagore. An after-thought made him decide to blend the knowledge of East and West in his works. Though balancing both the ideologies seemed to appeal to Raja Rao, it was difficult to reveal his soul in an alien language. Yet, Raja Rao created more authentic "voice" by recreating the ideologies and technicalities of both the East and the West.

Kanthapura was his first major work in English. In his Foreword to the novel, Raja Rao claims that it is quite a different job to articulate the subjectivity of the 'colonized' in the language of the 'colonizer':

> There is no village in India, however mean, that has not a rich sthala-purana, or legendary history of its own. Some God or God-like hero has passed by the village—Rama might have rested under this pipal tree, Sita might have dried her clothes, after her bath, on this yellow stone, or the Mahatma himself, on one of his many pilgrimages through the country, might have slept in this hut, the low one, by the village gate. In this way the past mingles with the present, and the Gods mingle with men, to make repertory of your

> grandmother always bright. One such story from the contemporary annals of my village I have tried to tell. (Raja Rao, *Kanthapura*, Orient Paperbacks, 2001)

The soul of Indianness is bound to get lost when the various hues of a particular thought process are expressed in an alien language.

Kanthapura works at two different levels which are entwined together. The form of a transcribed or 'literary' oral tale about the Indian Independence movement as experienced in a single village, a village which is a generic one in South India and has been carefully mapped out and restored in a textual form. Gandhi is introduced as a mythic figure to deliver humanity form its state of servility. Moorthy is replica of Gandhi in the village and he moulds the psychology of the villagers firing their senses in a way so that each one of the 'illiterates' joins the struggle movement for freedom. The political scenario of India has been compressed and concentrated in a small village, encompassing the canvas of Kanthapura; a village in slumber is awakened to awareness by 'our very own Moorthy.'

The reinterpretation of Gandhian principles by Moorthy through oral narrative is told in nostalgic pastoral mode. At the same time, the story of the community efforts to withstand the exploitation of workers on the nearby Skeffington Coffee Estate can be read as a parable about Gandhian 'passive-resistance' policy. Pastoral romance, Hindu myth and traditional narrative technique (grandmother's folklore narrative songs) blend with the contemporary tale of nationalist struggle.

The resistance to the programme of mass agricultural production enforced by the British by the local, illiterate villagers led by Moorthy relates the 'pastoral' in Kanthapura to its politics. In the context of Gandhian resistance, efforts to champion old village ways bear an explicitly political edge.

The technique of oral folklore is innate to the return to traditional ways and as a result legitimates the more insurgent aspects of Gandhian policy. The presence of 'female narrator' juxtaposed to "Waterfall" Venkamma and 'feminist' Rangamma symbolizes the different aspects of the Indian sensibility characterizing the position of women in society. The former represents the feminized Gandhian approach of submission and the latter refers to the modern contemporary women who came out of the restraining confines of society norms and self-imposed 'purdah' to actively participate in freeing the slumbering soul of the Indian women.

The feminist perspective, pivotal to the plot, has been adapted from the Indian mythology where the 'ideal family' of Lord Rama, Lakshmana and Sita posits the perfect conduit to outreach the simple villagers. Goddess Sita, epitome of self-abnegation, a woman of substance, who faced the world and its atrocities by remaining silent and who drew her strength from her will-power, is juxtaposed to Goddess Kenchamma (the local Goddess), the self-empowered one who kills the demon to deliver man from his atrocities. The 'demon' is symbolic of the British from whom the Indians have to be expiated by the 'Noble Cow,' Moorthy. Moorthy leads the villagers to purgate themselves of their profane beliefs which makes them servile to their English masters. Moorthy's modus operandi conforms to feminized principle of protest, i.e., resistance through silence and non-cooperativeness. It is ironical that this movement brings out the tiger-balls in the unpretentious women, the weak mutating into self-empowered Goddesses. The cohesion is complete with cognizant villagers following Moorthy's instructions with a fervour and zeal.

This deliberate mythicizing in portrayal of women mutating into embodiment of power brings out the fact with aplomb that Raja Rao is very much acquainted with the Indian sensibility prevalent in the village which is suddenly exposed to the outer world. The slumbering villagers are awakened to hard realities at the soft hands of enigmatic Moorthy, with his folklores and *Harikathas*.

Rangamma and Ratna display 'fervour' and 'force.' Rangamma joins the galaxy of great women of India by the sheer force of her contribution to the movement. She is described as 'a tight-jawed' person who could speak vociferously like a man but never acts like one. Ratna soars to a level of understanding where sex is insignificant and a desire for one's fellow being is dominant. Rangamma's perseverance in supporting Moorthy, offering her house for political meetings puts her on a pedestal where her sister-in-law Waterfall Venkamma can look up, shout raucously and spit with no effect. Rangamma tolerates rapacious Waterfall Venkamma, who has a vendetta against everyone in the village, making all her efforts to insult ineffectual by her 'silence.' Being a widow does not present any hindrance to her as she goes on doing her work with an equipoise leading the home-ridden women to their freedom of 'voice.'

She sponsors Ratna as a substitute-reader to Ramakrishnayya, to read the texts and she herself blends politics with legends and religion bringing the British in every line and word. She refurbishes her links with the outer world by getting the newspapers. The more she discourses, the more she displays the inner strength. To stir up the home-ridden women, she conjures up the pictures of Rani Lakshmi Bai, and deeds of Kamaladevi, Sarojini and Annie Besant. She carves out a Sevika Sangha and grooms the members like a commander. She comes out of the threshold and makes the men sit together for a grand feast and makes the women fall in line, irrespective of their caste and creed. Widowhood provides the freedom of soul and an inner strength to break the norms of the society, and add a feminine strength to the struggle of freedom.

Ratna, another child widow, the defiant niece of Rangamma, shuns the norms of society. She is educated and has progressive views. She refuses to dress like a widow and live a life of self-abdication. She dresses like a young girl with all the fineries of a married woman and in spite of the criticism hurled on her she deals it with defiance. Not even Waterfall Venkamma with her waspish tongue can stop her. She joins hands with Moorthy, not for marriage but for the emancipation of motherland.

Different forms of Shakti are manifested through the women of Kanthapura. Shakti's indomitable spirits possess them in their Satyagrah (non-violent struggle) against the British government. When the police ill-treats them with sticks and boots, the women think, move and act as one, for they are more distinct and pervasive in the devotional aspect. The enduring quality of the Indian village women is represented as ensuring an internal pertinacity that resists the 'Other,' the external crisis, its relationship to past contributing a sense of unity and continuity. Woman is the External Devotee. Shakti kneeling in rapt attention in front of Siva, reveals herself through them (women), as they listen Jayaramachar retelling epic stories and to Ramakrishnayya reading passages from the scriptures. The most touching example of their ennobling faith is Achakka's musings on the ruins of Kanthapura. She dreams of a happy end to a modern Ramayana where Rama (Mahatma Gandhi) will return from his exile (visit to England) with Sita (India) who has been captured by Ravana (the British), and as he returns to Ayodhya (Delhi) Bharata (Jawaharlal Nehru) who had been acting as regent will welcome him and celestial flowers will be showered upon his chariot.

The narrator Achakka's style is characteristically Indian; feminine spontaneity is coupled with a raciness and native vigour; a rich sense of drama is shot through with impromptu humour and lyricism.

> Waterfall Venkamma, it appears, has gone to stay with her new son-in-law, and Concubine China still remains in Kanthapura to lift her leg to her new customers. I drank three handfuls of Himavathy water, and I said, "Protect us, Mother!" to Kenchamma and I said, "Protect us, Father" to Siva of the Promontory, and I spat three times to the west and three times to the south, and I threw a palmful of dust at the sunken wretch, and I turned away. But to tell you the truth, Mother, my heart it beat like a drum. (184)

Raja Rao's narrative is a version of the Harikatha and its characteristics include digression, repetition, and a leisurely circular movement. The novel seems to work with the notion of 'Rasa,' with Moorthy as an idealized figure, a devoted Laxmana to a Rama-like Gandhi, and other characters, from Lakshmana to Akkamma, symbolizing various forms of 'Bhava.' The work is conceived mainly as an allegory, with colonialism as analogous to the abduction of Sita. As the novel moves to its end, the honesty of author demands an ambivalence. Moorthy has second thoughts about his political struggle and non-violent resistance and the supremacy of Gandhi is made deliberately ambiguous. It's only Rangamma who stoically follows the Gandhian principles to the end.

Kanthapura straddles two worlds, the mythical and the political, which explores the ambivalence of both the worlds instead of concentrating on the mimetic or the archetypal. If the notion of "Rasa' requires totality and is a dominant motif, the complexity and plurality prompts an ambivalent atmosphere. Kanthapura has been explicitly modelled on the promotion of emerging national culture with 'Khadi' as a predominant, metaphor. The romantic vision of Khadi is translated into the fabrication of the Indian national identity, and Raja Rao posits a glorified and unified cultural tradition, which survives despite political setbacks and caste differences. Change is more than a simple romance of a village, stand-in for a nation and nation achieving autonomy. Kanthapura farm plots are taken over by urban industrializing Indians and Indian economy, irrespective of colonial rule, is already a part of global circuits of capital and labour.

Raja Rao is good at the medium symbolist stream of consciousness incorporating Hindu philosophical discussions to produce a different kind of modernist text. The subtle delineation of troubled and complex characters presents the overall romanticizing of classical and rather conservative vision of India.

Raja Rao does not marginalize the role of women in the freedom movement. He highlights their individual contributions. Rangamma and Ratna form women volunteer groups despite opposition from the orthodox society. The novelist has deftly handled the various aspects—the identity of the 'colonized' slavery, the plantation system, political scenario, the 'voice' of freedom intertwining each thread meticulously and turning the complex story into a perfect painting like the Mughal miniature which projects through several stories painted in a single canvas.

Standing up /Stepping out: The Women in/of Kanthapura

NEERU ANAND
Dyal Singh (Eve.) College, University of Delhi

Do you realise what you ask
Do you realise what it means
To the small folk drawn into the pattern of fate
The small folk who live among small things?

ask the agitated women of Canterbury to Archbishop Beckett as they feel that their stupor of "living and partly living" and "avoiding notice" is about to shatter in a vortex of events (Eliot 244). Perhaps the women of Kanthapura too, had they the opportunity, asked the same question to Gandhi.

At the beginning of the novel *Kanthapura*, we see the women in the narrative "living and partly living," indulging in their small acts and trying to keep their "household in order" (Eliot 240). At the end we find them scattered all over the countryside, their homes in disarray: "The corner-house was all but fallen, except for the byre, and Rangamma's house was tile-less over the veranda, and Nanjamma's house doorless and roofless and the hearthstones in every corner." (259) And yet rather than being crushed and broken, they say, "But there is something that has entered our hearts, an abundance." (256) This paper discusses this affirmation of change in the women as they move from the private sanctuaries of their homes to the public arena of nationalist politics.

The participation of women in India's freedom struggle remains largely ignored. Barring a few works on women belonging to the elite, "The lives and conditions of the large majority of women, or their responses to the changing historical forces have consistently been unexplored and thus marginalised in history"

(Kasturi and Mazumdar xxvi). Raja Rao's *Kanthapura* which elucidates the changes that took place in a group of rural women because of their participation in India's freedom struggle, thus, is not merely a landmark in India's literary history, it is also the chronicling of an important chapter in India's political and social history.

Kanthapura, one of the sleepy, forgotten hamlets of India ("Our village—I don't think you have ever heard about it—Kanthapura is its name" [1]—begins the narrative), where the only contact with the outside world is through the carts of the tradesmen, *awakens to new life and freedom* through the coming of Gandhian ideals. It is a cloistered village where every caste and community has a separate quarter—there is the brahmin quarter, and the Potters' Street and the weaver street, the shudra street, the pariah corner—and the boundaries are rigidly maintained. The women too maintain their own hierarchies: the brahmin wives and widows at the top, followed by the wives of potters and weavers, the shudra women, and at the lowest rung, the pariah women. In a world thus defined by borders and boundaries, transgression is either morally condemned—Barber Channav's wife Sankamma died despite prayers to Kenchamma because, "it was not for nothing her child was born ten months and four days after he was dead. . . . Such whores always die untimely"—or regarded with fear as in the case of rebel figures like Ratna who not only fuels uncomfortable thoughts in Bhatta because of her "modern ways" but also in the other women (3). Despite her defiant subversive manner, they lack the courage to defy her at her face, and can only (in a gesture that completely defines them, at least initially) spit at her back.

Further, the feeling of maintaining their status-quo rules over them all. Even in similarly economically impoverished circumstances, a brahmin remains superior to the 'lower' castes. When the Skeffington Estate manager, for instance, tries to molest a brahmin girl, her father protests, "I'm a brahmin. I would rather die than sell my daughter." (81) Though the father is shot dead, the manager too learns his lesson: "now he'll never touch a brahmin girl." (81) As also when Moorthy asks the pariah women to spin khadi, and they make excuses, the brahmin narrator's tone turns totally superior: "And Moorthy feels this is awful and nothing could be done with *these* women." (103, my italics) She conveniently forgets that the brahmin women too had initially protested against spinning because they felt it would lower their prestige, "brahmins do not spin, do they?" (24) Thus "fundamental elements of social conservatism such as the maintenance of caste distinctions, and patriarchal forms of authority in the family, acceptance of the sanctity of the shastras," are accepted and embraced by the village community at large. (Chatterjee 241)

Totally outside the pale of 'moral' society is the prostitute Chinna, who ironically is the only woman who still stays at Kanthapura at the end of the novel. The rest, brahmins and pariahs alike, have all been pushed out, by their joining the mainstream of a nationalist struggle that takes not only them from the margins to the centre, but also makes Kanthapura one in the chain of cities that stretches from Peshawar to Lahore to Calcutta to Bombay to Madras. . . . It is significant that the earlier hymns in praise of Goddess Kenchamma, a local deity, have by the end turned into songs of revolution where it is the image of Bharat Mata that is evoked, and not only the Mahatma but revolutionaries like Jatin Das and Bhagat Singh are also extolled. This is a moving from the local to the national, from being concerned only within to concerns without, so that the "representative self that is the object of the [nationalist] narrative [attains] a secular nationalist consciousness as its defining characteristic." (Mufti 11)

Right from the time Gandhi returned to India from South Africa, he urged the women to join the national movement. In speech after speech, citing the virtues of the legendary Hindu heroines like Sita and Draupadi, he extolled the women to take up cudgels against the British Raj, which he repeatedly compared to Ravana. This intermingling of religion with contemporary politics was one of the high points of Gandhi's political strategy. It is not surprising that in Kanthapura too the awakening against an unjust foreign power begins with the pooja ceremonies and Harikathas: "But the *Harikatha* he did, which I can never forget in this life and in all lives to come, is about the birth of Gandhiji," gushes the narrator (14). And once Gandhi is established in the Hindu pantheon, Moorthy's task becomes that much the easier.

The next step is to ask them to spin khadi. Spinning was something that Gandhi felt could solve India's and women's problem.[1] He launched the khadi movement as it offered "to the masses of women an immediate open channel for their participation in the national struggle. . . . It brought the women an income basic for their survival, forced men to acknowledge women's higher skills in this activity, and unleashed women's aspirations to break through purdah and other barriers of inequality" (Kasturi and Mazumdar lii-liii). For the women of Kanthapura too, it is not merely the spinning of a yarn, it is the spinning of a bond. For all the women, cutting across lines of caste and community, are doing the same thing. It is a labour shared, and through this they discover a new, emancipated identity for themselves. In the euphoria of spinning khadi and discovering a more productive role for themselves, a branch of the Congress opens in the village, and because of her efforts, Rangamma is chosen as a member of the committee.

So far so good. The Harikathas, the spinning can be done in the enclosures usually seen as a woman's domain—temple, home etc. The problem arises when the women are asked to take on the roles traditionally assigned to men. Thus when Rangamma, who because of Moorthy's incarceration has been to the towns and is in the know of what is happening outside, suggests that they form a cadre of their own, there is a veritable howl of protest: "Nay, nay, we are not men Rangamma." (148) Because truth to tell, though the presiding deity of Kanthapura, Kenchamma, is an avatar of Shakti, the women of the village are content to just gossip, do household chores, and arrange and organise marriages for the young ones. Rangamma by narrating stories of ancient, modern, and even coeval heroines like Annie Beasant and Sarojini Naidu, shames the women to think of something more than "the blowpipe, and the broomstick and the milking of the many cows." (150) And thus is formed the Sevika Sangha. Once the Sevika Sangha is formed, the fight is not merely confined to protest against the British Raj, it extends its frontier to come up against the notions of Indian womanhood that men and women alike have internalized over the centuries—of the home being the designated space of the women.

Partha Chatterjee in his essay, "The Women Question," has argued how with the turn of the century, the difference between home (*ghar*) and world (*bahar*) became all the more problematic: "The world is the external, the domain of the material; the home represents our inner spiritual self, our true identity. The world is a treacherous terrain of the pursuit of material interest where practical considerations reign supreme. It is also typically the domain of the male. The home in its essence must remain unaffected by the profane activities of the material world—and woman is its representation." (245) And the problem is whether the extension of female space, through her entrance into the domain of public affairs, will have repercussions on her role as a 'home-keeper' and the custodian of the spirituality of the East. In fact now there is a special burden on the women, because as participants in the national struggle they have to take to the streets, yet at the same time keep the 'essential spiritual feminity' of the East intact, uncorrupted by their contact with the outside world. They can venture outside but only after fulfilling their household duties, and all the time making sure that the materialism of the world outside does not enter the sacred space of their home. Outside they are encouraged to challenge the authority of the White master, but back home they are supposed to accept demurely the authority of the man of the house. Any challenge to the patriarchal order at home is seen as an acceptance of a decadent western culture, and betrayal of their duties towards both their home and the motherland. Walking on such a razor's edge, the women not only have a dual responsibility but also have to bear the brunt in case they neglect their duties. Thus Radhamma's husband beats her up though she is seven months pregnant and Satamma's husband declares that he wants his home in order and meals served to him at the proper time.

It is significant that Rangamma despite her education and awareness does not think about forming a committee to assess and provide solutions to the problems faced by the women in the village: child marriage, child-widows, widow remarriage, the issues for which reformers in India had agitated violently in the previous century. The grand narrative of the Nationalist movement subsumes within it the problems and questions relating to gender. Geraldine Forbes puts it explicitly: "The political movement engaged women who . . . belonged to different worlds but who shared the burden of social norms that inhibited their autonomy. Women leaders wanted to mobilize their less sophisticated sisters for political action and they knew this would be impossible without the permission of husbands and fathers. Therefore it was expedient to concentrate on nationalist issues and leave (aside) feminist issues." (149) All Rangamma can do is to advise them all to look after their husbands and homes first.[2] But as the narrator asks, "But how can we be like we used to be?" (159) And the women are more than eager to go "picketing cigarette shops and toddy shops." (152)

A police report of 1930 states how Gandhi talked to the village women regarding their patriotic duties: picketing liquor and toddy shops, boycotting taxed salt, and spinning and wearing khaddar. Historian S. Chandrashekar remarks: "What is most remarkable is the expression of discontent by the unlettered, who except for the mythical name of Gandhi knew nothing of Colonialism or non-co-operation." (129) Thus forgetting "blow-pipe and the child's cradle and the letting-off of the morning cattle" (170) the women of Kanthapura "with their sari fringes tied to their waists" march out to Boranna's toddy grove (181) and experience for themselves what it means to step out. The lathis rain on them mercilessly, "the wounds fresh as burns," but the heart overflowing with the fact that "You've done something big." (186) The police of course, resort to their usual manoeuvre and the women are taken to distant places and abandoned. "The long walk home was meant to cool their fondness for demonstrations" (Forbes 139). A lesser artist than Rao would have made the women march back in triumph, singing songs of victory. But here the women wilt and their steps falter. Nanjamma cries out, "We are hungry. We've not had a meal since morning." (188) But the hero's welcome that they receive in Santhapura, with people falling over each other to have their darshan and piling foodstuff on them, acts like such a balm, that they can declare (with what charming conceit) "but this is what we should do to drive the British out." (190) This from the women who dared not look at the coffee-estate road lest the sahib cast a lascivious eye on them!!!

The spoils of victory—five twigs of toddy trees and a toddy pot—are planted in the temple. And Venkamma's ridicule only strengthens their inner conviction that the path they have chosen for themselves is the right one.[3] And this resolution is tested severely in the coming days. As their agitation increases—from picketing toddy booths to non-payment of taxes—so does the atrocity of the Raj. And the passages where the police step into the village is like stepping into an inferno. The breathless rush of the narrative (as though the narrator relives the entire scene while narrating it) further adds to the effect: the lathis, the blood, the smashed heads, the cracking of bones, the wails and the cries, the screams, the molestation and the rapes. It is a world gone totally mad and where a law-enforcing agency like the police indulges in wanton lawlessness and violence. However in the midst of all this violence the women also learn something about each other and themselves. When the women huddled together in the temple sanctum are 'rescued' by Rachanna's wife, it is an epiphanic moment, and not merely because a pariah woman has entered a space earlier denied to her. For the first time she is called by her name, Rachi. Till now only the brahmin women had been called by their names; the pariah women were always so and so's wife. By naming her, the narrator sees her as an individual in her own right and realises a kinship with her. The police violence has demonstrated to them that for the brutal force of the State, they are all alike. Whether brahmins or pariahs, women (bodies) are vulnerable, spaces which can be invaded, defiled and violated. The sites where the colonist regime contests with the nationalists, and through forcible entry, subjugates them and hence brands them forever with its victory and the (corresponding) defeat of the nationalists. As Ivekovic and Mostov put it, "according to patriarchal consensus . . . the other's women should be violated as the other's borders/ territories." (12)

After this high point of revelation, the text falters. One feels, as the women try to pick up the reins of their lives in Kashipura, that Rao should have shown a more positive affirmation of the change they feel within themselves. They are busy with the Harikathas and prayers, and household chores, and waiting for Rangamma to come out of the jail and lead them again. It is almost like what they were at the beginning of the text. But after having constructed a more active role for themselves, how could they lapse into this kind of inertia? No doubt they are still following the Mahatma who had constructed "a new ideal for Indian women that rewrote passivity and self-suffering as strength" (Forbes132). However, rather than accepting this kind of Gandhian conception they should have written a more dynamic role for themselves. Bewildered by the Mahatma's truce with the Viceroy[4] which would ensure that "the peasants will pay back the revenues, the young men will not boycott the toddy shops," they still do not question the decisions taken by the leadership at the top (256). Perhaps a few more women should have acted like Ratna who went to Bombay to chart a new destiny for herself. It is these women who left their homes and families, and ventured out all alone in alien cities, who turned the next page for Indian womanhood. But except for the fact that she went to Bombay we are told nothing about her. But this is not to underestimate what the women of Kanthapura did. Rooted in a religio-cultural tradition that valorized self-denial and subjugation, content with their simple ways of living, resigned to ennui, they yet stood up against the might of an empire. Keeping in mind the gender assigned roles in our society, this in itself becomes quite revolutionary.

"Maybe he would remember us?" they think at one point in the text. (109) Substitute he for anything—the name of a big leader, the eminent historians, the coming generations, or the nation—and the question reverberates with poignancy.

NOTES

1. Gandhi repeatedly, in his speeches and writings, drew the connection between spinning khadi, the emancipation of women, and the freedom of India. At a public meeting in Karaikudi, 24 September 1927, he says: "I do not know how much men in India will have to pay for keeping you, the women of India, in darkness about so many things of the highest importance in life both to men and women. But thanks to god that since the advent of the movement for reviving the spinning wheel thousands of women have learnt to come out of their homes." (*CWMG*, Vol. 35, pp. 38-39). Again, in a speech in Olpad taluk on 30 March 1930, he says: "whether we wish to boycott foreign cloth through the means of khadi or through mill-made cloth it is women who are the spinners." (*Ibid*, Vol. 43, pp. 154-55). In an article in *Navajivan*, "To the Women," on 6 April 1930, he writes: "The entire khadi movement would collapse today if the women were to refuse to extend their co-operation to it." (*Loc. cit.*, pp. 189-91)
2. The women of India too felt that their ideal place was home. Satyavati Devi, the daughter of a prominent freedom-fighter family spoke to the women thus: "Ordinarily my place was in my home. But at a time when my motherland is passing through a life and death struggle, I am one of millions of India's women . . . who have left their hearth and home and their traditional seclusion to muster under Mahatma Gandhi's standard to fight." (Qtd. Geraldine Forbes, p. 148)
3. "The women of India certainly demonstrated in 1930 that they were second to none in strength and tenacity of purpose. Women who had never stepped unescorted out of their homes, women who had stayed in purdah, young mothers and unmarried girls, became a familiar sight as they stood from morning to night outside liquor shops, and opium dens and stores selling foreign cloth, quietly but firmly persuading the customers and shopkeepers to change their ways." (Bipan Chandra, p. 276)
4. The Gandhi-Irwin pact has had its share of controversies, and not only because Gandhi did not make the release of Bhagat Singh, Sukhdev, and Rajguru (already sentenced to death) as a condition of the pact. (Amongst other things) the pact was also seen as a betrayal of peasant's interests because it did not restore confiscated

land already sold to a third party. Also not all the political prisoners were released from jails.

Works Cited

Chandra, Bipan, et al. *India's Struggle for Independence*. New Delhi: Penguin, 1995.

Chandrashekar, S. *Colonialism, Conflict and Nationalism: South India: 1857-1947*. New Delhi: Vishwa Prakashan, 1995.

Chatterjee, Partha. "The Nation and Its Women." *A Subaltern Studies Reader 1986-1995*, ed. Ranajit Guha. New Delhi: OUP, 2000. 240-62.

Collected Works of Mahatma Gandhi, Vol. 35, New Delhi: Publications Department. Abbreviated *CWMG*.

Eliot, T.S. *Murder in the Cathedral. The Complete Poems and Plays of T.S. Eliot*. London: Faber and Faber, 1969. 237-82.

Forbes, Geraldine. *The New Cambridge History of India: Women in Modern India*. Cambridge: Cambridge UP, 1996.

Ivekovic, Rada and Julie Mostov, ed. *From Gender to Nation*. New Delhi: Zubaan, 2002.

Kasturi, Leela and Vina Mazumdar, ed. *Women and Indian Nationalism*. New Delhi: Vikas, 1996.

Mufti, Aamir R. "A Greater Story-Writer than God: Genre, Gender and Minority in Late Colonial India." *Subaltern Studies XI: Community, Gender and Violence*, ed. Partha Chatterjee and Pradeep Jaganathan. New Delhi: Permanent Black and Ravi Dayal, 2000. 8-20.

Rao, Raja. *Kanthapura*. 1938. London: OUP, 1974.

The Women of Kanthapura: From Slumber to Awakening

RANU UNIYAL
University of Lucknow

Emergence of Women

This particular theme in the novel is bound up with the need to reassess rites and traditions both within and outside the family. It curiously invokes the severance of bondage both from past traditions and colonial legacy. Moorthy is one such revolutionary spirit whose movement in the temporal sequence of the novel leaves a blazing trail behind. The growth of the women is a result of the continuous repression by the Red-man's government. Ratna, Rangamma, Narsamma, Venkamma, Achakka, Puttamma, Rachi and several others react differently to the same socio-historical problem. Each reaction is different and of vital importance, for it is these characters which are held responsible for the emergence of unrest and chaos in Kanthapura.

Towards Self-Reliance

The remorseless and inhuman forces lie at the root of conflict and human struggle in Kanthapura. The people in the village were living an uneventful life. The celebration of religious rituals like *Sankara-jayanthi* and the rendering of *Harikathas* begin in Kanthapura. With the *Harikathas* comes Jayaramachar. He not only tells them the story of Bharata, the motherland, but also of the sages who had graced the land with their birth. He then speaks of the birth of Mahatma to fight against evil just as Krishna had come to kill the demons on this earth. The arrest of Jayaramachar by the policemen signifies the growing unrest in Kanthapura. The arrest signifies that whosoever raises his voice against the existing authorities will be crushed.

Moorthy becomes the enigmatic force in the lives of the women who had earlier lived a life of passive indifference. Kanthapura presents a panoramic picture of exploitation. It is in the landscape of Kanthapura that the coolies, men and women fight against the oppressive structure of society. Moorthy, by making these women aware of their state of dependence, urges in them the need to break away from bondage.

The Red-man's government signifies the presence of the being which has not only profited financially by suppressing the others but has become extremely callous after declaring its superiority over the others.

The British think that they are born to rule and the Indians to be ruled. Import of consumer goods from England, especially cloth, has not only made Indians too dependent on the others but has also made them forget their own potentiality for weaving cloth. Moorthy contacts the women of Kanthapura and makes them aware of the major need for self-dependence. He brings them out of their homes and inculcates in them the desire to be self-sufficient. His providing the women with the spinning wheel and free cotton to spin is a code of action which signifies the desire to act according to one's needs:

> "Sister," says he to Nose scratching Nanjamma, "sister, the Congress is giving away free spinning-wheels. Will you spin, sister? . . if you spin just one hour a day, you can have a bodice-cloth of any colour or breadth you like, one bodice-cloth per month, and a sari every six months. And during the first month, the cotton is given free." (28)

And when asked:

> "And why should the Congress give it free?" Moorthy says: "Because millions and millions of yards of foreign cloth come to this country, and everything foreign makes us poor and pollutes us. To wear cloth spun and woven with your own God-given hands is sacred, says the Mahatma. And it gives work to the workless, and work to the lazy. And if you don't need the cloth sister—well, you can say, 'Give it away to the poor,' and we will give it to the poor. Our country is being bled to death by foreigners. We have to protect our Mother." (29)

This is the essential revelation of the paragraph: the inevitability of protection. For good or ill, one must protect the 'Mother,' for she is slowly being tortured to death by the foreigners and this, according to Gandhi, can only be possible if there is a total boycott of foreign goods. Moorthy, the protagonist of the novel, becomes an ardent follower of Gandhi and he tries to build up this faith in others. He asks the women to spin and says even Mahatma does it: "Why, every morning he spins for two hours immediately after his prayers. He says spinning is as purifying as praying." (32)

Earlier they lived a secluded life inside their homes. A growing awareness of the problems being faced by the world outside not only makes them conscious of their existence as mere objects but creates in them a powerful desire to seize their individuality.

Rangamma and Transcendence of Being

Rangamma as an individual has not only defied the norms of society but by living according to her wishes, she has asserted her existence over the others. Her silence at what the others say about her is a significant code of protest, for by not retorting, she creates an acute sense of hostility in others. Though the orthodox Indian society has imposed several restrictions on widows, she fights consciously against them. Trying to fashion her life in her own way, she refuses to be treated as a mere object. Rangamma lives in a big house, wears Dharmawar saris and gold belt despite being a widow which gives rise to strong conflicts in Venkamma's mind. Her desire to kill Rangamma and her family with lizard-poison signifies the fear of her own loss of identity. Venkamma, afraid of her own insecure existence feels that Rangamma has no right to live. We can witness one trying to analyze the others' right to exist. Venkamma sees Rangamma's behaviour as a menace to her own solidity and durability.

To the women of Kanthapura, Moorthy appears as a guiding force. What occurred in the lives of these women underscores a tension which couldn't be resolved easily, because the tension was between two contradictory forces which is life at home and the life outside. After Moorthy's arrest, Rangamma emerges as the most powerful influence over the villagers. Not only does she go to Karwar from Kanthapura and stay with Sankar helping him in Congress business, she also makes her first speech from the platform. Her exposure to reality outside home makes her more conscious of her passive existence at home. Once out into the open, she refuses to go back and resists all attempts of the other to suppress her. Her going to the prison with other freedom fighters and their continuing the struggle against the other signifies their urge to be free from dominance.

Not only did she learn yoga, an act of self-control but she also encouraged the other women to practise it daily. Life in the city has not only made her conscious of her existence but has created a new awareness in her. Her objective subsequently becomes the complicated and contradictory one of trying to establish courage and will to struggle among the women as is visible in the following ensemble:

> In the city there are groups and groups of young women, girls, married women, and widows, who have joined together and have become Volunteers—Volunteers they call them—and they practise exercises like the Police, and when meetings are held they all get together and maintain order. (149)

Rangamma's act of encouraging women to be ready to respond to Mahatma's call and fight for him creates some doubts in the minds of the other women. They feel that only men have the right to fight. Taking examples from the history of India, Rangamma refers to the valour of Rani Lakshmi Bai who had fought against the Red-men. This fight would mean not fighting for personal achievement but for a wider cause i.e. for the freedom of the motherland. The formation of Sevika Sangha in Kanthapura shows the need to be consecrated for a greater cause i.e. freedom.

The women after being filled with a sense of purpose are motivated to action. Their practising of yoga and other exercises are codes of action enacted with full awareness of the goals to be achieved. Their excited chatter about how they are going to dress for the occasion when Moorthy is released from prison expresses their admiration for Moorthy. It also signifies the desire of the women to look beautiful and feminine.

We see that the women are better prepared than men to meet the atrocities simply because they had realized it as an eventuality from which they could not get away. The men had disapproved of their preparing themselves for action saying that they should confine themselves to their homes: "was there nothing left for our women but to vagabond about like soldiers? And every time the milk curdled or a dhoti was not dry, they would say, 'And this is all because of this Sevi business,' and Radhamma's husband beat her on that day he returned from village inspection, though she was seven months pregnant." (151-52)

Several men raise voices of discontent and disapproval. It is mainly because they feel that the women have specific roles to perform and that is of serving the family within the confines of the house and the way in which they had begun transcending the limits of their being was disapproved by them. Rangamma tries to influence the men of Kanthapura. The men feel it is not for a woman to affirm or impose herself and when she tries to do so they beat her, thus trying to restrict her from further action. The apparently unending waves of conflict and the struggle at home between men and women are also due to the neglect of work at home by women. Rangamma asks the women to give first priority to their family and then to the Sevika Sangha. Revolutionary spirit of the women is filled with a sense of revolt. The conflicts at home and outside serve to tighten their bonds with the Sevika Sangha. The women feel that for them going back to their kitchen is not possible: they are now better informed and more conscious of their existence as human beings. They have been so weighed with troubles created by the Other that this need to continue the struggle becomes all the more intense. The given ensemble reveals their state of mind: "But how can we be like we used to be?" (152) The will to struggle against the oppressive forces becomes active in the minds of the women. Their practising yoga and preparing themselves for action through the Sevika Sangha are significant codes of action which signify their decision-making power and urge to resist. Rangamma's being able to influence both men and women projects the command she has over the others. She receives the assent of men to plunge intc action when required. Her determination and tenacity of purpose enable her to maintain an identity of her own.

Rangamma's getting blue paper from the city and informing women about different places and things signify her wish to broaden not only her own horizon of thought and knowledge but also that of others. Being open to new ideas, she refuses to accept ready-made principles and values and tries to transcend the limits of her being by using her power to reason and question the action of others. Reading of blue papers makes her aware of the status of women in other parts of the world. Socialism in Russia had given women equal rights and they were being treatcd as men's equals in every sphere:

> And there in that country there were women who worked like men, night and day, and when they felt tired, they went and spent their holiday in a palace—no money for the railway, no money for the palace—and when the women were going to have a child, they had two months' and three months' holiday, and when the children were still young they were given milk by the Government, and when they were grown up they were sent free to school, and when they grew older still they went to the Universities free, too, and when they were still more grown-up, they got a job and they got a home to live in and they took a wife to live with and they had many children and they lived on happily ever after. (47)

This desire to radically reorganize the Indian society along socialist lines is too deep-seated in Rangamma. The wish to fight for equal rights for women is too strong and therefore creates in her a necessity to intensify the struggle.

Rangamma is one character in the novel who not only retains the sanctity of religious traditions even after the death of her father but also interprets the texts by bringing in Gandhian ideology into each and every page. Gandhism had become deeply rooted in the ancient traditions of India and therefore the women did not find it difficult to identify themselves with Gandhi. Gandhi had been able to establish an affinity with the Indian masses and it is in this affinity that the secret of his influence lay.

Ratna: From Defiance to War

Ratna is another very powerful individual in the novel who despite being a widow lives a most unconventional life. She defies the norms imposed on widows by society and her refusal to accept society as it is, is a strong form of protest.

Ratna lives life according to her wishes. She "not only went about the streets alone like a boy, but even wore her hair to the left like a concubine, and she still kept her bangles and her nose-rings and ear-rings, and when she was asked why she behaved as though she hadn't lost her husband, she said that that was nobody's business, and that if these sniffing old country hens thought that seeing a man for a day, and this when one is ten years of age, could be called a marriage, they had better eat mud and drown themselves in the river." (49)

Ratna's keeping 'nose-rings,' 'ear-rings,' and 'bangles' on her body is a gesture of assertion. She questions the social norms imposed on her as a widow, and that too when she had hardly known what marriage was. By refusing to bow down before societal norms, she poses several important conflicts in the minds of the others. She refuses to accept what fate has assigned to her. She is reprimanded for being outspoken and rebellious. She remains undeterred by what people say about her. According to people like Bhatta and Venkamma, Ratna's behaviour is most shocking. Bhatta feels uneasy in her company because Ratna is forever setting herself off as "different" from the others 'and when her sari fell over her shoulders, and bared her bodice it always made him feel uncomfortable.' (49-50)

Her spontaneous love of life, her unconventional living style, her bluntness of speech and her honesty make the others feel uncomfortable in her presence. The manner in which Ratna counters their protestations makes her more conscious of her existence. Her exuberance of life is unrestrained and her vigour makes others fearful of her. The sphere to which she belongs in the society is an enclosed one, limited and dominated by the socio-religious barriers. Certain rules which have been imposed on widows, have also been placed before her, but Ratna tries to raise and transcend herself from such societal barriers which impede her way to self-realization. She refuses to let others rape her wishes and thus, in trying to be herself, is in some way refusing to accept things as they are.

Ratna has a soft corner for Moorthy. This is quite apparent from her behaviour towards him. Ratna's praying for his release after he had been arrested, and later on, her plans to welcome him after his release show her attachment towards him. The desire in her to be loved by him is intense and that is why we see her actions directed towards pleasing him. The day Moorthy sits on fast, she promises to do as per his wishes. Her prostrating before the Gods and praying for Moorthy's welfare is an act signifying the love and respect she has for him:

> "God, God," she said, "keep him strong and virtuous, and may he rise out of this holier and greater; God I shall offer ten coconuts and a kumkum worship. God, keep him alive for me." (98)

The above ensemble reveals the fact that Ratna's world centres around Moorthy. She is willing to submit to him without any resistance and this reveals the other aspect of her personality. On the one hand, she defies norms imposed on widows by the society and on the other the desire to be loved and admired is strong in her. Though the writer has not brought forth any development in Moorthy's relationship with Ratna, it is quite apparent that the two are emotionally attached to each other.

The struggle for freedom becomes too intense and everything else except the resistance by the people recedes into the background. Ratna undergoes gradual transformation in her entire outlook on life. Earlier she did what Moorthy said. "She could hardly grasp his idea. She was but fifteen. Praying seemed merely to fall flat before the gods in worship." (95)

Ratna's naivete shows her inability to understand things at a young age. But despite being young she does not become what others ask her to. Despite being asked to follow certain rules and forbidden from certain things, she does not repress her spontaneous movements and lives as she wishes. As the struggle for freedom in Kanthapura gains momentum and Moorthy, after his arrest, is not present physically in the village any more, a new Ratna can be seen emerging from this particular background. She is the one who takes the movement ahead. She along with the other women goes picketing the toddy booths and the Estate. Later on, a policeman tries to assault her and fortunately she is freed from his clutches by the other women. Ratna becomes their leader and guide. She had begun reading the religious texts, which Rangamma had started interpreting after her father's death. The women find something very powerful and strong in Ratna: "and somehow we said there's the voice of Rangamma in her speech, the voice of Moorthy, and she was no more the child we had known, nor the slip of a widow we had cursed." (251)

The above ensemble reveals the gradual change in the opinion of the other women. To them she is no longer just a young widow but a woman with courage and resilience. The others tend to look up to her for guidance. They seek her advice and act accordingly:

> and Timmanna turns to her and says, "Oh where shall we go, daughter, with this new mother and child?" and Kamalamma says, "Why, to the temple," and Ratna says, "Wait, I shall go and see if the path is safe." (217)

The faith which she has in the Congress is projected in her dealings with people. It is this faith which takes her to Bombay after her term inside the prison is over. She goes from the village Kanthapura to Bombay to fight for freedom and equality. She has refused to become a prey and she tries to seize freedom by striving for it. Not being confined to a conjugal sphere, her reality is no more concentrated inside the house. Just like her, the other women too fight against oppression. War provides a chance to fight against the oppression of society at home and against the British rule outside. Gandhian struggle, which Ratna later joins wholeheartedly, becomes a collective movement drawing young village widow to a new level of experience and outer space.

Narsamma's March towards Extinction

Besides Ratna, Rangamma and the other women, there are Venkamma and Narsamma who have not been able to adjust to the changing patterns of the society. Narsamma had nurtured high hopes for her only son but his coming back to the village without completing his studies in the city leaves her distressed. His refusal to marry and his continuous mixing with the pariahs are responsible for the growth of unrest and despair in her. Mother and son stop communicating with each other. This snapping-off of communication signifies the unrelenting attitude of both the mother and the son. There lies a conceptual opposition between what Narsamma had expected her son to do and what he really does in life. His not having been able to fulfill her specific needs is the cause of frustration in her. Being a brahmin, the thought of excommunication is unbearable to her. The possibility of her son being excommunicated destroys something in her and she becomes too distant a person: "From that day on they never spoke to each other, Narsamma and Moorthy. He sat and ate his food by the kitchen threshold and she in the kitchen, and everybody saw that Narsamma was growing thin as a bamboo and shrivelled like banana bark." (65)

Narsamma's not speaking to her son, her 'growing thin' and her 'shrivelled' appearance are the semantic codes which signify her not being able to accept things as they were at that time. The clash between the old and the new is an important one. She becomes isolated and detached from her own son. When she hears the news of her son's excommunication, the desire to live is completely crushed in her.

> 'Oh!' moaned Narsamma, and that very night, when the doors were closed and the voices had died away, she ran through the Brahmin Street and the Potters' Street, and standing at the village gate, she spat once toward the east and once towards the west, once towards the south and once towards the north, and then, spitting again thrice at the pariah huts, where the dogs began to raise a howl, she ran over the Fig-Tree field bund, and she had such a shiver at the thought of all the ghosts and the spirits and the evil ones of flame, that she trembled and coughed. But there was

> something deep and desperate that hurried her on, and she passed by Rangamma's sugarcane field and by the mango grove to the river, just where the whirlpool gropes and gurgles, and she looked up at the moonlit sky, and the winds of the night and the shadows of the night and the jackals of the night so pierced her breast that she shuddered and sank unconscious upon the sands, and the cold so pierced her that the next morning she was dead. (65-66)

Her desire to die is partly defensive and partly an attempt to endorse the crushing sense of wrong. Her entire self has split and lost its integrity and identity. She has become too oppressive and frustrated. The above ensemble clearly reveals her anguished state. Her mental setup has been totally shaken and she, having lost all interest in life, ends it. It is simply not a question of how she would have lived after hearing such a news, more disturbing has been the fact that she, after having realized the futility of her existence, had stopped eating for days. Death to her was the only situation beyond which lay no other. The simple fact that she lived alone and the other, that is, Moorthy could do nothing for her reveals that his act is cause neither for regret nor for sorrow. It is the outcome of two forces genuinely opposed to each other. Hope had long been frustrated in her by the rebellious attitude of her son. Therefore her demise is a sign of protest against the manner in which the world is proceeding. Her death does not come as a surprise since she had been haunted by the fear of being excommunicated and therefore doomed forever. From 'moaned,' to 'ran,' 'spat,' 'trembled,' 'coughed,' 'hurried,' 'looked,' 'pierced,' 'shuddered,' 'sank' and 'dead' all these codes in succession reveal that in her case there was no way out. All these codes create a frequently recurring image of extinction. She no longer fears being crushed, engulfed, since she has been long dead. Clinical death has come days after the death of her personal being. Death as an ultimate possibility in Narsamma's case is the final form of protest and rebellion.

Venkamma: The Unrelenting Other

Venkamma as the Other in the novel resents the changes taking place in society. So concerned and scared has she become of her existence that she openly criticizes the other women. For Venkamma women's protestation is just another cause of shame, another of those forces which come to shake her up without having received her approval. Her major concern is her family and therefore whenever she feels her existence being challenged she retorts venomously. Her demanding to live in a big house only because she has children and Rangamma has none shows the tendency in her to assert her supremacy. She feels that Rangamma, being a childless widow, has no right to exist. It is only a woman with children who can and should live: "I've two sons and five daughters, and that shaven widow hadn't even the luck of having a bandicoot to call her own." Important signifiers being 'have' and 'hadn't' signify what one has and the other has been deprived of. The very fact that she has children and Rangamma has none fills her with a sense of achievement and makes her conscious of her status in society.

She argues with others over the 'Gandhi-business' and tries to convince them that Moorthy alone is responsible for breeding trouble in Kanthapura. Her hatred for Moorthy is due to one major reason—Moorthy's refusal to get married to her daughter: 'And, as everybody knew, she had no particular love for Moorthy. He had refused her second daughter, for whom bridegroom after bridegroom was being sought—and she was nearing *the* age." (28)

Venkamma exists only for herself and her family. Her main wish is to see her daughter married. She tries to curb all actions which demand any kind of participation, which would result in hindrance of personal aims. Her daughter's marriage to an old advocate is significant of the fact that she wants to get rid of that burden as soon as possible. The daughter represents the Other to her. She is no more than an object which has to be given away in marriage. Any act or conflict which demands change terrifies Venkamma. She seems rather contented in her shell of brahminical upbringing and dreads to see any kind of change. Life to her means stability and rigidity in every possible way. Therefore she rejects Gandhi and whatever Moorthy strives for. The kind of warm treatment the people receive at her daughter's wedding reveals the strange and different facet of her personality. To her, happiness means fulfillment of material needs, and the fact that her daughter is going into a rich family is enough to make her proud of herself. Later on, her going to stay at her son-in-law's place once the village is destroyed, seeks to project some kind of security which Venkamma had always been looking for. It is the fear of being left alone and isolated with her unmarried daughters that makes her resist any change in society.

Spirit of Rebellion in Women

Gandhian movement in 1930s had taken the people under its spell and collectively the individuals resorted to action. The struggle for equality which the women insisted on, persists not simply as a conflict but also as an idea. It is a projection of the fundamental hostility between the one and the other. All the women, except for a given few under the influence of an outside force, that is, Gandhi, become conscious of reality and of their existence in a group with a common concern. The struggle goes on not only between the British and the Indian but also between the pariahs and the brahmins, the widows and the non-widows, the coolies and their masters, and more than that it is a struggle between man and man.

The way these women are uprooted from their lands and driven to alien places shows the effects of the struggle. The aftermath has left them as refugees and even as refugees the women continue to sing bhajans and hold readings of Vedantic texts. Even though they are estranged from their lands, complete alienation does not take place in their case for they have still retained their old traditions. Their singing of bhajans and listening to Vedantic texts even in Kashipura is an indication of the fact that they have refused to accept the oppression of the government. The wish to fight, to reflect, to oppose and to revolt is still kindling within their hearts despite their complete uprooting from home. The women have been responsible for a temporary dislocation of the Other. They know that they have committed themselves to Gandhian ideology. They accept Gandhi as their leader. He conceived of spinning as a religious principle to be followed by all. The women's commitment to Gandhian ideology keeps their hopes alive. Though this commitment has not been able to dispel either confusion or complexity, yet it is that force which keeps them moving with a burst of hope.

of Raja Rao is the outcome of a very deep urge, very instinctive. It is a meditation and a mode of prayer.

Kanthapura provided the 'free form' as well as a new dimension of sensibility recognizably Indian and contemporaneous. It is work in which the fictional form is endowed with the freedom of romance, the amplitude of the epic, and the symbolic centrality of the fable. It is 'itihasa' and 'Purana' both unified into a 'Kavya.' As 'Itihasa' it is packed with historical action and covers the span of nearly a decade of the Indian struggle for freedom. The novel begins with the nineteen thirties, tracing the emergence of the national consciousness and the disconcerting campaign against the British rule and ends with the Gandhi-Irwin Pact. As a 'Purana,' it appeals to legendary memory and enshrines archetypal experience. The divine and the sacred processes mingle freely with the ineffable socialites on the historical and secular plane at which all mundane human action is projected as a ritual continuum. As a 'Kavya,' the novel integrates experience and contemplation into a vision of human destiny possessed and clarified by art. Basic to Raja Rao's achievement in the novel is his total awareness of the Indian tradition and Indian personality and his readiness to go beyond the surface and sound the depths of experience. As C.D. Narasimhaiah observes, "Raja Rao is fully conscious of the fact that he is telling story of a story. So viewed, the story is only a story, the story is a story is a story. . . . This is a breathless story, or stories illustrating a story, in the old age tradition of story telling."[1]

Raja Rao's expatriation to France at the young age of nineteen has its impact on his creative talent and fictional technique. The French novels succeed in penetrating deeply into the nature of human experience in that age, torn by successive global wars. His long sojourn helped him in making fiction an instrument of spiritual edification. So he is well equipped with knowledge of the two entirely different worlds—India, the land of his birth and inheritance and France, the land of his acquisition, where he spent almost equal number of years as in India. The simultaneous awareness of the Indian metaphysical creative mode and the French way of narrative expression makes him an heir of the two worlds. He is as much aware of the struggle of Valery, Malraux, Gide and Rilke as he is of poetic significance of Valmiki and Kalidasa. The Joycean fictional method of obtaining metaphysical effects by rhetoric devices has also attracted him, as the interior monologue or the stream-of-consciousness becomes an inescapable part of his narrative technique. In the Indian tradition, narrative technique and vision are not alien but mutually integrating forces shaping the structure and texture of the novel. The comparative influences of the Sanskrit and French traditions are highlighted on the creative processes of Raja Rao's novels.

Raja Rao energetically involves in forging a medium to express his apprehensions of life. There is a wilful departure from the conventional Western conception of a well-made novel. However he does not make experiments with new techniques for evolving a style worthy of carrying the burden of his metaphysical quest. It is in no way conscious or artificial effort. Form comes naturally and spontaneously to him. The aesthetics of Raja Rao as a novelist is as much a part of his sadhaka as is his spiritual quest. Though on 'Kanthapura' the impact of Silone's *Fontamara* is decisive, the stream-of-consciousness has been gainfully employed.

At the same time, the methods of narration are resilient, effective and approximately very close to the 'Puranic' mode. The characters and the goings on in that resurgent village are viewed through the camera eye of the old woman narrator gifted with an extraordinary memory. She succeeds with the help of her essentially reminiscent tone of narration in transmuting contemporary reality into novelistic configuration. The assimilation of the Joycean technique into the puranic form is indeed a technical achievement of a very high order. Harish Raizada rightly opines, "while using the old technique of ancient myths and legends, Raja Rao makes use of the innovations in the style of Conrad, James Joyce and Virginia Woolf to suit the narrator's rambling and reminiscent speech." The art of employing a narrator to tell the story is an essential aspect of Raja Rao's fictional technique and he employs it uniformly in all his novels. This helps the novelist in presenting his "point of view," through monologues.

Except in *Kanthapura*, the narrator in other novels is either the novelist himself or his surrogate. The old woman narrator in *Kanthapura* enables the readers to hear the pistol shot, transforming the land and vulgar din of political life into organic element in a "symphony of fiction." Raja Rao speaks of the technical difficulties involved in recreating the tempo of the Indian life in a language, which is alien to the creative writer, in his foreword to Kanthapura where Raja Rao pleads for Indian English as distinct from English. But he himself has shown the compatibility of English with the spirit of the native languages and has proved that "English is flexible enough to accommodate any experience."

In *Kanthapura*, Raja Rao has exhibited a rare originality and an uncanny ambidexterity in attempting to communicate the materials of Indian life and scene through a language, which superbly conveys its theme and the amplitude or vision. This he achieves without lapsing into "babu" English or grossly transgressing the syntactical or grammatical patterns of the normal English. It is no doubt an earnest attempt to transmute into English a local idiom with its distinct echo of regional speech and reflection, of local colour without slipping into awkward and unconventional 'Indianism.' It is more a matter of verbal possession of experience and its aesthetic register rather than the use of vocabulary at the level of lexis. *Kanthapura* also picks up the 'puranic' spirit and rhythm and there is a deliberate novelist and old-world whimsy in all its progressions and digressions. The classical stories and legends are skilfully woven into the novel, thus lending it the flavour of an Indian discourse (katha). For instance, the Kenchamma legend is used as a chronic refrain to ritualize the pattern of events affecting the lives of the villagers. Sidda's serpent lore is full of hyperboles and digressions, which are of the very essence of the old narrative. The descriptive passages have a classical flavour. There are breathless involutions and elaborate passages of lyrical beauty suffused with epic vividness and splendour. The description of the Kartik festival of lights is an instance where the folklore is elevated to the grand myth of seasonal renewal and cyclic returns. The passage describing the coming of the first rain is accurate, evocative and incantatory.

Raja Rao in *Kanthapura* is not interested to be merely a chronicler of events, but in projecting the 'localised myth.' He must tell the story and tell it effectively, the truth and untruth, the beauty and ugliness of the life, which he knows the best. The technique of story telling is Indian and like the technique of the *Mahabharata* and the *Ramayana*, it tells an interminable tale without punctuation and preposition, but exhaling the tempo of Indian life. It is not incidental that he chooses a grandmother, who herself has had the shared experience to narrate the story for the edification of the other village women who gather to hear the annals of their history. In a way she is a folk artist entering a hundredth time into the smithy and furnace of creative passion to forge the uncreative conscience of the race. The story can thus be narrated only in a language intimately passional to herself. She is said to be speaking the Kannada language and if she were to speak English, she would exactly speak in this way and no other.

> What are policemen before Gandhi men? Tell me does a boar stand before an elephant? Or a jackal before a lion?[2]

And again:

> If you are the sons of your father do what this learned boy says. (110)

Here, the intention is sunk in art. The dialogue is free from the pitfalls one often finds, for instance, in Anand's novels. In its verbal economy coupled with an elusiveness of the spirit, which reflects the inwardness of Indianness, the novel has superbly conveyed it. Raja Rao has equally exhibited an uncanny skill in adapting a flexible style demanded by the traditional pattern of the narrative. Any passage from the novel testifies to this fact.

In order to make his narrative authentic and self-consistent, Raja Rao introduces several other indigenous devices, which are in keeping with the theme on hand. He introduces and bodily transports the Kannada words into English expressions (as in 'Dasarahavu,' 'ayyappa,' 'ayyayyo' etc.), which establish an immediate correspondence or intimate approximation with Kannadiga ethos.

The very images, proverbs and pictures are Indian and show the Indian sensibility at its best. These images are drawn from Indian mythology, legends, myths and the natural phenomena. The exploitation of the economy and the gradual depletion of the country's wealth are shown through the image of "granaries as empty as measuring house," of one who is being "bled to death." The plight of the Skeffington coolies is shown through the image of the helpless animals juxtaposed with preying animals of the whispering cries. The Indian flora and fauna figure either to illustrate a person or to highlight a problem. Moorthy is a holy bull, elephant and cow; Rangè Gowda a tiger; Rangamma a kid; the use of violence against an enemy is like pulling out a lantana bush; the army of the Mahatma is an increasing garland. Abusive phrases, idioms, literal translation and use of Indian words are common features of the novel. It is this Indian sensibility, "tempo of Indian life infused in English expression" which may account for the unabating popularity of the novel. Iyengar, summing up his assessment of *Kanthapura*, draws our attention to the successful blending in the novel of several areas of experience and ranges of expression: "It is the singular fusion of poetry and politics, the perennial with the present that makes *Kanthapura* a distinctive novel, almost a new species of fiction."[3]

Even the linguistic experiments of Raja Rao are as original as the experiments of the West African writers like Amos Tutuola, Chinua Achebe and Gabriel Okara who have all tried to introduce the rhythms of their narrative speech in English, thus giving it an autochthonous foundation. Critics have praised this aspect of Raja Rao's originality. C.D. Narasimhaiah rightly comments: "While Raja Rao captures the magnificent mythical imagination of Indian antiquity successively in the three novels and short stories he has written to date, he has at the same time, to use T.S. Eliot's words 'altered' the 'expression' to accommodate a distinct, profoundly Indian sensibility."[5]

NOTES

1. Shiv Narayan, "An Interview with Raja Rao," p. 28.
2. Raja Rao, *Kanthapura* (New Delhi: Orient Paperbacks, 1971), p. 123.
3. K.R.S. Iyengar, *Indian Writing in English* (Second Edition, Bombay: Asia, 1973), p. 394.
4. C.D. Narasimhaiah, *The Swan and the Eagle* (Shimla: Indian Institute of Advanced Study, 1972). Qtd. Introduction, p. 4.

The Stream-of-Consciousness Technique in Raja Rao's *Kanthapura*

ALKA SAXENA
D.A.V. College, Kanpur

Kanthapura is Raja Rao's first novel and it was published in 1938. Even after almost seven decades, no Indian English novel has come close to the style and narrative technique of *Kanthapura*. It has been rightly described as the most satisfying of modern Indian novels. The success of *Kanthapura* lies in its impressive and unique narrative technique. The greatness of Raja Rao can be assessed by the manner in which he has skilfully combined facts and fiction, i.e., Gandhian ideologies and Indian legends and myths, in this novel. This combination is an original idea which heightens the dramatic element in the novel. The story of the struggle for independence is dramatized by combining Indian legends along with the main theme.

The story is narrated by Achakka, an old brahmin widow. The narrative technique used in *Kanthapura* has been described by Raja Rao in the following words, "Episode follows episode, and when our thoughts stop our breath stops, and we move on to another thought. This was and still is the ordinary style of our story-telling. I have tried to follow it myself in this story."[1] Hence we have Achakka who narrates an interminable tale and provides native humour and irony to enliven the narrative. The action moves steadily despite various digressions. The manner in which Achakka relates the story evokes the spirit of traditional Indian folklore, puranas and epics. Of the two elements, facts and fiction, the former is well known. It is in the interweaving of legendary fiction that the whole charm and artistry of the novel lies.

The brief but important Foreword by Raja Rao begins by saying: "There is no village in India, however mean, that has not a rich sthala-purrana, or legendary history, of its own. . . . In this way the past mingles with the present, and gods mingle with men to make the repertory of your grandmother always bright. One such story from the contemporary annals of my village I have tried to tell." Thus, as Raja Rao has stated, the legendary history and contemporary situations mingle to make an interesting story—*Kanthapura.*

The narrator of *Kanthapura* is very important. The whole impact and style of the novel would have been different, had the narrator been someone else and not the typical Indian grandmother. We as Indians can easily visualize the wrinkled, old, expressive face of the grandmother who narrates the story in an uninhibited, natural manner. Raja Rao has admitted that the telling of the story has not been easy because "one has to convey in a language that is not one's own the spirit that is one's own." He feels that the tempo of Indian life should be infused into our English expression. He has made a very correct observation: "we, in India, think quickly, we talk quickly, and when we move we move quickly. There must be something in the sun of India that makes us rush and tumble and run on." In order to make the narration more authentic and natural, Raja Rao has chosen the narrator to be a chatty, garrulous, old grandmother who rushes, tumbles and runs on with the story. Thus through the intelligent use of style, language and narrative technique, Raja Rao has successfully woven the political, religious and social strands of the novel into one excellent story of Kanthapura.

Raja Rao has used the ancient Indian way of narration. It is a breathless story, with long sentences, digressions and Indian expressions which are very meaningful and important. Episodes follow episodes in a smooth manner and the narrator comes back to the main point and develops the story further. The digressions are not boring or irrelevant. They are gossipy and therefore sustain the interest of the readers. The detailed account of episodes and characters are integral to the story because they reveal a lot about the social and religious aspects of the Indian village life.

The episodes are related in long sentences and paragraphs, which is a striking feature of this novel.

The old lady unfolds the story through the memories of the days gone by. Hence the story is in the form of the stream-of-consciousness method. Raja Rao has combined the western art form, the stream-of-consciousness technique with an Indian theme and treated it in an entirely Indian manner. It is important to mention here, that the stream of consciousness technique is not commonly used by Indian writers. Very few novelists like G.V. Desani, Shakuntala Shrinagesh, Anita Desai and Kamala Markandaya have experimented with this form, but these novelists have yet to reach the excellence acquired by Raja Rao. In this technique there is a jumbling of past, present and future to charge the novel with suspense and thrill. The juxtaposition of the past and present, of men and gods is set from the beginning of the novel and is maintained right upto the conclusion.

The novel opens with a detailed description of the village, Kanthapura. By the end of the second paragraph, the readers are introduced to Kenchamma, the goddess of the village. From describing the geographical location, the narrator almost glides into the description of Kenchamma. Keeping the traditional storytelling style, the old grandmother informs the readers of how the villagers sing, clap and dance around the fire and sing to Kenchamma:

> Kenchamma, Kenchamma,
> Goddess benign and bounteous
> Mother of earth, blood of life
> Harvest queen, rain crowned
> Kenchamma, Kenchamma
> Goddess benign and bounteous.[4]

From here, Achakka again proceeds to describe the houses and people of the village. She describes the Brahmin quarters, Pariahs, Potters, Weavers and Sudras quarters later on. The Skeffington Coffee Estate which symbolizes the impact of industrialization and alien rule on the innocent villagers of Kanthapura lies beyond the village. While describing the brahmins quarter, the narrator makes reference to Corner House Moorthy, Coffee planter Ramayya, Gold-bangle Somanna, Nose Scratching Nanjamma, Waterfall Venkamma and others. The use of such adjectives prior to the names of the characters is the characteristic quality of the Indian grandmother. Such epithets give certain vitality to the characters.

The story begins by the unearthing of a half-sunken lingam by Moorthy, and after the consecration ceremony is performed, *Sankara-jayanti* is celebrated and later *Harikathas* are held. Thus the past and present are freely mixed up, gods and goddesses, heroes and heroines of epics freely mingle with contemporary personalities. When the Harikathas are held, we find that Gandhi is already the subject matter of these Kathas. Jayaramachar, the Harikatha man, mixes traditional myths with contemporary politics, with great ease and in a natural manner. Before narrating the Harikatha, he informs the villagers in a very straightforward manner that the story related would be of Siva and Parvati as follows: "Siva is the three-eyed," he says, "and Swaraj too is three eyed. Self-purification, Hindu-Moslem unity, Khaddar. And then he talks of Damayanti and Sakuntala and Yashoda and everywhere there is something about our country and something about Swaraj. Never had we heard Harikathas like this." (14)

The effect of this blending of fact and fiction was so immense that it kept the villagers "rapt in tears for hours." (14) Achakka still vividly remembers the Harikatha about the birth of Gandhiji. The Harikatha man talks of Gandhi's birth in as divine a manner as the birth of Krishna. "But, O Brahma you who sent us the Prince propagator of the Holy law and sages that smote darkness of ignorance, you have forgotten us so long that the redmen have come across the seas and the oceans to trample on our wisdom. . . . O Brahma deign to send us one of your gods so that he may incarnate on Earth and bring back light and plenty to your enslaved daughter. . . . Siva himself will forthwith and incarnate on Earth and free my beloved daughter from her enforced slavery." (16) Continuing, with this story Jayaramachar describes the birth of Gandhi, "And lo when the sage was still partaking of the pleasures offered him in hospitality, there was born in a family in Gujerat a son such as the world has never beheld. (16) Throwing light on the life of Gandhi, the Harikatha man again merges myth and fact. "You remember how Krishna, when he was a babe of four, had begun to fight against demons and had killed the serpent Kali. So too our Mohandas began to fight against the enemies of the country . . . more and more men followed him as they did Krishna, the flute-player, and so he goes from village to village to slay the serpent of the foreign rule." (16)

In this manner Gandhi is glorified and compared to Rama and Krishna, who fought the Demons. By using this mythical technique, Raja Rao mixes the past with the present to glorify the present. The effect of such Harikatha was soon visible when the villagers threw away their foreign clothes and became Gandhi's men. They started spinning the charkha religiously and read the newspaper as the sacred *Gita*.

The whole story of *Kanthapura* bears religious overtones. Gandhi is elevated to the position of Rama, Bharat Mata is seen as Sita, the Redman is no doubt Ravana. Ordinary facts are emphasized and made significant when they are related to a myth. The illiterate grandmother's imagination can illustrate only from the epics. Adhering to the true Indian style of story-telling she feels that Swaraj is Sita and Jawahar Lal is Bharata. The satyagrahi in prison is the divine Lord Krishna in Kansa's prison. For her, the Mahatma is as large and blue as the Sahyadri mountain, while Moorthy is like the small mountain. For her, the satyagrah becomes a religious ceremony to which she is completely dedicated and devoted. Thus, simple and common incidents acquire larger than life dimensions by the chatty, talkative and gossipy narrator Achakka. Elaborating this point, Iyengar comments: "Events gather significance after the passage of some years the humdrum becomes the unique, the trivial becomes the heroic, and the hectic excitement of a day becomes a permanent communal possession. The political revolution is thus transcended and assimilated into the racial heritage as myth and legend."[2] The theme of *Kanthapura* is no doubt Gandhi and the impact of his teachings but the manner in which Achakka remembers and narrates the story through the stream of her memory, turns the story into a Gandhi Purana. Gandhi is the omnipotent, invisible God and Moorthy is his representative or avtar on earth.

When the scene shifts to the Skeffington Coffee Estate, 'Don't-Touch-The-Government Campaign' becomes very strong. Moorthy's fast, arrest and release, all these events are heightened and made important through the narrator's vivid description. Badè Khan, the policeman, is recruited at the Coffee Estate but the villagers are not frightened of him. They feel: "What is a policeman before a Gandhi man? Tell me, does a boar stand before a lion or a jackal before an elephant?" (81)

Soon the Kanthapura Congress Committee is formed. This evokes the anger of Bhatta, who could not appreciate the respect and popularity that Moorthy was getting. Despite the excommunication of Moorthy, he was still respected, honoured and loved by the villagers. In order to weaken the movement, Bhatta had to win the support of some important villagers. He decided to do a favour to Waterfall Venkamma by arranging the marriage of her daughter Ranga, with a widower Advocate Senappa. Bhatta assures himself by saying that every squirrel will have his day. The thought of Venkamma brought an idea to his mind, "I shall find a bridegroom for her daughter, and she will always be with us, and what with her tongue and her tail, she will set free where we want." (111)

The main story of the novel is interrupted by the digression that describes in great detail the marriage of Ranga and Senappa. Immediately after this digression, the narrator comes to a very serious incident i.e. the arrest of Moorthy. Achakka mentions another tale of Sankar, a saintly lawyer. This digression serves to build up the character of Sankar, who does not undertake false cases. He is a staunch Gandhian, and is therefore highly respected and honoured in Karwar.

Some critics are of the opinion that such digressions do not contribute to the action of the novel. But their contention is not correct. The digressions are an important part of this novel, because we must not forget that the novel is based on the stream-of-consciousness technique. The old grandmother deviates from the main story, whenever any incident comes to her memory. After giving a detailed description of that incident, she goes back to the main story with the words "so, as I was saying" or "I tell you." Through the digressions Achakka is not only seen as a narrator but also as a commentator. Her comments are not biased. They show the true traits of the characters. For example, although Bhatta is projected as an anti-Gandhiman, Achakka's comment, "I tell you, he was not a bad man," places him in the correct perspective. Achakka's evaluation of characters and situations helps the readers to understand them. Those readers who are familiar with the circumlocution of the style of Indian speech, will certainly appreciate Achakka's gossipy digressions.

Despite the digressions, the story develops further. When the Non-Cooperation Movement gains momentum, the villagers plan to escape from the village. They decide to escape under the cover of the Satyanarayan procession. Once again religion and politics combine and amidst chanting of Satyanarain Maharaj ki jai, Vande Mataram and Gandhiji ki jai, the villagers are able to flee Kanthapura and reach Maddur and finally to Kashipur. Here they are garlanded and called the pilgrims of the Mahatma. When they hear of the Round Table Conference, they accept the truce and wait patiently for positive results.

Gandhi's visit to England to attend the conference is made more dramatic by giving it a puranic effect, "they say the Mahatma will go to the Red-man's country, and he will get us Swaraj. . . . And we shall be happy. And Rama will come back from exile, and Sita will be with him, for Ravana will be slain and Sita freed. And as they enter Ayodhya there will be a rain of flowers. Like Bharat, we worship the sandals of the Brother saint." (258)

Kanthapura is in fact a Gandhian epic, a mini Ramayana. Raja Rao has written in the preface to the novel that the meandering, repetitive manner of story-telling is part of India's literary tradition. "The *Mahabharata* has 214,778 verses and the *Ramayana* 48,000. Puranas there are endless and innumerable. We have neither punctuation nor the treacherous ats and ons to bother us—we tell one interminable tale." (vi) *Kanthapura* is accepted as Raja Rao's *Ramayana* and it certainly has a distinct epic quality. Just as myths and legends form the integral part of Eliot's *Wasteland*, similarly they are the central core of *Kanthapura*. Thus instead of being surely a *sthala-purana*, *Kanthapura* takes the dimension of an epic.

There are various advantages of adhering to this style of story-telling. It gives full play to the use of Indian idioms, proverbs, expressions and imagery. For example, our hearts beat like the wings of bats, every squirrel has his day, as honest as an elephant, you cannot straighten a dog's tail etc, are typical Indian expressions. There is a fine fusion of poetry and politics and the lyric quality is heightened. The objective of the novel to combine religious, political and social strands has been successfully accomplished. Raja Rao has modified the English syntax to express emotions which are typically Indian. The novel is Indian in theme as well as treatment. A western art form has been transformed into an essentially Indian theme and style. The mythical technique used successfully by English writers like Virginia Woolf, T.S. Eliot, James Joyce, and others has been modified by Raja Rao and consequently *Kanthapura* has emerged as an exceptionally unique, remarkable and new species of writing. It is a rare, effective and satisfying synthesis of Eastern and Western literary techniques.

NOTES

1. Raja Rao, *Kanthapura* (Madras: Oxford University Press, 1989) Foreword, p. vi.
2. K.R. Srinivasa Iyengar, *Indian Writing in English* (New Delhi: Sterling, 1990), p. 390.

people from the West could not understand it completely. India remains incomprehensible and unapproachable to them: an enigma, a mystery. "India has no history, for Truth cannot have history." There is a gradual progression from Raja Rao's earlier treatment of struggle in *Kanthapura*, the struggle there was against colonial forces and to some extent Moorthy tried to analyze the basic cause of repression. The final truth which haunted him was:

> As long as there will be iron gates and barbed wires round the Skeffington Coffee Estate, and the city cars that can roll up the Bebbur Mound, and gaslights and coolie cars, there will always be Pariahs and poverty. (181)

He protests and says: "it is the way of the masters that is wrong." (180-81) The protagonists in the novels of Raja Rao strive to collectively destroy the forces that threaten and undermine their existence. India to them represents the truth. Moorthy in *Kanthapura* emphasizes the value of truth. Truth is that strong weapon in the hands of an Indian which alone can bring change: 'Between Truth and me none shall come.' (86)

The whole of the Gangetic plain is one song of saintly sorrow, as though Truth began where sorrow was accepted, and India began where Truth was acknowledged.

Raja Rao believes in truth being God and according to Ramaswamy, who voices Rao's opinions, this truth resides in India. India to him symbolizes an abode of knowledge and nothing exists beyond this truth.

The quest for knowing himself is too deep-seated in Moorthy and Ramaswamy. In *Comrade Kirillov*, we come across an individual Padmanabhan Iyer who becomes a Communist after being appalled at the state of existence of men in Indian society. The presence of pariahs and the inhuman treatment meted out to them pricks his consciousness. Like Moorthy who was made to think: "how is one an outcaste?" (80) 'P' too thinks of the evils present in society and turns towards Marxism for a solution. The novel aims to show the protagonist in sheer confusion: 'a communist can be very sincere but his sincerity is confused. There is intellectual confusion,' states Raja Rao. (Niranjan, 58). P is caught between two opposing forces; on the one hand he believes that a revolution like the one in Soviet Union alone could solve the problems of Indians; on the other he feels proud of India's cultural heritage, for it has much to offer.

There is a desire in him to revive the Indian classics. Comparing the rich East with the shallow West, he says:

> Unlike Europe, it is not sincerity that goes a-begging in India—we are not yet that corrupt. But we shall soon reach the requisite standards. We are human like all. But one thing I felt sorry for when I was in India—the neglect of our classics. I forgot my politics for a time and jumped into the classics. It was such a joy to go back to *Uttarramacharita*, and to Kalidasa. (75)

Kirillov too, like Moorthy and Ramaswamy is very fond of India "his Indianhood would break through every community chain." (81) His being a communist did not in any way loosen his bonds with the Indian culture. There is a desire in him to see India free. Like Moorthy he pines for its freedom, but unlike him, he regards Marxism as the greatest possible weapon on earth. Future for him shall be bright only if one follows Communism and not Gandhism. He does not see eye to eye with Gandhian Ideology yet he extends blind support to him and is unable to hear a word uttered by the other against Gandhi:

> Kirillov was an Indian, and he had peculiar reactions which no dialectic could clarify. . . . He could not bear a word said against Mahatma Gandhi. (26)

This implies his subconscious love for Gandhi. Gandhi to him remained an epitome of goodness and love. There remains an affinity between Kirillov and Gandhi. He calls him:

> Friends and fool of the poor, the sadhu reactionary who still believed in caste and creed and such categories, and whose birth in this world had set history many centuries backwards. (53)

The protagonist Padmanabhan Iyer, later known as 'P' is torn between several conflicts. Raja Rao's three protagonists are Brahmins, Moorthy, Rama and 'P' who consciously try to bridge the ècart which existed between them and the others, yet are unable to give up their age-old beliefs. They are making vigorous attempts to realize their being and in this process undergo gradual transformation. To Ramaswamy 'Brahmin is he who knows Brahman.' (5)

A true Brahmin is one who seeks the ultimate truth and this can be attained only if he negates the other reality and probes into the inner one. There continues a constant search for the realizations of this truth. *Comrade Kirillov*, by becoming a communist, resorts to a new programme of action and hopes for a better India. He chooses to be a follower of Marx, just as Moorthy had chosen Gandhism as his form of action. His being a communist implies that he is on the side of the proletariat:

> Marxism had given a strange ascetic incision to his Brahminic manners and his sweetness had that unction, the theological compassion, of a catholic priest. (30)

But even the Marxian influence had not destroyed his faith in the concept of non-dualism. During moments of despair and crisis he would sing:

> Manobuddhi ahankara cittani naham
> cidananda rupah shivoham—shivoham. (86)

Uttering of 'I am Siva, I am Siva' provided him with strength. "Shivoham, Shivoham" as chanted by Moorthy, Ramaswamy and Kirillov, signifies the strong faith in the powers of the Supreme. Brahmin through the strong force of non-dualism, attains the highest state and in doing so realizes his entire being and thus knows perfect bliss, that is, himself. As we see Moorthy encouraging people to read Vedantic texts, Ramaswamy trying to explore the residues of meaning of life through them and Kirillov too showing interest in them we can feel Raja Rao himself trying to attain 'moksha' through non-dualistic approach. The entire thrust of the chanting of mantras is the supreme significance of a ritual action, through which the protagonist tries to assure himself of his existence on the earth. There is an underlying assumption that these individuals are torn between several conflicts and that the meticulous performance of several rituals like singing bhajans, reading religious books, going to the temple and discussing philosophy are essential to the proper understanding of one's self. The struggle becomes intense as the cultural affinity is established among people.

In his novels Raja Rao has also done a detached analysis of the relationship between the being and the other. The conflicts arise in the protagonists' mind due to several reasons. The struggle ensues not only between the British and the Indian, the East and the West, the brahmins and the pariahs, but it is also a struggle between man and woman to understand one another. Their inability to understand each other leads to several doubts and conflicts. The protagonist in Raja Rao's novels, through his relationship with the women, tries to analyze himself. All the female characters emerge as powerful individuals and their attitude towards life also brings a change in the behaviour of the protagonist. Woman is the other to him, and caught between the desire to possess the other and also to be free from the other, we find the protagonist going through several phases of uncertainty and confusion.

In *Kanthapura*, Moorthy's relationship with his mother is snapped off because of his progressive ideas. She, being an orthodox brahmin, is unable to accept the fact that he had begun mixing with the pariahs. The dreams which she had built around him had no chance of being realized in the near future. He had given up his studies and his refusal to marry aggravates the tensions in her mind. Life to her becomes overshadowed with ennui and disappointment. The news of her son's ex-communication leaves her distressed. She accepts death as a consolation because she has nowhere to go. The unrelenting attitude of one leads to the complete destruction of the other.

As we analyze Moorthy's relationship with Ratna, Ramaswamy's relationship with Madeleine and Savithri, and Kirillov's relationship with Irene, we find the men in Raja Rao's novels unable to comprehend the mysterious other. Woman has always been revered and held in high esteem by these protagonists. She is a part of the reality on this earth, yet appears unreal and dream-like to the protagonist at times. Moorthy had loved Ratna but never disclosed his love for her. He realizes the power she has over him. Afraid of his being possessed by her, he refuses to be an object in his own eyes and the relationship takes a spiritual turn: 'she seemed something so feminine and soft and distant.' (64)

As she comes to see him, he realizes the impact of her presence on him. The struggle goes on in the mind of the protagonist. She appears to him as someone soft yet aloof. In his attempt to realize what feelings he had for her, we find Moorthy drifting away from the other. This distance, which gradually develops between the two on a physical level, does not separate them mentally. Moorthy, by refusing to succumb to his physical desires, is able to continue the freedom struggle and yet maintain an affinity with Ratna by writing to her. His writing a letter to her signifies the urgent need in him to be remembered and understood by the other.

The conflicts which arise in the mind of Ramaswamy due to his confrontation with the women are also responsible for creating the need for self-exploration in him. He marries Madeleine and even the strong bond of marriage does not let him penetrate the depths of her being. It was the Brahmin in him that had appealed to her. Ramaswamy tries to see himself in her: 'Madeleine was like the palace of Amber seen in moonlight . . . such a luminous mystery the deeper you go, the more you know yourself.' (14)

Ramaswamy has become so dependent on Madeleine that her absence makes life meaningless to him. On his return from India, Ramaswamy is unable to see Madeleine immediately and this leaves him estranged from the outer world:

> It makes all the difference in the world whether the woman of your life is with you or not; she alone enables you to be in a world that is familiar and whole. If it is not his wife, then for an Indian it may be a sister in Mysore, or little mother in Benares. (57)

It is her presence that makes the world a happy place to live in. The man in Raja Rao's novels discovers that he is helpless without her. Ramaswamy is attracted to the silence which makes her so different and yet so loving. Comparing Madeleine to his little mother he says, "they both had the same shy presence, both rather silent and remembering everything; they loved, too, more than is customary." (20) Of Savithri he says, "she never says anything that really matters and, her presence never said anything, but her absence spoke." (31)

The mutual passion between Ramaswamy and Savithri creates their own world, separate from others: "for her, I could see, everything was gesture and symbol . . . all was secret to her but herself—so all was a legend, and every event a wonder." (126)

During her visit to France, Savithri's relationship with Ramaswamy takes on a spiritual aspect. He gives her the toe rings of his mother. The spiritual marriage between the two signifies their desire to remain rooted to their innermost self. Even his sister Saroja appears as an unknown being to Ramaswamy. There was this desire in her: 'to hide something of her own.' (49) The silence of the woman as a significant sign can be conceived as a bearer of meaning. Through her 'silence' one can give meaning to several other actions of hers. A woman is that incomprehensible other and in Madeleine we find a desire to own Ramaswamy. She treats him like a god and worships him: "To amount oneself in worshipping another is the basis of all love. We become ourself by becoming another." (81) Just as Ratna worshipped Moorthy and was willing to do anything for him, we can see an attitude of subservience visible in Madeleine. Deep down in her heart lies the wish to possess him. This realization that she understands him far too well grips Rama with fear: "I could be bent by the knowledge she had of me—the knowledge of my silences, the vigorous twists of my mental domain." (92) As Sartre has also pointed: "There is a relation of the for-itself with the in-itself in the presence of the other." (92) She loved him and was conscious of the desire to grab hold of his being. Love becomes an enterprise to her. It is an attempt at realizing herself and this leads to her alienation with the other.

She talked of him to the others like Tante Zoubie and Catharine and says:

> I spoke especially of the respect you show to me—for you, a woman is still the other, the strange, the miracle. You could never show the familiarity European men show, towards their wives. You worship women even if you torture them. But I like to be tortured and to be your slave. (98)

This confession of Madeleine reveals her inner sight. Analyzing this sort of relationship, Sartre says: "in love the lover wants to be 'the whole world' for the beloved. This means that he puts himself on the side of the world." (479) The protagonist on having realized the incompatibility between him and the other refuses to become an object for what he wants is different from what the other can give: "No, of course I did not want a slave. I wanted a companion of pilgrimage." (98)

Gradually we see the protagonist Rama trying to understand the philosophy of life. He severs all connections with Madeleine and decides to come back to India. He feels: "Life is made for woman—man is a stranger on this earth." This realization, that a woman is intimate to another woman in a way a man could never be to another man, fills Ramaswamy with a sense of isolation. His entire being finds itself alienated from the material world and the search for the unknown persists. He finally comes to a conclusion that what separated him from Madeleine was India. India he feels stands "vertical to space and time, and is present at all points."

'India' to Ramaswamy represents that whole beyond which lies no other truth. 'India' as a socio-cultural code represents not only Brahmin but also the absolute. The protagonist after having been unable to identify himself with the West pines to go back to his roots. It is the Indianness in him which makes him accept the superiority of woman over the other. She represents an entirety to him.

The woman, therefore, to Ramaswamy represents not only the 'Panch Tatvas' but also the entire universe. It is only through his contacts with the other that Ramaswamy realizes the final truth. Life and death to him appear as the two integrated forces and there remains continuity between the two. The revelation to the protagonist comes as a surprise. He discovers his inner contradictions. As a being he knows he possesses the capacity to transcend his present situation and its possible limitations. Yet part of his individuality is infected with a desire to be loved and this seems paradoxical. He accepts what he wants and says in his diary: "5.5.54. 'No' not a God but a Guru is what I need." (34) To such a Guru he was taken. The Guru, he tells Madeleine can let him distinguish the Serpent from the Rope. He alone would be able to light his path and lead him towards perfect bliss i.e. attainment of the absolute. For him: 'India is the Guru of the world.' (332)

Thus we see that the protagonist in *The Serpent and the Rope* is in quest of the ultimate reality. He discovers at last that the problems he is facing have a spiritual connotation and this unrest due to spiritual conflict in the mind cannot be easily resolved. His pilgrimage ends with the discovery of truth, the Guru. Self-knowledge being the goal of his life, he decided to return to India for complete discovery of oneself.

This crucial need to understand, results from a slow evolution in Raja Rao's thought. In *Kanthapura*, Moorthy, after having understood that change alone would result in proper freedom, raises his voice against the inequality which exists in society at several levels. In *The Serpent and the Rope*, Ramaswamy's predicament and his ultimate realization of what he wants from life resulted from his ties with his past, the irresistible urge in him to go back to India from France and his incapacity to give up his Indian identity. The implication being that his quest for knowledge could never be fulfilled unless he found a Guru an epitome of truth and this truth resides only in India.

Comrade Kirillov is much more than the chronicle of an Indian turned Marxist. The book reveals the conflict of commitments. In *Comrade Kirillov*, we find Padmanabhan Iyer trying to adhere to the communist programmes. By doing so he tries to break away from the old order and bring in a revolution. In communism lies an answer to all human problems. He derives his conviction from Marx but this alone does not fulfil his being in totality. We see 'P' caught between several unsolvable dilemmas. Even communism is unable to give an answer to his questions. His love for India draws him back to its roots. Proud of its cultural heritage, he finds it difficult to break away from the familiar grounds. The protagonist in *Comrade Kirillov* is unable to set himself free from all bonds of Indianhood. 'He was ever conscious of his skin' in England. After having been treated as a mere object of ridicule by the British,

> The brahminic sensibility of Kirillov had such antennae inward and outward that a fierce anger rose in his belly. And he cursed the British race, wished it a sepulchral fire, and the red, ruinous tongue of Hell. (52)

Comrade Kirillov's hatred towards the British is too intense and he wishes their complete extirpation. Both Moorthy and Kirillov strive for a change in society. Nevertheless they differ in their ideologies. Moorthy, a follower of Gandhi, believes in non-violence and hopes to transform the enemy through love. *Comrade Kirillov* however feels contempt for British race and believes:

> The communist, the true Marxist, is above all a realist. . . . Mahatma Gandhi should have been born in the Middle Ages, and he should not have bothered us with his theology in this rational age of ours. (37)

Like Moorthy, he craves for a classless society where all individuals would be their own masters and wealth be equally distributed among them. To him communism is a genuine resolution of the conflict between one man and the other.

A brief survey of *The Cat and Shakespeare* reveals that it is a sequel to Raja Rao's other novels. Raja Rao calls it 'a metaphysical comedy.' The author has tried to give a comic flavour to serious philosophical issues. The protagonist Ramakrishna Pai is advised by Govindan Nair not to worry for:

> Life is a riddle that can be solved with a riddle. You can remove a thorn with another thorn, you solve one problem through another problem. Thus the world is connected. (37)

The woman to the protagonist always remains 'a puzzle.' The novel is full of symbolic allusions from the Upanishad and parables taken from the Puranas. The life to Govindan Nair is 'a rationshop' and "Shakespeare knew every mystery of the rationshop." (83) Shakespeare's penetrating soul had looked deep into the recesses of human thought. The 'cat' in the novel is a symbol with multiple implications as the *Prakriti* or the Mother or the Guru or the Divine. The brief narrative while trying to grapple with a wide range of ideas has become too complex and obscure to an ordinary reader.

The protagonist is seen in search of an answer to his existential predicament. Various questions haunt him. However, all of them have only one answer and that lies in the discovery of the divine. His final realization is that God alone can save the world from peril and complete resignation to him can provide salvation to the searching souls. He realizes that "the unknown alone resolves the unknown." *The Cat and Shakespeare*, as Naik puts it, "has its moments of dazzling brilliance and sudden glory, but the brief blinding lighting flash, with its searing white splendour, though impressive, can never take the place of the midday sun." (142)

The most striking feature in the novels of Raja Rao is his use of a variety of signs and symbols which embody a vast network of meaning. Through the use of signs and symbols not only has he probed the personal and cultural relationships which form the basis of our social codes but also hidden, secret recesses of the human psyche.

The characters in his novel come alive through the narrative process. In *Kanthapura*, an old woman is narrating the villager's struggle for freedom. The narrator's style may seem tediously repetitive to the hasty reader, but this is not so: the manner in which she unfolds the story forms the very essence of the novel. The narrator, Achakka, subtly draws our attention to an interminable tale where one episode follows another and gradually the problematics is unfolded. Raja Rao tries to justify his technique when he says: "Our method of expression therefore has to be a dialect which will some day prove to be as distinctive and colourful as the Irish or the American. Time alone will justify it." (Author's Foreword to *Kanthapura*)

The people in *Kanthapura* after having launched a struggle against existing inequalities try to strengthen their political consciousness by seeking socio-cultural integration. Raja Rao has focussed on several important problems of the society. Raja Rao successfully highlights certain socio-economic issues which have been responsible for cultural and political estrangement.

The characters in *Kanthapura* strive to eliminate certain social evils like untouchability, social inferiority of women, suppression of widows, those rites and practices which hinder the national character of the struggle. The protagonist Moorthy is seen pondering: "how is one an outcaste?" The women of *Kanthapura* refuse to be submissive and fight vigorously for their upliftment. Once an awareness of their state of suppression is created in them they begin questioning themselves: "How can we be, like we used to be?" Moorthy realizes the futility of freedom as long as there is economic disparity among men. His final question: "What is the goal?" leaves one disgusted with the ruling class.

The Gandhian struggle brings about many profound changes in the life of the people. Once they discover their rich cultural values they acquire a clearer awareness of the economic realities of the country and the sufferings of the common people. Thus we see people in Raja Rao's *Kanthapura* striving for political independence which would also include their economic, social and cultural progress.

The final realization dawns upon Moorthy that no political liberty can come without the inner being achieving freedom. The novels of Raja Rao portray such protagonists who try to resolve their inner turmoil. Their psychological upheavals are caused by forces both within and without. They begin their journey, the exodus towards the realm of self-knowledge. Ignorance of the self as well as the tentacles of society are the sources of man's misery. The means to resolve such issues appear too idealistic; we notice that the author's protagonists embody the futile meanderings in a labyrinth of darkness that occasionally admits a streak of hope.

Works Cited

Naik, M.K. *Raja Rao*. New York: Twayne, 1972.

_____. *A History of Indian English Literature*. Delhi: Sahitya Akademi, 1982.

_____. *Perspectives on Indian Fiction in English*. Delhi: Abhinav, 1985.

Niranjan, Shiva. *Novelist as Sadhaka*. Ghaziabad: Vimal, 1985.

Raja Rao. *Kanthapura*. London: George Allen and Unwin, 1938; New York: New Directions, 1963.

_____. *The Serpent and the Rope*. London: John Murray, 1960; Delhi: Hind Pocket Books, Orient Paperbacks, 1968.

_____. *The Cat and Shakespeare: A Tale of Modern India*. New Delhi: Vision Books, Orient Paperbacks, 1971.

_____. *Comrade Kirillov*. New Delhi: Vision Books, Orient Paperbacks, 1978.

Sartre, J.P. *Being and Nothingness*. New York: Washington Square Press Pocket Books, 1968.